THE INDUS AND ITS PROVINCES

D1879851

Owing to the antiquity and rarity of this book, certain pages are regrettably absent, and readability is compromised due to the blurring of the original text. If you possess any insights regarding the availability of these missing sections, kindly inform us. Your assistance is crucial in ensuring the completion of this significant work for the benefit of future generations.

THE INDUS AND ITS PROVINCES

W. P. ANDREW

GYAN

Published by

GYAN

Gyan Publishing House
5, Ansari Road
Daryaganj, New Delhi-110002
Phone: 011-47034999, 9811692060
E-mail: books@gyanbooks.com

Distribution Network
gyanbooks.com
India, USA, Canada, UK, Australia

© Publisher
All rights reserved. No part of this work may be reproduced, stored, adapted, or transmitted in any form or by any means, electronic, mechanical, photocopying, micro-filming, recording or otherwise, or translated in any language, without the prior written permission of the copyright owner and the publisher.

ISBN: 978-93-7133-872-1 (PB)

First Published, 1857

2nd Impression 2025

Printed at: Gyan Press, Delhi.

The book is sold subject to the condition that it shall not, by way of trade or otherwise, be lent, resold, hired out, or otherwise circulated without the prior publisher's written consent.

THE INDUS AND ITS PROVINCES
Author: W. P. ANDREW

THE INDUS AND ITS PROVINCES,

THEIR

POLITICAL AND COMMERCIAL IMPORTANCE

CONSIDERED IN CONNEXION

WITH

IMPROVED MEANS OF COMMUNICATION.

ILLUSTRATED BY STATISTICAL TABLES

And Maps.

BY W. P. ANDREW,

CHAIRMAN OF THE SCINDE AND PUNJAUB RAILWAYS, AND INDUS STEAM FLOTILLA.

Author of "Indian Railways as connected with the Power and Stability of the British Empire in the East,"
&c. &c. &c.

"It is a solecism of power to think to command the end and yet not to endure the means."—*Bacon's Essays of Empire.*

LONDON:
WM. H. ALLEN & Co., 7, LEADENHALL STREET.

From the "LAHORE CHRONICLE, *August*, 1857.

RAILWAYS FOR INDIA.—Now is the time to impress upon the Government the vital importance of establishing a net work of Railways in this country (India.)

The absolute necessity of establishing rapid communications, has been amply proved by the present crisis. Even with forced marches, troops take 24 days to get over the distance they would be carried by rail in 12 or 18 hours ! !

On economical grounds alone, the Railway ought to be extended and ramified without delay and regardless of the immediate outlay. This may seem a paradox, but we will explain. Ten thousand men with a rail to travel by, are fully equal in this country to thirty thousand with the existing means of conveyance, and the cost of the difference, viz., 20,000 European troops is a matter of pounds, shillings, and pence, that we leave for financiers to calculate.

What a glorious thing it would have been, had the Euphrates Valley Railway and the Scinde and Punjaub Railway been accomplished facts at the time of the present insurrection. How it would have "astonished the Natives" to have seen a gallant British Army landed at Lahore, within a month of the outbreak taking place! and yet such a thing would have been possible, supposing the Electric Telegraph to have been also completed so as to establish an electric messenger between the Indus and the Thames.

But we are a people of slow perception in spite of all that may be said of our superiority. It is only when we are severely punished that we awaken from our lethargy.

The British Lion, terrible when once aroused, requires a good shaking before he can be awakened, but once up, his vigour is as great as ever. At present, however, months must elapse ere the punishment can be dealt out.

Prompt chastisement carries terror and fear with it, and unhinges the plans of the conspirators, whereas, delay in punishing the guilty, gives them confidence and adds to their strength.

Let us hope that one of the good things to result out of this great evil may be RAILWAY AND STEAM COMMUNICATION ON A LIBERAL SCALE.

CONTENTS.

CHAPTER I.

INTRODUCTORY.

CHAPTER II.

THE INDUS VALLEY AS A MILITARY HIGHWAY.

CHAPTER III.

KURRACHEE.

CHAPTER IV.

KURRACHEE

CHAPTER V.

SCINDE RAILWAY.

CHAPTER VI.

THE INDUS STEAM FLOTILLA.

CHAPTER VII

THE PUNJAUB RAILWAY.

CHAPTER VIII.

PROVINCES OF INDUS.

CHAPTER IX.

PROVINCES OF INDUS.

CHAPTER X.

INDIA AND CENTRAL ASIA.

CHAPTER XI.

PRODUCTIONS OF VALLEY OF INDUS.

CHAPTER XII.

PRODUCTIONS OF VALLEY OF INDUS.

CHAPTER XIII.

PRODUCTIONS OF VALLEY OF INDUS.

CHAPTER XIV.

PRODUCTIONS OF VALLEY OF INDUS.

CHAPTER XV.

PRODUCTIONS OF VALLEY OF INDUS.

CHAPTER XVI.

COLONIZATION IN INDIA AND AUSTRALIA COMPARED.

APPENDIX A.

APPENDIX B.

APPENDIX C.

APPENDIX D.

APPENDIX E.

APPENDIX F.

APPENDIX G.

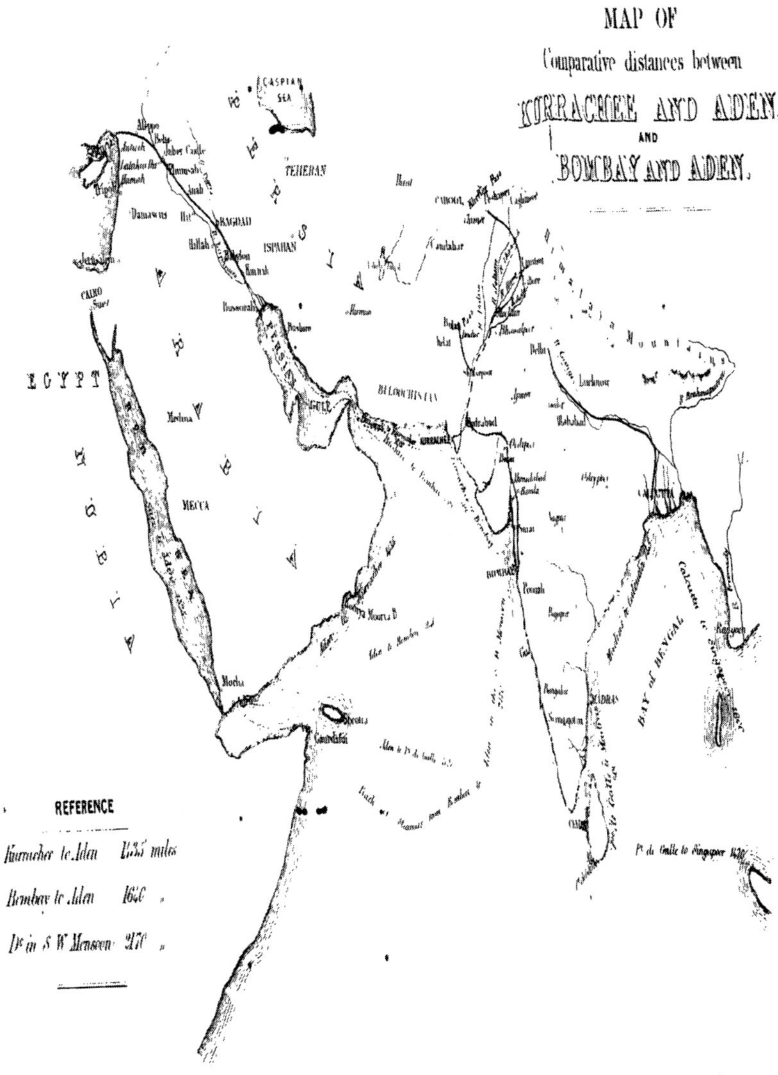
MAP OF
Comparative distances between
KURRACHEE AND ADEN,
AND
BOMBAY AND ADEN.
REFERENCE
Kurrachee to Aden 1435 miles
Bombay to Aden 1640 „
Do in S W Monsoon 2170 „
CASPIAN SEA
TEHERAN
ISPAHAN
BAGDAD
Aleppo
Damascus
Jerusalem
CAIRO
Suez
EGYPT
Medina
MECCA
Mocha
Busserah
Bushire
BELOOCHISTAN
KURRACHEE
Hydrabad
Candahar
Delhi
Lucknow
Allahabad
CALCUTTA
BOMBAY
Poonah
MADRAS
BAY of BENGAL
Rangoon
Socotra
Guardafui
Pt de Galle to Singapore 1430

THE INDUS AND ITS PROVINCES.

CHAPTER I.

INTRODUCTORY.

THE RETURN OF COMMERCE TO ITS ANCIENT ROUTES.—THE INDUS ROUTE TO CENTRAL ASIA AND EUROPE USED IN THE SEVENTH CENTURY.—SIR A. BURNES ON THE INDUS ROUTE.—OPINION OF SIR CHARLES NAPIER.—THE INDUS VALLEY PECULIARLY SUITED TO THE COMBINED SYSTEM OF RAILWAYS AND STEAMBOATS.

FEW facts bear more conclusive testimony to the sagacity of the ancients, when the limited amount of their geographical knowledge is remembered, than the tenacity with which commerce adhered to the direction given to it by them, and the readiness with which it returns to any of those channels when temporarily diverted by political events or geographical discoveries. The overland route from Europe to India, by the Isthmus of Suez and the Red Sea, is certainly as old as the days of the early Phœnician navigators. The navigability of the Euphrates was tested long before Trajan ever sailed on its waters, and was revisited by the Italians in the eleventh century, and our own merchants in the days of Elizabeth as the best way to the East;* whilst the value of the Indus, as the shortest and easiest route for the commerce of India, not only with Central Asia and the north of Europe, but with the whole of the West, was fully recognised by the later Romans in the seventh century. Necessity, in their case, was the mother of invention. When the rapid progress of the Mohammedan arms had wrested Egypt from the Byzantine power, and thus closed the overland route of Suez to the Greek merchants, they forthwith turned to other means and sought out a new channel, by which the productions of the East might be transmitted to the great emporium of the West. The route thus discovered was that by the Indus. The rich and easily-stowed products of India were carried up the great river as far as it was

* "Various causes concurred in restoring liberty and independence to the cities of Italy. The acquisition of these roused industry and gave motion and vigour to all the active powers of the human mind. Foreign commerce revived, navigation was attended to and improved. Constantinople became the chief mart to which the Italians resorted. There they not only met with favourable reception, but obtained such mercantile privileges as enabled them to carry on trade with great advantages. They were supplied both with the precious commodities of the East, and with many curious manufactures, the product of ancient arts and ingenuity still subsisting among the Greeks. As the labour and expense of conveying the productions of India to Constantinople, by that long and indirect course which I have described (the route by the Indus, the Oxus, the Caspian, and the Volga) rendered them extremely rare, and of an exorbitant price, the industry of the Italians discovered other methods of procuring them in greater abundance and at an easier rate. They sometimes purchased them at Aleppo, Tripoli, and other ports on the coast of Syria, to which *they were brought by a route not unknown to the ancients*. They were conveyed from India by sea up the Persian Gulf, and ascending the Euphrates and Tigris as far as Bagdat, were carried by land across the desert of Palmyra, and from thence to the towns on the Mediterranean."—Robertson's America, Book 1.

navigable; thence transported to the Oxus, down whose stream they proceeded as far as the Caspian Sea. There they entered the Volga, and sailing up it, were carried by land to the Tanais (the Don), which conducted them into the Euxine Sea, where ships from Constantinople waited their arrival.* The discovery of the long, but easy route, by the Cape of Good Hope, combined with the deadly feuds between the Christians of the West and the Mohammedan nations that held the countries of the Nile and the Euphrates, for a time diverted the stream of commerce from those routes. It has not been so, however, with the Indus, to the same extent. If the revival of the overland route and the impending re-opening of the Euphrates as the highway to the East, are evidences of a return to old paths, the continuance of a commerce with Central Asia and northern Europe, by way of the Indus, and the two great gates of India, the Khyber and Bolan Passes, is a pregnant proof of the tenacity with which trade adheres to its old channels, and of the sagacity which originally selected that direction for the produce of the East. However great may have been the changes of masters and manners in the territories between the Indus and the Bosphorus, a portion of the tide of commerce has flowed, and does still flow, as it did in the seventh century. When the late Sir Alexander Burnes was in Lahore in 1831, he found English broad cloth sold in the Bazaar that had been brought, not from Calcutta, but from Russia; and when he penetrated further into Central Asia, met, at Bokhara, with a merchant, "thinking of taking an investment of it to Loodhiana, in India, where he could afford

* Robertson's America, Book 1, quoting from Ramusio, vol. i., p. 372.

to sell it cheaper than it was to be had there, notwithstanding the length of the journey."†

The traffic between India and Central Asia, described so fully by Sir Alexander Burnes, as existing at the period of his visit, was carried on in a slow and most expensive manner either by camels or by the badly constructed boats of the country on the Indus and the tributary streams of the Punjaub, despite accumulated difficulties. Besides the labour of tracking, so often required to stem the stream of the river, the rude character of the boats employed, and the exactions of each petty prince through whose territory the goods passed, there was the serious impediment offered by the selfish policy of the Ameers of Scinde, who unavoidably arrested the development of trade when they carried their devotion to field sports so far, as to think nothing of devastating a large tract of populous and fertile land in order to secure greater quiet and more secure cover to a particular species of antelope, whose destruction was "a royal sport." The occupation of the whole valley of the Indus by the English, and the consequent introduction of security of property and encouragement to commerce and agriculture, have swept away every political and social impediment to progress, and given to us a magnificent region of land and water that invites the agency of modern science, capital, and enterprise.

Speaking of the upper portion of this great valley, Sir Alexander Burnes bears full testimony to its great capabilities. "There is," he says, "perhaps no inland country of the globe which possesses greater facilities for commerce than the Punjaub, and there are few more rich in the pro-

† Burnes's Travels, vol. ii. p. 432

ductions of the mineral, vegetable and animal kingdoms. Intersected by five navigable streams, it is bounded on the west by one of the largest rivers of the old world. To the north, it has the fertile and the fruitful vale of Cashmere to limit its sceptre; so placed, that it can export without trouble its costly fabrics to the neighbouring kingdoms of Persia and Tartary, China and India. Situated between Hindostan and the celebrated entrepots of Central Asia, it shares the advantages of their traffic, while it is itself blessed with an exuberance of every production of the soil that is useful and nutritious to man. The productions of the Punjaub relieve it from any great dependence on external resource. Its courtiers and chiefs may robe themselves in the shawls of Cashmere, and the strong and beautiful silken fabrics of Moultan. Its citizens and husbandmen may wear the cheap textures of the native cotton. Every animal may be bounteously fed on the grains indigenous to the country; and a range of mountains, entirely composed of salt, furnishes that necessary ingredient of food, while the upland parts yield condiments and fruits to season the daily bread."* The writer then goes on to enumerate the chief products,—the shawls, silks, cottons, minerals and vegetables, and to show the advantages of opening the Indus to the Punjaub trade. At that period, from the exactions of the native Governments, he anticipated but little opening for our manufactures, but rather looked for advantages to us from the liberal exports we might expect from the valley of the Indus. Could he have looked forward to the present day, he would have seen that the gain to be expected by improving the navi-

* Burnes's Travels, vol. ii.

gation of the great river was mutual. In 1843, the value of the exports was £1,010, and that of the imports through Kurrachee £121,050. In 1856, through the same port, exports to the amount of £734,522 were met by imports to the value of £685,665.

At the time (1833), however, when Sir Alexander Burnes wrote of the Punjaub and Scinde, steam navigation on rivers was little more than in its infancy; and the idea of a railroad for any part of India, if projected, was laughed at as an absurdity. It is interesting, therefore, to remark, that though without hope of aid from the rail and with the prospect of but little assistance from the steamboat, our traveller saw at a glance the real want of the province, and suggested a combined system of land and water carriage as the best means for improving and opening the communication with the countries at the head of the Indus. He was decidedly against encouraging navigation upward above Moultan, except by smaller boats, on the Chenab and Jhelum, and regarded the tortuous course of the Ravee to Lahore, and its decided inferiority in depth and size to any of the other rivers, as a fatal objection to its being made the channel of commercial communication.

Nine years after the visit of Sir Alexander Burnes, Sir Charles Napier recognised with "his eagle eye" the commercial importance of the line of the Indus. "If any civilized man were asked" he wrote, in 1842, before, be it remembered, railroads were seriously entertained for eastern countries, "were you ruler of Scinde, what would you do? His answer would be, I would abolish the tolls on the rivers, make Kurrachee a free port, protect Shikarpoor from robbers, make Sukkur a mart for trade &c. on the Indus.

I would make a track-way along its banks. I would get *steam boats.*" * Again wrote the same eminent authority, "in a commercial point of view, Shikarpoor is of considerable importance. It offers a depôt for goods from the north and west with the countries of which it has long possessed channels of communication. Adverse circumstances may for a while interrupt these. But under a firm government they will soon be re-opened. Shikarpoor goods would be sent to Sukkur, there to be shipped on the Indus, and they would also pass by land to Larkaana, and thence to Kurrachee. These seem formerly to have been the lines of trade. They are geographically and naturally so, and will therefore quickly revive. . . . . Shikarpoor and Sukkur naturally support each other in commerce." †

It was with this object that during his government in Scinde he constructed a mole at Kurrachee, in order to enable ships to load without delay, opened the channel between that port and the Indus by Ghisree Bunder—and obtained from the Government four war steamers, with which he commenced the navigation of the Indus for commercial purposes. The line of commercial communication by the Indus was, in his opinion, "pointed out by nature—the best, the quickest, the safest, and the cheapest." ‡ The Punjaub not being then in our possession, Sir Charles Napier not unnaturally regarded Kurrachee in the light of a western port of Bombay. Hence it was that he so strongly advocated a railroad from Hydrabad via Oomercote and Deesa to the latter city, § now

* Conquest of Scinde, by Sir W. Napier; p. 128.
† Ibid; p. 125.
‡ Life of Sir C. Napier. Vol. 4; p. 355.
§ Ibid. Vol. 3; p. 6.

recommended for survey as a most important branch of the Scinde line, and that in speaking of the future of Kurrachee, he generally coupled it with that of the older port. It was in this view of things that he wrote in 1847.

"I am taking or rather trying to take advantage of our lull to push a steamer up to Feroozepore with good and cheap things for the troops from Bombay, instead of dear from Calcutta. I hope to draw down commerce to Kurrachee.

"The whole of the Calcutta interest is at work to run down Scinde and the Indus because they will ruin the trade of the Ganges; all will come down the Indus to make Bombay and Kurrachee." *

Again in 1849 he writes, "India should suck English manufactures up her great rivers, and pour down those rivers her own varied products. Kurrachee, you will yet be the glory of the East! Would that I could come alive again to see you, Kurrachee, in your grandeur." †

These views, which he had never ceased to urge on the authorities, he once more advocated in a masterly memoir, published in 1852, in consequence of statements caused by the movement at Manchester, in favour of forwarding rules for trade with Central Asia, through the means of the fairs of Scinde. After showing what he had endeavoured to effect on this score, and how, after a delay of several years, his projects had been warmly adopted by Mr. Frere, the then commissioner of Scinde, he says :—
"The whole commerce of the countries north-east of Scinde will finally descend upon Kurrachee; and the march of Alexander the Great from the Beas to the ocean

* Life of Sir C. Napier. Vol. 4; pp. 71, 72.
† Ibid. Vol. 4; p. 202

with the voyage of Nearchus, marks the coming line of European trade with India."

Speaking from our present knowledge of what steam can do, both on land and on water, the valley of the Indus—as the united territories of Scinde and the Punjaub may well be called—seems in an especial manner marked out for the successful application of that combined system of river and rail which I had the honor of suggesting for the valley of the Ganges as far back as 1846, and which might have been long ago in efficient operation.*

* "We have already stated our decided preference for that plan of *commencing* improved transit, which would only supersede the river navigation where it was most defective, and co-operate with it where it was always available, *i. e.*, a railroad from Calcutta to deep water in the Ganges at Rajmahal; from this point, river steamers to Allahabad, at the confluence of the Jumna and Ganges, where deep water ceases, and a railway from Allahabad to Delhi and the Sutlej. This would be nearly one thousand miles of railroad, exclusive of branches, traversing the easiest, the richest and most densely peopled portions of our dominions, where the river transit is either dangerous or tedious, as by the Nuddea rivers and Sunderbunds, or only applicable to the smaller country craft, and closed entirely to steamers, as the great rivers are beyond Allahabad. Above this point it is impossible, by land or by water, to move military stores or merchandize in any quantity beyond the average of twelve miles per diem. No Utopian ideas of a railroad system, starting at once into complete perfectibility, should divert enterprise and capital from so fair and inviting a field."

"Our opinion remains unchanged, notwithstanding that the Railway Commissioners have enunciated propositions, and proposed projects in exact accordance with the views entertained by the East Indian, or Mirzapore Railway Company; but which they have failed to demonstrate, not even supplying the requisite data, on which to found the demonstration of the plans and propositions proposed and enunciated by themselves—we say that our opinion remains unchanged, as to the impolicy of *commencing* the railroad system by an attempt to supersede the river navigation where it is

From the sea coast to the head of the Delta, some 30 miles below Hyderabad, the course of the Indus is tortuous in the extreme, the delays unavoidable, and the losses most serious. From the nature of the channels of the Delta, the trade can only be pursued by steamboats of such a construction, as to render them as unfit for the sea voyage to Kurrachee as a first-class sea steamer would be for the shallow, shifting, twisting channel of the river. The country, however, between the sea board and Hyderabad is all but a dead level, offering every facility for a short line of railway of little more than a hundred miles, from Kurrachee to Hyderabad; and thus overcoming the delay, the losses, and the danger incident to the navigation of the Delta. From Hyderabad again, up to Moultan, five hundred and seventy miles, the river is broad and suffi-

comparatively free from obstruction, and is always available for steam navigation, as is the case between Rajmahal and Allahabad. The former is situated at the head of the Delta of the Ganges, and the latter at the confluence of the Ganges and Jumna, the distance between the two towns, by the river route, being 500 miles. But should a line be determined on for this portion of the country, an extension of the Rajmahal line up the Gangetic valley to Mirzapore and Allahabad, would have many advantages over the direct route indicated by the East Indian, or Mirzapore Railway Company. These advantages we shall notice in detail when we come to review the report of the Railway Commission. It may, however, be mentioned now, that although the actual, or lineal distance between Calcutta and Mirzapore by the valley of the Ganges, would be 100 miles longer than by the direct route, yet taking the difference of gradients into account (assistant power being required on the latter, and *pro rata* to the power required so is the distance) the gain in which would be too trivial to be an element in any calculation of the comparative merits of the two lines, in a country, where time occupied in travelling is estimated by months instead of hours."—Indian Railways, in connection with the Power and Stability of the British Empire in the East, by An Old Indian Postmaster. 2nd ed., 1846.

ciently deep for a flotilla of powerful steamboats, capable not only of drawing large flats, but of carrying passengers on board. At Moultan, again, the advantage is once more with the land,—another level plain invites the construction of a railway to Lahore and Umritsir, and which will speedily be extended to Peshawur, near the mouth of the Khyber, on our extreme north-western frontier. These means for perfecting the communication with the countries at the head of the great river, as well as for providing for the enormous traffic of the territories through which it and its tributaries flow, have been sanctioned by the Indian Government, in the form of the Scinde Railway, from Kurrachee to Hyderabad, the Indus flotilla between Hyderabad and Moultan and the Punjaub Railway from Moultan to Lahore and Umritsir.

The importance of these three associate works cannot be overrated, especially when considered in relation to the extensive commerce* and present position of our empire in the East, and the urgent necessity that exists for carrying out, without a moment's delay, every project capable, not only of increasing the means of intercommunication in India, but of shortening the distance from England to the most important and most vulnerable

* 1856–57.

Imports into British India from United Kingdom (value)	£16,734,898	
,, ,, other parts	11,873,387	
		£28,608,285
Exports from British India to United Kingdom (value)	£10,635,606	
,, ,, other parts	15,956,275	
		£26,591,881
Total Trade of British India (value)		£55,200,166

portions of her eastern empire. That they would serve this latter purpose most fully, in connection with the proposed Euphrates Valley Route to India, I have already shown in my Memoir on that undertaking and elsewhere.* I now propose to regard them more as a means of intercommunication,—a great military and mercantile highway —to northern India† and Central Asia, and to show their

* Memoir on the Euphrates Valley Route to India, with Official Correspondence and Maps. Dedicated to the Earl of Clarendon, K.G. By W. P. Andrew. W. H. Allen and Co.

Letter to Viscount Palmerston, K.G., on the Political Importance of the Euphrates Valley Railway. By W. P. Andrew. With Reports by General Chesney and Sir John Macneil, and Memorandum by Sir Justin Shiel, K.C.B. W. H. Allen and Co.

† "But it was not only against enemies beyond the mountains that the Imperial Government had to guard; they had to battle with the natives of India on their own soil; and the establishment of steam transit along the Valley of the Indus must prove a most valuable auxiliary in preventing or crushing rebellion in our own territories. In addition to other considerations which recommended the opening up of a line between the westernmost port of India and our north-western provinces, it was important to draw attention to a suggestion which had been made to him by a gentleman of considerable experience in Indian affairs, namely, that there was no route by which we could pour in troops into the north-western provinces so short or so rapid as by Kurrachee and the Valley of the Indus, besides the additional advantage of avoiding the humid heat and disease of Bengal; and, moreover, that by sending our European reinforcements by the Indus route, we should prove to the Sikhs, who were now our allies, and fighting bravely under our flag, that we did not entirely depend for the maintenance of our authority upon *their* thews and sinews."—Extract from Speech of the Chairman at the Meeting of the Scinde Railway, December 17th, 1857.

The following address of Sir Colin Campbell to the Punjaub Cavalry will show the estimation in which those gallant troops are held by their veteran Chief. It is dated Camp, Nowgunge, 11th November, 1857:—

"Tell your men, sir, I remember them when, five years ago, they importance by selections from official and other communications, illustrating at once the political requirements and capabilities and the commercial resources of the valley of the Indus.

served under me at Eusufzye. I saw then what admirable soldiers they were; and though, since then, I have travelled over many countries, seen many armies, and fought in many battles, I have never had occasion to change the opinion I formed of them then, viz., that finer Light Cavalry could not be found. I have mixed since then in many military circles, and wherever I have been I have spoken of them, and had my opinion confirmed by every one, for the Punjaub Cavalry I found had been heard of everywhere. What I admire of them is, that intrepidity that makes them go at their enemy wherever they see them, regardless of numbers. It is not the common pluck that most soldiers have, but that intrepidity, sir, that wins one's admiration. I do not say this to flatter them, for when I formed my opinion of them I never expected to return to this country; but now I have returned, I find that they have turned out to be what I always thought them, and beyond that. Through the whole of these trying times, when nearly all the native army has mutinied, they have shown the greatest loyalty, as well as zeal and courage. I shall take care that the Government know of their services, and that they shall not go unrewarded. Tell them that I have spoken before to her Majesty the Queen of England about them. I shall let her Majesty and the people of England know of their loyalty and courage. Her Majesty will be proud at having such subjects, and England also will rejoice at their conduct."

CHAPTER II.

THE INDUS VALLEY AS A MILITARY HIGHWAY.

THE INDUS AS A BARRIER AGAINST INVASION.—M. FERRIER ON THE PRACTICABLE ROUTES FROM THE CASPIAN TO THE INDUS.—THE MOVEMENTS OF RUSSIA.—PRINCE BARIATINSKI.—PROJECTED RUSSIAN RAILWAYS.—MR. BARTLE FRERE ON THE INDUS AS A DEFENCE.—SIR JUSTIN SHEIL ON THE INVASION OF INDIA BY RUSSIA.—LORD DALHOUSIE ON IMPROVED TRANSIT BY THE INDUS.

Though the importance of improving the inland communications of India, as a means of defence against invasion, has long been recognised, the full value of such improvements, in the event of internal disorder or mutiny, has not, until late, been so fully appreciated. To say that the late mutiny would have been crushed before it assumed its gigantic proportions, had the proposed railways in India been completed, is to underrate their effect. Had the steam communication from Calcutta to Delhi, and that from Kurrachee to Lahore, been connected by the indispensable portion between the capital of the Punjaub and Delhi, the knowledge that European troops could be poured in on all sides with vigour and promptitude, instead of finding their way up, after months of exhausting marches, *would have prevented the outbreak.* "What a glorious thing it would have been," said a writer in the 'Lahore Chronicle' of August last, "had the Euphrates Valley Railway and the Scinde and Punjaub Railway been accomplished facts at the time of the present insurrection. How it would have 'astonished the Natives' to have seen a gallant British army landed at Lahore, within a month of the outbreak taking place! And yet such a thing would have been possible, supposing the Electric Telegraph to have been also completed so as to establish an electric messenger between the Indus and the Thames." The immediateness of the danger in this case has at last fully opened our eyes to the important part good roads and speedy transit play in the government of kingdoms. But though the danger from invasion is more distant, is it after all less certain? The minute and accurate information on the available military routes between the Caspian and the Indus, furnished by M. Ferrier, sets the possibility of the invasion at rest; and no one who knows what Russian perseverance is, can doubt that she will never cease trying to carry out that policy to which she has been pledged for centuries. Without any apology for its length, I proceed to quote M. Ferrier's conclusions on the much-mooted point —the invasion of India.

"The difficulties attending an invasion of British India by a Russo-Persian army, or Russian only, are, without doubt, serious; but they may be said to exist far more in the character of the people of Afghanistan and the Tartar states than in the scantiness of the resources of the countries through which the expedition would be obliged to pass—their poverty and the difficulties of the ground have been greatly exaggerated. The statements of Macdonald Kinnear and Sir Alexander Burnes have, it is true, generally served as the basis upon which public opinion has been formed. Both one and the other have taken pains to bring these difficulties very prominently forward, and this with considerable tact, though it must be admitted that Burnes only saw that road which presented the most unpromising features. Nevertheless, his manuscript, which was for several years in my possession, in some things contradicted that which he printed; and he admitted in it, as I now do, the possibility of marching an invading army across the deserts and steppes of Turkistan and Afghanistan. This was not likely to escape his superior intellect; but it would not be easily accomplished, however possible, at several points. Let me add, however, that the English have a chance of victoriously repulsing the attack, although to obtain this success, incessant vigilance is imperatively necessary, and an European war might endanger the whole question. In the meanwhile the Russians have not abandoned the long-cherished plan of extending their conquests in Southern Asia; and they seek to advance more and more every day towards the Oxus and Khiva.

"The various military expeditions which they have organised having failed from privations and the effects of climate, they have for the last seven or eight years adopted a system, once that of the Roman tacticians,—namely, to proceed but little at a time, slowly and surely. After having descended the course of the Oural to the Caspian Sea, they reached the mouth of the Embah, situated a little lower down to the south-east, and ascended that river to the point at which, turning south, it approaches the Aral Sea. Here they have established a military colony, and dug wells at short distances in the desert, between the Embah and the sea; they have also placed around these wells settlements of Cossacks, who cultivate the soil in the neighbourhood, and create resources which never existed before; so that in a few years an army will be able to obtain sufficient food and forage in all their encampments, and will reach the Aral without serious difficulty. Two other lines of wells have been also dug by the Russians; one on leaving the river Ourloo Irghiz, tending towards the northern end of the Aral Sea; the other commences from two points, Ming-kishlak and Dash Killeh, on the eastern shore of the Caspian, which unite in one line half-way, and is thence laid down in the direction of Khiva.

"By means of these chains of posts the Russians intend to advance to that town and the Oxus, and when they shall have reached that point, it will be impossible to say where they will stop. The possession of that river is of as much importance to them as that of the Indus is to the English; it is the artery which vivifies the territories of the great Tartar hordes through which it flows, who are otherwise unapproachable on all sides by reason of the steppes and deserts of shifting sand. Once masters of this river it would be easy for the Russians to subjugate the tribes on its banks, from the Aral to Badakshan. The Russian army could readily ascend the Oxus in the boats of the country, within two parasangs of Balkh, where it first ceases to be navigable. Burnes is on this subject a competent authority, and the following is a passage from his work, very much to the point:—

"'Facilities in the navigation of a river rest much on the supplies of the country through which it flows; in particular of the nature and quality of wood which is there procurable. The number of boats on the Oxus is certainly small, since they do not amount to two hundred, but there is every facility for building a fleet, the supply of wood being abundant, and fortunately found in single trees along the valley of the river, and not growing in forests in any particular spot. There are no cedar or pine trees brought down by the inundation, which I hold as conclusive proof that the mountains from which the Oxus and its tributaries flow are destitute of that wood. The only other trees which I saw on the river were mulberry and white poplar, which last is floated down in quantities from Hissar to Charjooee, and applied to purposes of house-building. In any increase of the tonnage on this river the immediate resources of the neighbouring country must therefore be called into action, but these are highly important. The nature of the build in the boats of the river requires no skill in naval architecture; the wood is not sawed, and it does not require seasoning, so that the utmost dispatch might be used at all times in forming a flotilla, whether it were desired to navigate, cross, or bridge it. I believe that one hundred and fifty men might be embarked on a boat of the size which I have described. The river could only be bridged by boats, for the wood is too small for an application of it in any other way; and furze and tamarisk which grow on its banks would supply the place of planks, and make it at once complete and practicable. . .

" 'The advantages of the Oxus both in a political and commercial point of view must then be regarded as very great: the many facilities which have been enumerated point it out either as the channel of merchandise or the route of a military expedition; nor is it from the features of the river itself that we form such a conclusion. It is to be remembered that its banks are peopled and cultivated; it must therefore be viewed as a navigable river, possessing great facilities for improving the extent of that navigation. This is a fact of great political and commercial importance, whether a hostile nation may turn it to the gratification of ambition, or a friendly power here seek the extension and improvement of its trade. In either case the Oxus presents many fair prospects, since it holds the most direct course, and connects, with the exception of a narrow desert, the nations of Europe with the remote regions of Central Asia.'

"Burnes might have added that water carriage was not in this country the only available means of transporting an army, and that in following the course of the river by and with its *matériel*, it would also be ready to meet an attack, and avoid many inconveniences. A Russian army might thus direct its march as it thought fit either to Khulm, or withdrawing from the river on its arrival at Charjooee, reach Merv by the desert, and marching along the fertile and populous banks of the Moorghab gain Herat. There would not be any obstacle of a serious nature to stop an army on its way to the river, and the desert situated between it and Merv offers no difficulties that cannot be surmounted; the Khans of Khiva and the Emirs of Bokhara have sufficiently proved this in their almost annual expeditions to seize upon Merv, some of which have been made at the head of ten to twelve thousand horse. Would they have exposed themselves to the dangers mentioned by Burnes, if they had been of his opinion?

"Wherever it was impossible to skirt the Oxus the army might without inconvenience keep five or six parasangs from the river on either side, for here they would be sure to find enough water for the troops in the numerous wells dug by the shepherds for the use of their flocks; similar wells might also be made with little labour, and in a very short time; water is generally found at a depth of nine or twelve feet, and the soil is of a silicious nature, easy to work, but it must be supported by planks or wattles. Brushwood or brambles for fuel are readily met with, and in the winter and spring the steppes are covered with sufficient herbage to meet the requirements of an army. I mention these facts in reply to the opiniated arguments of some persons, who affirm that nothing is to be found in these deserts except sand, and if this were so the obstacles would not even then be insurmountable. The Russians themselves are well aware how and where they can obtain supplies. The following quotation from Mouraviev's work is evidence on this head :—'In our days, with the knowledge we have of these countries, the success of such an enterprise is certain. A corps of three thousand Russians, under a resolute and disinterested leader, could subdue and keep this country, so necessary to Russia by reason of her commercial relations with the East. . . . Even at Khiva we augment our force by the addition of the three thousand Russians who are in slavery there, and the thirty thousand Persians who suffer with the same impatience as the Russians the miseries which they are obliged to support. . . . As to supplies, where are they to be obtained? At Khiva itself, where they are in abundance.'

"Thus the Russians, as well as the English, admit the resources of this country, and yet the latter like to indulge the illusion that it is impossible for the former to cross the deserts of Tartary to get at them. They ought, however, to be well persuaded that when the Russians have made up their minds to attack India, *these* obstacles will not stop them; and, besides, their adversaries calculate upon avoiding them by interesting Persia in their enterprise; an expeditionary corps embarked at Badkooh and Astrakan would then land in perfect security south of the Caspian, and proceed to concentrate itself at Astrabad; Khorassan, which the Russian army would in consequence have to cross, is a fertile and populous country, and it would find a welcome everywhere if strict discipline was observed. As far as Kandahar the difficulties would be no greater for them than for the English, who would have to advance beyond it to dispute the ground with them. With few exceptions, the Russo-Persian army might always march through plains in which they would find water, food, and fuel; but if it was found more desirable not to draw the supplies for the whole army from one district only, they might march in three columns through this province.

"The first, to the north, on leaving Astrabad would follow the course of the Goorghan, cross the territory of the Kurdish colonies at Boojnoord and Koochan, and thence to that of the Seraks, and strike the Heri-rood at the spot where it loses itself in the steppes, following its banks up to Herat, through a well-cultivated country.

"The second column would direct its march to the south on Shah-rood Bostan; there it would be formed into two divisions; the first would follow the direct road by Sebzevar, Nishapoor, Meshed, and Kussan; the second would keep more to the right by Turshiz, Khaf, and Gorian, and the whole army uniting at one point by the routes we have indicated, would concentrate itself at Herat, where provisions of every kind abound or could be obtained from the rich districts of Meimana, Kaleh-now, and Obeh, &c.; here it might winter before advancing southward. The fortifications of this city should then be put into an efficient state, and the place properly provisioned and supplied with all kinds of military stores. Its central position within a line of fortresses, commencing at Balkh on the north, and passing by Akhcheh, Andekhooye, Shibberghan, Meimana, Kaleh-now, Sebzevar, Ferrah, and Laush Jowaine, renders Herat a particularly suitable point for this concentration.

"A glance at the map will clearly show that, adopting the routes I have mentioned, all the districts of Khorassan, and even some of Irak, such as Damghan and Tubbus, would contribute materially to supply the army. It would of course, be necessary for the Russians to form their magazines beforehand; the Shah of Persia never troubled himself much on the subject, and yet he has frequently marched an army of from thirty to forty thousand men into Khorassan, and always found the means of feeding them by simply making a decree for a tax in kind. When they hear the Shah is coming, the peasants expect these extortions, as well as being pillaged by the troops, who strip them of all they have; and yet they never try to evade them. On the great lines of communication the Shah's troops are never short of provisions. If the Persian peasant submits to this imposition so quietly, what might he not do from the Russians, who would pay punctually for what they took? If their army were to reach Kandahar by way of Jaberan, Giran, Bakooa, Washir, and Girishk, the road usually taken by the caravans, the end of winter or the commencement of spring would be the most propitious time for them to leave Herat; water would be then everywhere plentiful in the steppes, the temperature mild and the air pure, and supplies could be drawn from Meimana, Kaleh-now, Shibberghan, and Andekhooye on the north, if those of Neh-bindan, Ghain, and Birjan, &c., on the south did not suffice. The certainty of a trifling profit would bring the people to the camp with their productions; they take them without as good a chance to that of Yar Monamed's, and they would eagerly seek that security for themselves and their property which they could never hope to obtain from the native rulers of their country.

"If unforeseen circumstances should not permit the army

to move from Herat at the proper moment, the springs and streams would be dry on the road designated above; it would then have to lean more to its right by Sebzevar, and follow the Haroot-road, the Helmund, and the Urghend-ab, which leads up to Kandahar. The army could be easily subsisted in these districts. From the last-mentioned city to Shikarpoor they would have to traverse some desert steppes and get through the Bolan Pass, but these ought not, I should think, to be serious difficulties, though I had no opportunity of judging of them myself. The victorious march of the English army upon Kandahar, in 1839, is a sufficient proof of this; they had to ascend the pass, the Russian army would merely have to descend it. The English consider, and with reason, the Indus their best line of defence on that side of their Indian possessions, but would it stop the enemy? It may be permitted to doubt that fact, nay, almost to prove a negative to the question. When the Russians had reached this river, it would, if not impossible, be at any rate very difficult to prevent them from crossing it. The attention of military men has been directed to two points, which alone offer the necessary facilities for the passage of an army—Attok to the north, and Bukkar to the south; if this be so, it would be sufficient to erect *têtes-de-pont* and other important fortifications at both these places.

"But the Russians are as well aware as the English of the possibility of crossing the Indus at other eligible spots, and this in spite of the rapid current, the great width, and the precipitous banks of that stream. A pontoon train would not be required; with a few mule-loads of empty *mesek* skins, adapted to the purpose, a sufficient number of rafts might be constructed in twenty-four hours, and the whole army transported to the left bank. The points where such a passage might be effected are not rare, for there is ample choice on a length of upwards of two hundred miles. Two at once suggest themselves. One of these is to the south of Attok, on the line of road from Ghuznee and Kandahar,—namely, by the pass of Dera Ismael Khan, from whence Moultan could be gained; but there would be a disadvantage in choosing this route, inasmuch as after the Russians had crossed the Indus, they would also have to cross the rivers of the Punjaub; it would therefore be much better to take the Indus below their confluence with it by the pass of Dereh Ghazee Khan, from whence they would descend into Scinde and Guzerat, and raise the discontented populations of those conquered provinces, who would eagerly seize the opportunity to revolt—and this with the secret determination of subsequently getting rid of their new allies also. Before undertaking such an enterprise, it would of course be very desirable that Russia should be in possession of Khiva, Bokhara and Balkh; but it would not be necessary, as several writers have declared, to exterminate the Tartars before they could reach the Indus; their neutrality, which might be obtained, would be all that the Russians would require. If the neutrality were not observed, two small Persian divisions, posted at Surraks and on the banks of the Moorghab, would hold them in check."*

That Russia is always preparing for the realization of the darling object of her policy, cannot be doubted. Whatever benefits we may have gained by the late Persian war, Russia has gained far more, and has taken advantage

* Caravan Journeys in Persia, Afghanistan, &c., by J. P. Ferrier, pp. 457—464.

of the fears of the Shah to improve her position in the Caspian, and her communications with the Sea of Aral. The fact of the Russian territory lying so close to the capital of Persia, whilst our attacks can only take place on sea-board of the Persian Gulf, naturally gives additional influence to Russia at the Court of Teheran. Hence, too, the different mode by which she acts from us. During the late war with Persia, according to the *Augsburger Allgemeine Zeitung*, the greatest activity prevailed along the banks of the Caspian Sea. Transports and steamers were incessantly conveying troops or stores between Astracan, Schondrakow, Bakinks and Astrabad. It was not long since that Prince Bariatinski repaired to Tiflis, the seat of his government, from Astrachan to Fort Petrowski by water, and on this occasion inspected all the fortified places along the coast. Attached to his head-quarters and staff there is a special division entitled the '*Du-jour* Service of Marine,' consisting of a vice-admiral and several naval officers, and having under its concentrated command the flotilla in the Caspian Sea, the cruisers on the east coast of the Black Sea, and the rowboat flotilla of the Cossacks of the Sea of Azoff. It must also not be lost sight of, that not long back there was a Governor-general appointed to Kutais, also under the supreme command of Bariatinski, who has likewise under him Chruleff's army of observation on the Turkish Caucasian frontier and the troops occupying the Caucausus under Bebutoff. This extended, and, at the same time, concentrated command, vested in the hands of Prince Bariatinski, points very distinctly to preparations having been made with reference to the late critical state of matters in and connected with Persia.

Commenting on these facts, the *Warsaw Journal* of that day contrasted the secret system of Russia, with the ostentation and noise of our movements.

" While England, said the writer, with much noise and ostentation, prepares an expedition against Persia, Russia, unostentatiously and noiselessly, is getting ready to come to the succour of the Shah. The Orenburg *corps d'armee* has been considerably reinforced. It is commanded by Aide-de-Camp-General Peroffski. The outposts of this corps extend to the very limits of the country of Turan, upon the rivers Oxus and Jaxartes; and the military flotilla of the Lake of Aral, placed under the orders of the same general, is brought by the above-mentioned rivers to the frontiers of India. On another side, great activity reigns upon the Caspian Sea and in the army of the Caucasus. Transport vessels, having troops and war *matériel* on board, pass incessantly between Astrakhan and the port of Bakou, situated in the province of Shirvan, bordering on the Caspian Sea, belonging to Russia, and at the frontier of Persia. The new Lieutenant-General of the Caucasian provinces, Prince Bariatinski, has received fuller powers than his predecessors. He has lately inspected, on its way to its destination, the flotilla of the Caspian Sea, which has been considerably increased and partly left at his disposal. This flotilla can easily take troops on board either of the corps of Orenburg or the army of the Caucasus, and take them to the relief of Persia, disembarking either at Astrabad or upon the neighbouring coast of Teheran. The corps which forms part of the army of the Caucasus, cantoned at Shirvan and Erivan, and commanded by General Khruleff, who distinguished himself in the Eastern war, can also succour Persia by land as well as by sea.

Meanwhile the Russian Government neglects nothing in replacing the war *matériel* consumed during the late war, and continues to refill the exhausted magazines."*

The lately-projected Russian railways, however speciously put forward as new commercial roads, are only another step in the direction of the future invasion of India. Their influence, when completed, will, no doubt, be as commercially injurious to the interests of our merchants, as strategically dangerous to our supremacy in the East. The commercial effect of the proposed Russian railway system is fully discussed by Count de Gerebtzoff, a relation of Count Orloff's, in his late remarkable volume, "The Three Questions of the Moment." In discussing the second of these questions—Russian railways—the other two being free trade and communism, he endeavours to show that the construction of these lines will destroy the English monopoly of the trade with India, by opening up new channels of intercourse with *Persia, Central Asia, Afghanistan,* and *the North of India,* of which all Europe will take advantage ! ! ! At present, he observes, Asia is supplied with European Goods entirely by way of *Bombay* and *Calcutta.* Merchandise is transported from those English ports on camels' backs to Kandahar, Cashmere, Cabul and Afghanistan, at great expense and with much delay. Having to pass through many English possessions, no merchant other than an Englishman would undertake such a trade. The two routes to India, by the *Red Sea* and the *Cape of Good Hope,* are both practically in the almost exclusive possession of England ;—that of the Red Sea on account of the English fortress of *Aden ;* and that by the Cape, because every re-victualling port on the line is in

* The Warsaw journal, the Czas, of the 30th November, 1856..

the power of the English. He therefore arrives at the conclusion, that no European power, England excepted, has any direct trade with India. Count Gerebtzoff goes on to say, that in two or three years at farthest, when the line from Moscow to Nijni-Novgorod shall be finished, goods for Afghanistan may be sent direct from *Paris* to *Tach Kend,* at the door of Central Asia, in *twenty days!*

This is the route :—

	Days.
From Paris to the banks of the Volga	6
Thence by steamer to Astrakhan	4
Thence to the eastern coast of the Caspian Sea .	2
From the Caspian to the Sea of Aral, by rail . .	2
Thence by steamer to Tach Kend, less than . .	5
	19

The Russian government intends to unite the Caspian Sea with the Sea of Aral by a railway, 300 kilometres long, to be made across a perfectly flat country, flanked by wooded hills. This distance will be traversed in *two* days. The railway will abut upon *Syr Daria* at *Bainsk,* whence a steamer will tow the goods, in *less than five* days, to *Tach Kend.* Thence they will be forwarded by caravan routes to *Kandahar, Cashmere, Bokhara, Thibet, Cabul,* and *Afghanistan.* With regard to the trade with Persia, inasmuch as a steamer takes only *two days* to go from *Astrakhan to Astrabad,* it will be possible to send a bale of goods from *Paris* into *Persia* in *twelve* days; and from Astrabad there are caravan roads to the interior of Persia and all the *western* parts of *Central Asia.*

This route, the writer contends, would be as cheap as that by Bombay and Calcutta, while it would be much more expeditious; and by it, France, Germany, Belgium and Switzerland, would necessarily be led to compete with England in the eastern trade.*

Where a cargo of goods will pass, a batallion of men can follow; and all the more easily and effectively will troops be concentrated against our north-western frontier when masked under commercial movements. Most important therefore, in a strategic view, is every proposal to facilitate communication throughout the valley of the Indus, and to enable us to concentrate troops on any point that is threatened, or, if need be, to move in force to either of the two great Passes—the Bolan and the Khyber. Should, however, one of these be closed to our forces, they could be moved with rapidity to the other, and in either case the enemy would be taken in flank or rear.

In support of these views, I would refer to the following extract from the speech of Mr. Frere, Commissioner in Scinde, at the meeting of the Scinde Railway Company in February 1857. "Mr. Andrew," said that gentleman, "had adverted to the military and political importance of the line. For his own part, he (Mr. Frere) did not think it was possible to overrate its importance. They had just escaped the 'war ninepence,' and no doubt if the war with Persia had been destined to continue, the immense value of this undertaking, and those with which it was in connection, would have been singularly demonstrated. The practical value of the railway was to increase the available power of every ship, and of every man employed in military and naval operations. In reference to the Punjaub, the capacity of moving troops to a given point was of immense importance. If they looked at the map, they would see that they had a mountainous range, between which and our possessions the Indus formed a natural boundary, and the

* Bell's Weekly Messenger, July 18th, 1857.

Company proposed to make a line along its level plains. In a military point of view, the advantage would be this, that if the Khyber Pass should be closed to our forces, they could be moved with rapidity to the Bolan Pass, and in either case the enemy would be taken in flank or in rear. In the meantime, the Euphrates Valley Railway would give them the command of the sea board of the Persian Gulf, and not only this, but the completion of that railway would practically make Chatham nearer to the point of action in the Persian territory, than any military force that could be brought to bear upon it from Central Asia."

The same views had been powerfully advocated in 1856 by the author of "Our North-west Frontier," in the following passages:—

"It appears, then, that the means at our disposal for permanent success are not to be found in the Persian Gulf. And that, if we are to meet the coming struggle in the manner of statesmen entrusted with the destinies of the East, we must leave all petty aggression, all petty retaliation, and permit no power on earth to swerve us from the sole disposition that can and will secure, what is, in truth, the one and *sufficient object* of this, on our part, grand defensive war. We must, that is, at once and for ever, secure the North-Western Frontier of our Indian Empire. Unless all measures contribute, and are subordinated to this great line of defence, they can be no more than palliatives, increasing in cost, as the evil to be palliated approaches. But immediately the mind grasps the question in all its bearings, and, discarding all small measures and aggressive expeditions, realizes distinctly, that the object in view is not of an aggressive, but of a defensive nature, then it arrives at the just conclusion, that our preparations should be made at the gates of India, at the Passes of the Bolan and the Khyber. Establish a sufficiently large military body at some point immediately above the Bolan Pass, and a second at Peshawur; confide our diplomatic relations along the entire frontier to one good and able man, and then, mark what would be the result. The gates themselves would be closed and defended; friendly relations would be gradually extended throughout Afghanistan; that vast tract of country which lies between our frontier and the present position of the Persian army, along the line of Herat, would become our shield. Without assuming direct military control of the Afghan and Belooche Irregulars, we might so leaven their mass as to render them a most formidable host of light troops, or Eastern Cossacks, and capable of destroying in detail, by force or famine, among their own mountain passes, any army that could be advanced from the westward.

"Or should the invaders attempt to approach the head of the Khyber, the force at the head of the Bolan would quickly operate upon its flanks and rear, by a march along a line shorter, and capable of being rendered easier, than that from Herat to the Khyber. The invaders' supplies would be wholly cut off, and it would experience a fate similar to that endured by our own army in the same hostile tract.

"But should the invaders reach the head of the Bolan itself, they would fall under our force then established at the entrance of the Pass, holding free communication with the plain of the Indus, and capable of being easily and rapidly reinforced to any required extent. Such a position for an invading army would inevitably end in its absolute destruction. It could not possibly advance. Its supplies and communications would be cut off by the tribes in its rear. Not a man could stray a mile from its camp and live. It must either be starved as it stood, or it must retreat; but to do the latter would be to have the entire Afghan population down upon its flanks, and to have our own force close upon its rear. Those who remember the position of Napoleon's army at the fortress of Bourg, and can imagine to themselves what that position would have resulted in, had the fortress been really impassable—had the Austrian main body been close behind it, and had Napoleon's own supplies and communications been absolutely cut off by hostile mountaineers,—those may picture to themselves the dilemma of a Russo-Persic force at the head of the Bolan when wise precautions should have been taken by us, for rendering that head what it might and ought to become." *

Regarding the insidious movements of Russia towards the East, that eminent authority, Sir Justin Sheil, late British Ambassador at the Court of Tehran, makes the following pregnant and suggestive remarks in notes appended to Lady Sheil's recent and interesting volume, "Life and Manners in Persia."

"The Caspian Sea washes the coasts of the Persian provinces of Talish, Geelan, Mazenderan, Asterabad, and Persian Toorkomania. The inhabitants of these spacious territories carry on an extensive commerce, in part with the Persian ports on that sea, in part with the Russian districts on its northern and western shores. With a far-seeing policy, which anticipates all the possibilities of futurity, when Persia was gasping almost in the last throes, Russia humbled her to the dust, by forcing on her the renewal of a stipulation contracted at the treaty of Goolistan, by which she bound herself not to maintain

* *Vide* "Strength of Frontier Clans." Appendix E.

any vessel of war in the Caspian Sea. Upwards of a hundred years ago, an Englishman named Elton, a man of wonderful ability and resource, who had been brought up to a seafaring life, and who had previously been an officer in the Russian navy, was in the service of the Shah (Nadir), and not only commanded his naval forces in the Caspian Sea, but built ships for him on European models. The most unnautical nation in the world, with an Englishman as their leader, became dominant on the Caspian; and, as the author of the 'Progress of Russia in the East' says, '*forced the Russians to lower their flag,*' and the banner with the open hand* floated triumphantly through the length and breadth of the Caspian. To preclude a revival of this discomfiture, Persia was forced to sign her degradation, and the Caspian became a Russian lake. When the Czar rendered Persia powerless on this inland sea, he was heedless of the fact that the Toorkoman pirates of the eastern coast near the Goorgan and the Atrek were accustomed to make descents in their boats on the Persian shores, to kidnap the inhabitants and carry them into slavery. True, he was ready to make compensation, by sending his own vessels of war to 'protect' the Persian coast from depredation; but the real meaning of imperial protection is not unknown in Persia, and for a long time this proffer was regarded in the light of the Persian fable of the frog who invited the snake to guard his dwelling. Unfortunately an event occurred several years afterwards which placed them in the poor frog's predicament, and which, though not strictly bearing on the treaty of Toor-

* "The banner of Persia is surmounted by an open hand, of which the five fingers are said to express Mahommed, Ali, Fatma, Hassan, and Hoossein."

koman Chaee, as it refers to the Caspian, may be introduced here.

"The small sandy island of Ashoorada is situated in the gulf or bay of Asterabad, about twelve miles from the coast nearest to that city, which is twenty miles from the sea. In size it is about a mile and a half in length, and less than a mile in width. The water is deep in its vicinity; and its lee affords a secure shelter in a gale from any direction. Hitherto it has been uninhabited. Twelve or thirteen years ago it fell into the hands of Russia, by one of those protective processes of which we have lately heard so much. Its advantages as a naval station had not escaped the observation and cupidity of Russia. It commands the entrance to the bay, menaces that portion of the coast inhabited by the Yemoot Toorkomans, and intercepts the commerce with Mazenderan, on which the stationary tribes of that race chiefly depend for subsistence. The island possesses sources of sweet spring-water, together with a climate remarkable on that coast for its salubrity. The inner side has sufficient depth of water to float a brig-of-war, within a few yards of the beach. These are some of the inducements which led to the occupation of this spot of Persian territory by the Russian government, which act was perpetrated in 1841, immediately after the catastrophe of Cabul became known. At that time Persia was ruled by Mahommed Shah, a monarch of whose wisdom much cannot be said. He had for minister a man who was half mad and whole Russian. He was a native of Erivan, in Russia, and often proclaimed himself to be a subject of that empire. This was the notorious Hajee Meerza Aghassee, who, from tutor to the royal family, was raised at once to the vezeership. Russia was asked to lend Persia for a short time one or two small ships of war, to hold in check the Toorkomans residing between Asterabad and the Toorkoman settlement of Hassan Koolee, at the mouth of the Atrek. With the most amiable and neighbourly cordiality she replied that she would save Persia all trouble, and come herself to chastise the marauders. Two vessels of war forthwith appeared, and soon after established themselves at Ashoorada, from whence they have never since moved. Complaint and remonstrance were met by countercharges of ingratitude, and by indignant expostulation at this offensive display of distrust. It is not surprising that there should be a reluctance to depart. The position is a good one; for, besides overawing the Toorkomans, it also controls Mazenderan. The most complete possession has been taken of the island. It is covered with residences, hospitals, barracks; and soil has been conveyed to it for the construction of gardens. In short, there is every evidence of permanent occupation and retention.

"The sea-going Toorkomans have been brought under complete control. Some have been sent to Siberia, or to Russia Proper. Not a boat is allowed to move without a passport, under heavy penalties, and even Persian boats are under the same restriction; this, too, on the coast of their own sea! Since the occupation of the island a consul has been placed at Asterabad, so that, with the consul on one side and the commodore on the other, Mazenderan also is on a hopeful road to protection.

"True, the incursions of the Toorkomans have nearly ceased. But the Persians say, and with justice, that an occasional chepawool of these pirates was less irksome than the presence and interference of the consul and commodore.

"No attempt has yet succeeded for forming an establishment on the mainland among the Toorkomans. When the day for that arrives, the Goorgan will doubtless receive a preference. Its banks are on the highroad to Meshed, and are covered with the richest pastures; and the climate and the soil are suited for the production of abundant harvests of corn. No fitter spot could be found for subsisting an army, or for being made the basis of a plan of military operations to the East.

"The naval strength of Russia in the Caspian is not easily ascertained with correctness. It is believed to amount to four or five small steamers and a few brigs and schooners of war, the largest not carrying more than eighteen guns; but her supremacy is as complete as that of England in the Irish Channel."

"For more than a century Russia has been aiming at the possession of Khiva. Twice she has failed in attaining her object by force, by open force. The next attempt will probably secure the prize. Dissension at Khiva, steamers on the Aral and at the mouth of the Oxus, a fortress at the Jaxartes, invite an attempt and promise success.

"England has some concern with the establishment of Russia in this principality. There she would be inexpugnable. She is within two hundred miles of the Caspian, a space which, to minds accustomed to the vast distances of Asia, is as nothing. A Persian soldier thinks little of a march of one thousand miles from Azerbijan to Khorassan. Master of Khiva, the Russian government becomes supreme over the Toorkomans, and will find no insurmountable difficulty in establishing through the intervening level tract a permanent and available communication with the Caspian Sea The noble river Oxus, navigable to within a hundred miles of Hindoo Koosh, becomes Russian, and is covered with Russian steamers. At his choice the Emperor can fix the boundary of his empire on that river, for who is there to gainsay him? Khoolloom and Koondooz will doubtless then become the limits of the Russian dominions. The trade between India and those countries, now free and uncontrolled on the payment of not immoderate duties, falls then under the despotic rule of that government, and becomes subject to its protective and selfish commercial restrictions. Her near neighbourhood is not likely to strengthen our position in North-western India. And yet it seems impossible to avert these evils, or to prevent the downfall of Khiva, or its eventual occupation by Russia. Can nothing, however, be done to save the Oxus, to save at least the portion approximating to Afghanistan?"

"Without undertaking to decide the large question at issue (the invasion of India by Russia), I shall assume the feasibility of invasion to be established, and merely observe that now more than ever should we be on the watch, for the Russian and Indian dominions are twelve hundred miles nearer to each other than when the invasion of Afghanistan took place. Excluded from prosecuting her ambitious objects in other quarters, revenge, the desire of retrieving her prestige, all conspire to urge Russia to the East. She will await the favourable moment in patience, moving forward in the mean while by the wiles she is reputed to understand so well. On this occasion she has been opposed by four combatants; next time these conditions may be reversed. Let it not be forgotten that, when her railroads to Odessa and to Vladikafkaz are completed, her strength, particularly towards the East, will be doubled."

"Jonas Hanway says, 'the situation of Candahar renders it a strong barrier between the empires of Persia and India.'

"The town of Candahar commands the three roads to India: that by Cabul, by Shikarpoor, and the sterile routes across the Suleina range to Dera Ismaël Khan and Dera Ghazee Khan, on the Indus.*

"The above city is situated in the most fertile part of Afghanistan, in plains abounding with wheat, barley, and other grains. Here it is practicable to provide for the subsistence of an army during a certain time. It should be our care to secure these resources from being available to an enemy."

"The distance between Candahar and our outposts does not exceed 200 miles.† If the abandonment of this position is deserving of regret, its resumption should form an object of early effort. Established here, we may almost set invasion at defiance. A Gumri, a Sebastopol, in this spot makes us paramount, for it will be an announcement to all the world that the determination to remain is irrevocable."

"Our taking up a formidable position at Candahar will go far to deter even speculation on the chances of invasion.

"The cost of the plan offered for consideration, and the drain on the already encumbered resources of India, deserve reflection. Yet present expenditure is often real economy,

* "There is a mountain road from Herat to Cabul, but it is described to be impassable for guns, and to be through a thinly-inhabited country, consequently to be deficient in food."

† "It is assumed that Dader and Kelat are our frontier stations."

of which the war we are now waging is a notable example. It seems to be a national vice to prefer the most lavish outlay in prospect to present moderate disbursement. Whatever tends to avert an attempt to wrest India from our hands, and prevent the enormous consequent expenditure, is economy."

"Russia may be said to have already announced that she is even now preparing for her next encounter with Great Britain. Her railways have no other end than to transport troops. She found that in the last struggle her weakness lay in the impossibility of collecting her forces at the proper moment on the distant points of her empire. This weakness she has intimated shall disappear. But we, too, will not remain idle. Our railways in India will advance as well as those of Russia. Established and prepared in Candahar, *with a railway running the whole length of the left bank of the Indus, we may await any attempt in calmness.* The Russian grenadier now knows his inferiority to the English soldier. The Cossack will find a match in the Hindostanee horseman."*

Lord Dalhousie saw the importance of the route by the Indus, and in his Minutes on Railways in India, of April, 1853, he said :—

"I attach no great value to the connexion by railway of the several capitals and seats of government, considered merely as such. But it appears to be of the first importance to connect the several Presidencies by a line of rail, each with the other, and to unite Hindostan and the

* Glimpses of Life and Manners in Persia, by Lady Sheil. With Notes on Russia, Koords, Toorkomans, Nestorians, Khiva, and Persia. John Murray, Albemarle Street. 1856.

districts to the north-west with the western ports in the Peninsula.

"Whatever strength there may be in the arguments by which a general line through Hindostan has been urged on political grounds, they bear as strongly in favour of a junction line with the Presidency of Bombay. The military power of the government of India would be incalculably advanced thereby. The Presidency of Bombay may be said to have no foreign frontier, except in Scinde.

"*Heretofore, and until very recently, every recruit that joined his corps from England—every invalid that was sent back shattered to his home, was obliged to travel the long, slow, weary track to Calcutta, however distant the station at which he was placed. Within the last two years, the establishment of steam communication regularly on the Indus has enabled the Government greatly to lessen this evil. The dispatch of recruits by Bombay to Kurrachee for that large portion of the Bengal army that is stationed to the westward of the Jumna, and the conveyance of the invalids of the same portion of the army from Ferozepore to the sea, have been a vast improvement.* Furthermore, I hope before long, to see the cost of the conveyance of troops to India reduced by still another step, and the time occupied upon the voyage equally curtailed, by obtaining permission to convey them across the Isthmus of Suez.

"When Hindostan is connected by rail to the western coast of India, the conveyance by rail across Egypt will, I venture to hope, remove any objection which might be felt there to the passage of foreign troops; while, if the permission should be granted, a corps might leave England after the heat of summer was over, and might be quartered before Christmas upon the banks of the Sutlej, without any exposure in its way, and with four months before it of the finest climate under the sun; so that the men would enter the first heats of India with constitutions vigorous and unimpaired by the accident of voyage or march."*

More recently, Lord Dalhousie reiterated the above views in another Minute:—

"In the meantime, the channel of the Indus is becoming the great highway between Europe and the north-western provinces of our possessions. Troops arrive and depart from England by that route. Recruits are sent out, and invalids sent home, each year by its stream, thus avoiding the long and weary march which must otherwise be made by Calcutta. Great quantities of heavy stores follow the same course, and passengers in large numbers, now by preference seek a point of departure at Bombay." †

When these remarks were written the only available overland route to India was that by Suez, and the project for re-opening the old channel of communication by the Euphrates was in its infancy. Since then the superiority of the latter route to that by Suez has been admitted, thus giving additional force to the observations of Lord Dalhousie. Having in another volume fully explained the value of this line of Railway, I need only remark here, that, by it, India will be brought a thousand miles nearer to us, and within a journey of fourteen instead of twenty-eight days.

* Minute by the Governor-General of India, dated 28th April, 1853.

† Minute by the Marquis of Dalhousie, 28th February, 1856, reviewing his administration in India.

CHAPTER III.

KURRACHEE.

HARBOUR AND PORT OF KURRACHEE.—OPINIONS OF COMMODORES YOUNG AND RENNIE AND CAPTAIN BALFOUR, I. N.—DEPTH OF WATER ON BAR.—TONNAGE OF SHIPS.—GENERAL JOHN JACOB'S TRADE REPORT.—VALUE OF SEA-BORNE TRADE OF SCINDE.—KURRACHEE, THE EUROPEAN PORT OF INDIA.—THE GATE OF CENTRAL ASIA.—OPINIONS OF MR. J. WALKER. — CAPTAIN C. D. CAMPBELL, I. N.—COLONEL TURNER.—LIEUTENANT LEEDS.—MR. FRERE.—GENERAL PARR.—KURRACHEE, CHIEF SEAT OF TELEGRAPHIC COMMUNICATION BETWEEN EUROPE AND INDIA.

A GOOD port, capable of admitting ships of large burden, and at all hours and seasons, is indispensable to the success of the combined system of rail and river for the valley of the Indus, intended to be carried out by the Scinde and Punjaub Railways, in conjunction with the Indus Flotilla. Such an harbour is to be found in Kurrachee, the most western port of India, and the only land-locked harbour between Bombay and the Persian Gulf. This port is perfectly safe, and easy of access to large ships by day and night, and even during the monsoons. According to Commodore Young, of the Indian navy, who in 1854 took the steam frigate *Queen* twice into Kurrachee in the night time, during the south-west monsoon, though a bar-harbour, Kurrachee has depth of water, even in its existing state, for ships of from 17 to 18 feet draught at the high water of ordinary tides. At high spring tides the depth is from 20 to 21 feet, and at times even to 22½ feet. In this view, Commodore Young is confirmed by Commodore Rennie, of the Indian navy, who, during the preparations for the late expedition to the Persian Gulf, was constantly in and out of the harbour with troops, and became convinced that there was frequently more water on the bar than the port-register showed. As a proof of this, it may be stated, not only that the *Bussorah Merchant*, a large vessel drawing 20 ft. 6 in., passed the bar in May last, when the register showed only 21 ft. water; but that when, on the 5th of September last, the *Hugh Lindsay* went out of the harbour with the *London* in tow, the lead never gave less than 26 ft., though the signal at Manora marked only 21 ft. In the same month the *Ajdaha*, H.E.I.C. steam-frigate, and the *England*, one of Mr. Lindsay's Calcutta line of steam-ships, with the 4th regiment on board, ran up to the landing-place at Keamaree without difficulty. All that such a port requires to make it easily available to ships of heavy burden at all seasons of the year, is a good pilot establishment, a steam-dredge, and some moderate engineering improvements, all of which measures have already been ordered by the East India Company. The list of large ships that passed into the harbour, in 1855 alone, will be found below.*

* During the year 1855 the following ships, among others, entered the harbour of Kurrachee :—

		From London.	Tons.	Draught.
	Dec. 1,	Marion,	684,	18 ft. 6 in.
	Nov. 23,	Norwood,	850,	15 ft. 0 in.
	Oct. 19,	El Dorado,	841,	21 ft. 0 in.
	Sept. 24,	James Gibb,	813,	21 ft. 6 in.
Monsoon months.	Aug. 12,	Marmion,	388,	16 ft. 3 in.
	,, 6,	Kenilworth,	582,	16 ft. 6 in.
	July 30,	Granger,	878,	19 ft. 6 in.
	,, ,,	Sir James,	646,	
	,, 26,	Alex. Wise,	295,	15 ft. 0 in.
	,, 2,	Saxon,	526,	15 ft. 2 in.
	,, ,,	Tamar,	556,	17 ft. 10 in.
	June 30,	Semiramis,		large steamer.
	,, 14,	Agamemnon,	756,	16 ft. 3 in.

Lieut.-Colonel, (now Brigadier-General.) John Jacob, C.B., Officiating Commissioner, reports, under date the

I am indebted to Captain Balfour, I. N., for the following valuable information respecting the capabilities of Kurrachee harbour:—

14, St. James' Square,
1st *August*, 1857.

My dear Sir,

Since I had the pleasure of speaking with you on the subject of Kurrachee harbour, I have met a gentleman thoroughly acquainted with the subject, and one whose opinion is entitled to the fullest weight,—I refer to Commodore Young, I.N., whose name may be known to you as having commanded at the capture of Mohummerah.

Captain Young, when in command of the *Queen* steam frigate, took that vessel twice (in 1854) into Kurrachee harbour in the middle of the night, during the height of the south-west monsoon,—a feat which speaks for itself.

He is decidedly of opinion that it may be entered at night throughout the year, provided that lights are displayed on the buoys indicating the channel. And he would have no hesitation in taking in vessels of a much larger draught than the *Queen*.

In the existing state of the bar, he considers that vessels of from 17 to 18 feet draught may cross it at high water ordinary tides, and of 20 to 21 feet at high water springs: 22½ feet draught is his extreme point. And a ship requiring more than that depth would rarely be taken in by an *amateur* pilot, except on a great emergency, or on an extraordinary high tide during the fine weather season.

With reference, however, to this point, it occurs to me to mention that according to the latest official reports I have met with on the state of the Hooghly, the greatest draught at which even a *steamer* could with safety, and at all seasons, proceed to Calcutta, taking advantage of the springs, is 22½ to 23 feet, and that 24 feet is there the extreme draught, requiring a concurrence of very favourable circumstances.

Captain Young concurs with me in thinking that the first, and by far the most important requirement for Kurrachee harbour, is an efficient pilot establishment. This question came under his cognizance when recently master-attendant at Bombay; and he tells me that a proposal, similar to that I mentioned the other day, viz.,—to select one of the best of the Bombay pilots and send him up with a boat

30th April, 1856, that, during the year 1854-5, 1,086 vessels of the burden of 56,695 tons entered the ports of Scinde inwards; 39 of which, including steamers, were square-

of the most approved form—had, or shortly would receive the sanction of the Bombay Government, and be carried out. The pilot so selected is Mr. Brown, and the salary allotted to him is about the same as that of the seniors of the Bombay pilots, 250 rupees per mensem. With reference to this, it is to be noted, that the Bombay pilots derive very trifling emoluments from gratuities,—the practice is in fact prohibited; but I doubt the wisdom of extending this rule to a new harbour, and above all to a bar-harbour, when a pilot, without inducement to exert himself, can often plead "scant water" or high swell, as an obstacle to running in.

Captain Young informs me, that when he left Bombay in May last, the steam dredges for the bar were nearly ready for launching. He anticipates the most favourable results when they are set to work, and has no doubt, that with their aid and with an efficient pilotage, the harbour will be practicable throughout the year for the largest class of merchant ships.

Believe me,
&c., &c.,
(Signed) W. BALFOUR.

W. P. ANDREW, Esq.,
&c., &c.

P.S. The above statements are made on the supposition, that efficient steam-tug power is available to tow-in sailing ships.

From J. NEVILLE WARREN, Esq., Agent to the Scinde Railway Company, to W. P. ANDREW, Esq., Chairman, Scinde Railway Company.

(EXTRACT.)

KURRACHEE, *28th September*, 1857.

I think it is right to state that your publication of an extract from one of my letters respecting the depth of water on the bar, has excited attention again to that subject. A few days after that extract was seen, several merchant captains went on board the "Hugh Lindsay," while towing a ship out, and they never had soundings rigged, of a burden of 13,841 tons. The number that cleared outwards was 1,103 vessels, burden 58,194 tons, including square-rigged ships and steamers.

The increase of the import and export trade is still continuing, especially in the exports of the staple products of the valley. The steadiness of the rate of increase is not

less than 26 feet. And Captain Darke, of the "Hugh Lindsay," holds and expresses a very strong opinion, that it is impossible to find any high tide throughout the year when soundings would be less than 26 feet in the main channel. It has certainly been very gratifying within the last fortnight to see the "Ajdaha," H.E.I.C. steam frigate, come in and moor at Keamaree (the landing place in Kurrachee harbour). The "England," also one of the Lindsay line of Calcutta steam ships, came in on Friday last with part of the 4th regiment on board, and steamed direct up to Keamaree.

(Signed) J. NEVILLE WARREN,
Agent in India.

W. P. Andrew, Esq.,
&c. &c. &c.

From the "Sind Kossid," of September 8th, 1857.

On Saturday last, several nautical gentlemen had an opportunity of witnessing a complete and satisfactory corroboration of Mr. Warren's opinions, and we feel it our duty to lay the matter before the public.

The sea on that day had little or no swell on, and the wind was moderate. About 10 A.M. the *Hugh Lindsay* steamed out of harbour with the ship *London* in tow. The lead was kept going on board the steamer during the whole of the trip out, and there never was less than 26 feet of water found on the bar, whilst the signal at Munora only gave at first 21 feet! and subsequently 22 feet. The *Hugh Lindsay* took the eastern channel going out and the western one coming in, and in both the depth of water was nearly the same. There were on board the steamer several commanders of merchant vessels, who declared that they had noticed the same discrepancy between the Munora signals and the lead, as was apparent on this occasion.

less remarkable than its large amount, as the following tables show :—

Year	Imports.	Exports.	Total.
	£	£	£
1843-4	121,150	1,010	122,160
1844-5	217,700	9,300	227,000
1845-6	312,900	40,500	353,400
1846-7	293,400	49,300	342,700
1847-8	287,872	154,730	442,600
1848-9	344,715	107,133	451,849
1849-50	419,352	114,378	533,731
1850-51	425,831	196,461	622,293
1851-52	489,220	244,122	733,343
1852-53	535,690	376,337	800,000
1853-54	508,793	376,310	885.103
1854-55	575,196	346,893	922,089
1855-56	629,813	604,440	1,234,253
1856-57	685,665	734,522	1,420,187

VALUE OF STAPLE EXPORTS.

	1847-8.	1851-52.	1852-53.	Increase per cent. in 5 years.
	£	£	£	
Wool	18,159	75,716	160,000	800
Indigo . . .	2,825	21,595	24,000	750
Saltpetre . . .	8	4,323	9,600	12,000
Ghee	726	9,616	18,300	2,400
Piece Goods Silk & Cotton	1,288	3,921	4,750	260

Every increase in facility and safety of transport will give fresh impulse to all native products. The export of cotton, silk, wool, corn, oil-seeds, saltpetre,* and indigo, madder, and other dye stuffs, is capable of almost indefinite extension.

* The following shows the growth of the saltpetre export trade from Scinde :—

1847-48	Maunds	33
48-49	„	0
49-50	„	426
50-51	„	6,052
51-52	Cwt.	6,822
52-53	„	13,949
53-54	„	25,066

Colonel Jacob reported to Government that the total export trade of the province (Scinde), during the year 1855-6, was 50 per cent. in excess of the previous year; that the increase was most remarkable in oil-seeds and wool: in the former it was 900 per cent. and in the latter 60 per cent. increase. Col. Jacob further observes "The quantity and value of articles suitable for British consumption exported *viâ* Bombay to the English market, are estimated at 18,000 tons of produce, worth in round numbers £38,000; and if to this be added some 15,000 tons of flax and oil-seeds, which will probably be received from the northward, there will be a total of not less than 35,000 tons of produce, being a value of £500,000, available for export from this province during the next year adapted to British consumption." *

Besides the European and native troops, European travellers and native traders will, it is believed, largely avail themselves of the Indus Valley line of transit, when relieved of the obstructions of the Delta.

From the large number of passengers proceeding from the Punjaub and Upper India to Europe, and *vice versa*, there can be little doubt but that a direct steam communication will soon be established between Kurrachee, and Aden and Suez—this route being actually the shortest, until the opening of that by the Valley of the Euphrates, while it is the safest from the prevailing direction of the periodical winds.

The pilgrims from the countries on our North-west Border *en route* to Mecca, and other holy cities, would supply traffic to the railway and steam flotilla, and increase

* Appendix to the Reports of Col. Jacob, and of Mr. Dalzell, Collector of Customs, regarding the trade of the province during the year 1855-6.

the intercourse already established between Kurrachee and the ports of the Persian Gulf.

"From the Sutlej to the Oxus, whoever wishes to communicate with any place beyond the sea, must pass through Kurrachee. It occupies a position scarcely less favourable to commerce than that of Alexandria." *

The port is protected from the sea and bad weather by Munorah, a bluff rocky headland, projecting south-eastward from the mainland, and leaving a space of about two miles between the extreme point and the coast to the east.

The harbour is spacious, extending about five miles northward from Munorah Point, and about the same distance from the town, on the eastern shore, to the extreme western point.

" Kurrachee," says Thornton, " is a position of very great importance, whether regarded in a commercial, a political, or a military point of view. In a commercial point of view, it may be defined the gate of central Asia, and is likely to become to India what Liverpool is to England." " It has been officially reported that accommodation exists for the reception within the harbour, at the same time, of twenty ships of 800 tons (and any number of smaller craft). The climate of Kurrachee is cool in proportion to its latitude; and under British auspices, the town must speedily become a most important place." Lat. 24° 51″, long. 67° 2″.†

Its value was manifested and tested during the campaigns on the Sutlej, during which it became the grand depôt whence our field forces were supplied with all the munitions of war. Thousands upon thousands of tons of military stores were imported into its harbour. The population of Kurrachee is about 40,000,‡ and is rapidly increasing; and boats, as well as labour, in the harbour are abundant and cheap.

* Friend of India. † Thornton's Gazetteer of India.
‡ Cantonment, 15,000; town, 25,000.

Kurrachee, then, is not only the natural port of Scinde, but also of the Punjaub and central Asia; and the Scinde Railway, which connects it with permanently deep water in the Indus at Hyderabad, is only the first link in that chain of improved communication which must at no distant period connect Peshawur, on the borders of Afghanistan, with the sea.

The whole subject of improving the port of Kurrachee was referred by the Court of Directors to Mr. J. Walker, F.R.S., the eminent harbour-engineer, to whom detailed surveys, taken by Lieut. Grieve of the Indian navy for this express purpose, were submitted. Mr. Walker has officially reported to the Court his opinion in these words:—"It is satisfactory to me to be able to state, at the outset, that I think the objects which the Court of Directors have in view — namely, the deepening or even entire removal of the bar, and the general improvement of the harbour of Kurrachee—are not of doubtful execution; but that, on the contrary, there is good reason to expect, through the application of proper means, the accomplishment of both—and this at a moderate expense, when compared with what I understand to be the almost national importance of a safe harbour at Kurrachee, capable of receiving and accommodating sea-going vessels of large tonnage;" and "that Kurrachee is capable of being made an excellent harbour, and that there are no very great engineering or other physical difficulties to contend with in making it such." * The experienced harbour engineer sanctioned by the Court of Directors to assist in carrying out the plans of Mr. Walker, has arrived at Kurrachee.

To that able and excellent officer, Captain C. D. Camp-

* Report to the Court of Directors of the East India Company on Kurrachee Harbour, by James Walker, LL.D., F.R.S., L. and E. 1857.

bell, I.N., belongs the honour of having been the first to take in on his own responsibility a large armed steamer into the harbour of Kurrachee.

"Colonel Turner," said Mr. Frere at a public meeting at Kurrachee, "instituted a series of very careful experiments by boring, and showed most conclusively that there was not a particle of rock anywhere on the bar; that the whole was composed, to considerable depth, of soft sand. The establishment of this fact of course removed one principal ground of the fear which mariners before had—of approaching or touching on the bar.

"But the principal share of the credit of practically proving the absence of any danger in entering the port, was due to Lieut. Leeds, the port officer, who with great skill and judgment, and on his own responsibility, piloted in ships of considerable burthen, and had practically shown that this might be safely done, even without any aid from steamers. The result was, that during the monsoon just closed, four large steamers from Bombay and Aden, and eight sailing vessels of from 300 to 878 tons, had come in and gone out, and with one exception, it had never been found necessary to wait even a single day for any particular tide. And it must be further remembered, that each of these eight sailing vessels was towed in and towed out of the harbour by a steamer (the *Victoria*), which, no later than last year, was employed in conveying passengers at the most crowded season between Bombay and Suez.

"*Facts like these prove beyond a possibility of doubt, that there was no difficulty whatever in getting vessels, even of a considerable size, into and out of Kurrachee harbour during the south-west monsoon, the most unfavourable period of the year.*"

General Parr, when commanding at Kurrachee, stated, on

the occasion before referred to, that, "by the facilities for rapid communication with Suez and Moultan, which were glanced at in the Report, and which the statements they had heard showed to be strictly within the limits of what was possible, and he hoped practical at no distant date, it would positively take less time to move a brigade from Southampton to the Punjaub, than it would at present take to move the Kurrachee brigade from this camp to Moultan; in other words, *you might have Southampton, instead of Kurrachee, the base of your operations for any campaigns in the Punjaub, or any countries beyond it.* This facility appeared to him, as a military man, to afford advantages so enormous, that he was sure the meeting would excuse his dilating on the other aspects of the scheme."

To be the nearest point to Europe of all our Indian possessions, is important in many points of view, but more especially with reference to "the Euphrates Valley route," and every remark relative to the direct communication of Kurrachee with Suez is equally, if not more applicable to that with Bussorah, as materially reducing the sea voyage from India. The electric wire is now connecting Kurrachee with the Punjaub; and when the proposed telegraphic communication is established with Europe, whether it be by the Persian Gulf or the Red Sea, or as it ought to be, by both routes, the advantage will be great, of being the medium of disseminating the political and commercial intelligence of Europe to the most distant parts of our Indian possessions, and giving to Europe in exchange the most recent events in India and Central Asia. Hitherto beyond the pale of the electric chain that spans the empire, Kurrachee is destined, ere long, to become the chief seat of the telegraph in India.*

* For information regarding the port of Sonmeanee, *vide* Appendix C.

CHAPTER IV.

KURRACHEE

IN CONNECTION WITH IMPROVED MEANS OF INTERNAL COMMUNICATION.—OPINION OF SIR HENRY POTTINGER.—OF DEPUTY-COLLECTOR OF PORT.—OF MR. FRERE.—TRAFFIC BETWEEN PORT AND TOWN.—TRADE OF KURRACHEE FOR 1856-57

On the formation of the Scinde Railway Company early in 1855, Sir Henry Pottinger addressed the Chairman a letter, from which the following is an extract:—"From my long and intimate acquaintance with the province of Scinde, I most entirely and cordially concur in all that has been advanced in support of the proposed scheme, and I trust that early sanction will be obtained from the East India Company, to its being carried out, on the same terms that have been accorded to other railways in India.

"To the intended line of railway, over which I have travelled frequently, I am not aware of a single objection that can be urged, and of the Harbour of Kurrachee I have always had the highest opinion. I went there with a mission in 1809, in the cruiser "Prince of Wales," and the "Maria," country ship. These vessels entered the Harbour with perfect facility, and lay inside for above a month, when they were sent back to Bombay, owing to its being determined that the mission should return to India, through Kutch. This was in the height of the south-west monsoon, and demonstrated at that early period, the capabilities of the Port. I mention this fact, as I see it is not alluded to in the papers you have been so good as to send to me. I had a very complete journal of all the events and circumstances attending the first mission to Scinde in 1809, in which the dangers and difficulties of the navigation of the lower Delta of the Indus were fully described, and exactly tallied with what have now been brought forward. My journal and all my notes and papers were destroyed, on the breaking out of the war in 1818, when the residency at Poonah was burned by the Mahratta army.

"What I now state may be so far satisfactory, perhaps, to the Directors, as showing the views which were early forced on me, with regard to the important question now under discussion."*

The late Mr. Macleod, Deputy Collector of Customs of Kurrachee, in October, 1853, in writing to Lieutenant Chapman, the able engineer who surveyed the country from Kurrachee to Kotree, remarks that:—"The Indus, though nominally open to commerce since Lord Ellenborough's proclamation after the conquest of the country in 1843, yet was virtually sealed up to the beginning of last year, when river dues were finally abolished: we may therefore expect that the raw produce of the Punjaub and the North-west Provinces will now find its way continuously and uninterruptedly by the line of the Indus, in exchange for the manufactures of Europe — a trade which has already received considerable impetus from the establishment of the regular monthly steamer between Moultan and Kurrachee. And here I must not forget to mention the important fact, that the Indus is now the highway for

* From Lieut.-Gen. the Right Hon. Sir Henry Pottinger, Bart., G.C.B., to W. P. Andrew. Esq., Chairman of the Scinde Railway Company.

troops and military stores to the Punjaub and Upper India."

He further states :—"*The commerce of the port has been progressing during the past few years at the rate of 20 per cent. per annum, and there is every reason to expect a continuance of the progressive ratio. The residents in the Punjaub have shown a desire to procure their supplies by the Indus, in preference to the line of the Ganges, and in a few years their desire will in all probability be gratified to the fullest extent. An extensive Affghan trader, who has had dealings with Calcutta for years, having tried the Bombay market during the two past seasons, has given the latter the preference. Others will follow his example. These prospects of the Scinde trade lead me to believe, that by the time a railway shall be laid down, and be prepared for action,* OUR COMMERCE WILL HAVE DOUBLED ITS PRESENT VALUE, AND THE PASSENGER TRAFFIC BE TEN TIMES AS MUCH AS IT IS AT PRESENT."

The opinions of Sir Henry Pottinger and the late meritorious Deputy Collector of the Port, as to the value and importance of Kurrachee as a harbour in connection with the Scinde Railway, are entirely confirmed by Mr. Frere, Commissioner in Scinde, who expressed himself as follows when addressing a meeting of the Proprietors of the Scinde Railway Company, on the 18th February, 1857. "It was impossible to be in error in the adoption of the two great terminal lines of the great chain between Lahore and Kurrachee, on portions of country where the river was not navigable, but upon the intervening section of navigable water, the development of the traffic by river steamers, would enable them to arrive at a more just conclusion in determining the course which they should best take to fall in with the railway system of the country (hear, hear). Mr. Andrew had adverted to the military and political importance of the line. For his own part he (Mr. Frere) did not think it was possible to overrate that importance.

"He was quite alive to the great military and political importance of the line of the Punjaub; but if the permanent tranquillity of Central Asia was to be secured; if the triumphs of Great Britain were to be permanent, they must be rendered so by a mutuality of interests, by the material and civilising influences of expanding commerce. The great battle of the country for the tranquillity of Central Asia must be fought at Manchester and Liverpool (hear, hear). If we would command Central Asia, that dominion must be established by opening up a ready market for their raw produce, and subjecting them by the force of their own material interests. A curious illustration of the correctness of this view of the case came under his own observation. It was that of a ruler in Candahar, an old Afghan, who had of late years shown an increasing indisposition to hostilities against us. The British authorities were induced to inquire into the reason, and it was ascertained that the principal part of the wool came from his part of the country (hear, hear). It might be that he realised from this source a yearly revenue of 70,000 Rs., or, about £7000 a year, a sum which might not appear large to a manufacturer in this country, but which was to him equal to the revenues of a State, and which he wisely valued more than the irregular profits of predatory warfare. If they extended the application of this principle they would come to the conclusion that every extension of commerce added to our military strength (hear, hear). Without underrating, therefore, the military and political importance of the railway, he looked on its commercial advantages as calculated in an equal degree to strengthen and give permanence to our dominion in the East. Allusion had been made by Mr. Andrew to the extraordinary increase which had taken place in the exports and imports of the province of Scinde, and if the meeting would not think him tedious, he would read to them a few figures which would demonstrate this in a very striking manner (hear, hear). In 1843, the imports amounted in value to £121,000, and the exports to 1,010. Total, £122,000. In 1847, the imports were of the value of £287,000, and the exports £154,000; total £441,000. In 1851, the imports were £489,000, and the exports £244,000; total, £733,000. In 1854, the imports attained the value of £629,000, the exports £604,000; total, £1,233,000 (applause). Now, in these figures there was evidence of a very substantial increase in the unaided resources of the country, although it was a great reflection upon us that we had been talking a good deal about developing the resources of the province, but as yet in truth very little had been done. But with such figures before them, it must be obvious to every one, that if fostered and developed, the increase would have been much larger. Let them imagine, for instance, such a system of transit in operation as that in which they were now engaged in maturing, and the results must have been perfectly astonishing. Within the few last days he had received the Kurrachee financial returns for the past official year, from which he would, with permission of the meeting, read a few items. The value of cotton goods, plain and coloured, twist and thread, the produce of Manchester and Glasgow, was £294,000. The import of grain amounted to the value of £32,000. This was principally wheat and other grain consumed by the army at Kurrachee. Now, this would in due time be supplied from the upper country. There was also an import of raw silk from Persia and Bokhara—Bokhara standing for the value of £28,000. Sugar also, £28,000, which ought to be brought from the upper country; and, as soon as the line was open, instead of importing sugar, it would become an article of export. Horses and drugs were exported to the value of £14,000 Indigo, which in the first year of our possession figured in the exports to the value of £2,000 only, last year attained the value of £42,400. And this, it was to be observed, was without the aid of British capital as in Bengal, nor had the war anything to do with it. It was entirely a natural increase. The export of grain was put down at £66,000, but the whole course of the Indus from Scinde to Cashmere was a wheat producing district, and the remark of Mr. Andrew was not exaggerated, for the day would come, when with facilities of conveyance opened, Scinde would be found competing with Dantzic for the supply of grain to Mark Lane! Saltpetre was exported to the value of £21,000 which a few years ago was not exported at all. In oil seeds, the value exported was £137,000. The trade to which no limit could be assigned, was still in its infancy, but was destined to obtain a very considerable magnitude. Again, sheep's wool, which recently was not exported at all, last year was exported to the value of £221,000. The total imports and exports of the past year amounted to £1,095,000, the amount of the imports exceeding the exports only by about £20,000. He would here beg to draw attention to the fact that the principal business was now carried on through Bombay. But, by the last mail, he has learned that two firms in connection with Manchester, had settled at Kurrachee, and when the aggregate of cost in transacting such business at Bombay, was compared with the corresponding expenses of Kurrachee in carriage and transhipment, and if the trade was now profitable through Bombay, it was obvious that it must be more profitable if direct with Kurrachee! In reference to the Punjaub, he was not personally acquainted with the district, but he was well acquainted with several gentlemen of local experience, who assured him there was a total absence of what are called engineering difficulties, and that this was the case might be judged of from the fact, that a canal of irrigation was in operation between Moultan and Lahore without a single artificial means of elevating the water along the whole distance (hear, hear), a convincing proof of the level character of the country. The importance attached to the improvement of the harbour of Kurrachee by Mr. Andrew was exceedingly just. That gentleman had told them that the home authorities had sent out a properly qualified engineer to carry into effect Mr. Walker's suggestions, and he, (Mr. Frere), might add that he had since received letters from Colonel Turner and Captain Greene, entirely coinciding with the recommendations of Mr. Walker."*

I have elsewhere remarked that "Kurrachee is not only the port of the Indus and Central Asia, but, from its geographical position and other advantages, appears destined to become, if not the future metropolis of India, most certainly the second city and the European port of that empire." †

* Report of proceedings of Meeting of Scinde Railway Company of 18th February, 1857.

† Letter to Viscount Palmerston, K.G., on the Political Importance of the Euphrates Valley Railway, by W. P. Andrew.—W. H. Allen & Co., Leadenhall Street.

Return of Traffic passing the Kurrachee Bunder during the Year 1856.

Kurrachee Bunder.		Carts.	Camels.	Horses.	Donkeys or Mules.	Horned Cattle.	Sheep or Goats.	Porters with Loads.	Unladen Foot Passengers, Europeans.	Ditto, Natives.	Palkees or Litters.	Gares Carriage.	Artillery Gun or Carriage.
January,	1856.	2,977	482	3,836	463	3.135	165	4,154	1,512	77,843	98	1,352	
February	,,	12,402	2,242	3,810	466	4,047	179	4,848	1,830	70,209	104	1,440	
March	,,	13,610	324	3,872	280	3,902	155	5.259	811	78,121	68	1,412	
April	,,	4,122	418	4,222	433	4,596	227	7,074	899	94,001	90	1,458	
May	,,	14,365	360	4,258	336	4,935	153	5.586	788	70,758	86	1,480	
June	,,	6,206	266	3,240	202	2,715	61	3,064	599	35,975	56	1,256	
July	,,	3,124	400	3,006	590	2,206	57	730	666	26,001	38	1,206	
August	,,	6,754	512	3,574	1,295	2,635	99	3,327	879	67.333	70	1,362	8
September	,,	4,244	609	4,138	588	4,270	131	5,780	936	108.105	78	442	
October	,,	7,136	670	3,952	456	4,514	94	5,647	1.856	71,519	230	1,330	
November	,,	16,874	498	4,621	520	4,274	611	5,411	1,967	68,375	118	1,688	18
December	,,	15,252	354	3,722	246	4,206	105	4,446	1,074	65,309	32	488	
Total . .		107,066	7,135	46,251	5,876	45,435	2,037	55,326	13,817	833,549	1,068	14,914	26

Commissioner's Office, Kurrachee,

22*nd May*, 1857.

(Signed) H. B. E. FRERE,

Commissioner in Scinde.

The following abstract statement of the trade of Kurrachee for the official year 1856-57, is taken from an Indian paper :—

"We have been favoured with an abstract statement of the external trade of the province by its sea face during the past official year (1856-57), from which we gather that it amounted in value to Rs.142,01,879 against Rs.123,42,537 in the previous year. The increase amounts to Rs.18,59,342—of which Rs.5,58,523 are due to imports, and Rs.13,00,819 to exports.

"The details of the imports, compared with those of the previous year, are as follows :—*

IMPORTS.	1855-56.	1856-57.
Apparel	R.1,52,184	R.1,01,763
Cotton Piece Goods :—Coloured . .	4,51,554	4,47,360
Plain	22,17,957	21,72,070
other kinds . . .	75,545	59,109
Twist and Thread	2,03,227	1,91,481
Grain	2,32,947	3,37,569
Metals, raw	2,16,952	3,17,247
" manufactured	1,06,453	95,881
Silk, raw	1,47,794	56,575
Silk and Woollen Piece Goods . .	1,36,704	85,697
Spices	1,57,155	2,49,945
Sugar	2,15,959	1,64,776
Wines and Spirits	1,94,590	2,63,247
Treasure	3,00,378	2,09,488
Fruit	1,31,060	2,56,283
Railway Stores	———	5,63,462
Other articles	13,48,678	12,84,702
Total . . £	628,913 8	685,665 14

* Value of details in Rupees, and totals in Pounds Sterling, the Rupee being taken at the par value of Two Shillings.

"The principal articles of exports during the same period are as follow:—

Exports.	1855-56.	1856-57.
Horses	R.3,39,060	R.4,31,850
Dyes:		
Indigo	4,23,881	3,54,655
Munjeet	68,944	4,40,552
Other Dyes and Drugs	1,60,675	1,30,949
Grain:		
Wheat	3,08,299	10,672
Other kinds of Grain	2,56,193	1,57,337
Ghee	2,33,672	1,56,107
Saltpetre	2,12,004	3,75,472
Seeds:		
Jingly	5,91,215	8,37,621
Sursee	4,76,335	3,18,600
Other kinds of Seeds	3,32,013	94,606
Silk, raw	3,761	3,20,174
Wool, Sheeps'	22,13,107	31,15,903
Other Articles	4,25,244	6,03,873
Total . . £	604,440 6	734,522 4

"The following is a list of the countries holding commercial intercourse with Scinde, and the value of the trade with each during the past two years.

	Imports.		Exports.	
	1855-56.	1856-57.	1855-56.	1856-57.
Bombay	R55,81,212	R52,27,429	R53,74,320	R66,97,549
Calcutta	...	...	...	13,074
Kutch and Kattiawar	2,04,308	2,74,379	2,33,886	2,02,907
England	1,57,800	7,73,835	35,139	1,446
France	...	...	...	93,390
Goa and Demaun	4,532	10,064	...	231
Guzerat and Concan	60,072	1,46,297	11,747	15,647
Malabar	97,632	90,388	1,69,154	1,45,933
Mauritius	1,894	8,930	17,568	28,538
Mekran and Persian Gulf	1,90,684	3,25,335	2,02,589	1,56,507
Total . £	629,813 8	685,665 14	604,440 6	734,522 4

"These returns exhibit a very satisfactory progress in the trade of Scinde. The principal points of interest in them are the attempt to open a direct traffic with Europe and the Mauritius in country produce; the importation of railway material, and the large increase in the exports, particularly in wool, munjeet, saltpetre, jingly seed and silk, articles which are transmitted to Europe for consumption.

"To the large augmentation of sheep's wool we would draw the particular attention of the manufacturers in England. From holding a subordinate position in our trade returns in 1847, when the export of the article amounted to only £18,000—it has in the space of nine years risen to the chief place in our exports, and in the returns before us, the article is valued at upwards of £311,000 sterling.

"We need scarcely allude to the vast importance of this article, and however gratifying it may be to observe the gradual increase in the export of it, we have good reason for believing that it is susceptible of still further extension.

"At present this article is exported hence to Bombay; but after the hydraulic presses lately arrived from England, and for which a suitable building is now under construction, have been brought in use, we doubt not that it will be shipped direct to England at a saving of considerable expense, both to the shippers and consumers.

"Madder (Munjeet) and saltpetre have also made large progress since 1847. The export of the former article was in that year valued at £376; the present trade returns exhibit its value at £44,000. Saltpetre from being an article almost unknown in the Kurrachee market in 1847, the exports for that year being valued at only £8, has now risen to the value of £37,500. In fact, the history of almost every one of our articles of export, for which there has been a steady and permanent demand, is similar to the instances we have cited.

"Not only has the quantity of our staple productions been increased, but almost every year some new article has been added to our list of exports. Within the last few years we have brought forward as articles of export the following commodities, viz.:—Ooplate, sal ammonia, borax, linseed, silk, sugar and tallow, the demand for which we are glad to find is gradually progressing in foreign markets. It will be perceived by a reference to our returns that silk has at once taken a prominent position in the list of exports; the quantity exported last year being valued at £32,000 against £376 in the previous year. This article is said to have been brought down from Bokhara, *via* the Punjaub, and would appear to have been diverted to Kurrachee, instead of proceeding to Calcutta as heretofore. We have reason to believe that supplies of this article will continue to be brought to Kurrachee.

"It will be seen that in indigo the export has somewhat fallen off, but this decrease we think may be attributed to our recent dispute with Persia, to which country the article is chiefly shipped; the quality of that at present produced in the Province not being such as to suit it for the European markets. In Upper Scinde, about Moultan, and in Bhawulpore, the soil and climate are in every respect favourable to the production of this valuable article, and with due encouragement on the part of the Government, European capital and skill might be brought to bear on its cultivation; and an article produced, capable of competing in the English market with the general run of the Bengal dye, and at very much less cost.

"The absence from our list of the valuable article "Cotton" will probably be remarked; limited though the local consumption be, the province does not produce sufficient to meet the demand, and there is therefore necessarily a small amount imported, though the quantity is too trifling to admit of separate detail. The enquiry naturally forces itself upon us, why the province does not grow enough of the article to meet the local demand, and we wish some of our better informed readers would come forward to answer it. It can scarcely be that the country is unfavourable to its production, for we have always understood that the Delta of the Indus was particularly suited for the growth of cotton; and we must therefore suppose that the cause has been either the poverty of the land cultivators, or the indifference of the Zemindars, or of the district officers. *

* "A correspondent of an Indian paper says:—'In April last (1855), I brought to England a small quantity of cotton (the raw material) grown from *acclimated* American cotton seed in a district on the banks of the river Jhelum; this specimen I had shown to several cotton spinners in Manchester. They pronounced it to be the finest specimen of cotton they had seen grown in India, even from directly American seed, and to be worth from 6¼d. to 6½d. per lb. Along the banks of our Punjaub rivers lie tracts of land admirably situated for the growth of cotton. It only requires steady encouragement on the part of the local government, trouble and perseverance on the part of the district officer, to cover those lands with cotton of the finest quality. The cotton that could thus be grown might, with ease and at trifling cost, be conveyed in country boats (until we have, as we ought to have, steamers on those rivers) down the Indus to Kurrachee and there shipped for England. Kurrachee is a port of great importance; but, like many things of great

" In order that the progress which the trade of Scinde has made since 1847 may be seen at one view, we subjoin a statement of the chief articles of export in 1856, contrasted with their value in 1847. The improvement made since that period will afford our mercantile friends and others interested in the trade of the port, an idea of the future prospects of our trade, which Mr. Temple, the Secretary to the Punjaub Government, estimates as next in importance to the trade of Calcutta.

EXPORTS.	1847-48.	1856-57.
Horses	R.2,05,800	R.4,31,850
Indigo	28,252	3,54,655
Munjeet	3,765	4,40,552
Other Dyes and Drugs	1,08,234	1,30,949
Wheat	19,439	10,672
Other Grain	43,071	1,57,337
Ghee	7,268	1,56,107
Saltpetre	79	3,75,472
Jingly Seed (Sesamum)	...	8,37,621
Sursee Seed (Rape)	...	3,16,000
Other Seeds	22,383	91,606
Silk, raw	537	3,20,174
Wool	1,81,598	31,15,903
Treasure	7,73,719	98,816
Other Articles	98,163	5,05,057
Total . . £	154,730 16	734,522 4

importance, not heeded or taken advantage of. *The one article, cotton, if properly cultivated in the Punjaub and in Scinde, would afford export freight for a vast number of ships visiting Kurrachee, while Government stores for the Punjaub, private property and merchandize would afford endless import freight, to say nothing of the great number of passengers who would avail themselves of that route.* According to a Scinde paper—' Any one located on the banks of the river Indus might observe fleets of boats coming down the river in the winter months, all laden with cotton." The cotton brought to Scinde and shipped at Sukkur comes across the Jaysulmere Desert,

"These results in the progress of our trade have been achieved with very little aid or encouragement from Government in the construction of roads and other appliances to meet the wants of commerce. When the communication between this province and the Punjaub shall have been completed, by means of railroads and steamers, and the internal communications of the two provinces attended to, by the construction of roads from village to village, connected with the grand trunk road, the trade of Kurrachee will then exceed the present value by as much as the present exceeds the trade of 1847.*

Speaking of this Report of Mr. Dalzell, a copy of which will be found in the Appendix, a late writer says :—

"So much English capital is being embarked in railway and steam enterprise in the province of Scinde, that it may be useful to quote the following extract from a report on the External Trade of Scinde for the year 1856-7, furnished by the deputy Collector of Customs :—"

'"The external trade of Scinde for the past official year (1856-57) is distinguished by some encouraging features highly promising to the commerce of the province.

'"The value of the aggregate trade, exclusive of government stores, amounts to Rs. 1,42,01,879, showing an increase over the previous year's trade, valued at Rs.1,23,42,537, of rupees 18,59,342, equivalent to 15 per cent., and detailed as follows :—

from Rajpootana, and is either consumed in Scinde or exported to Afghanistan.—*Vide 'Scinde Railway, and its Relations to the Euphrates Valley and other Routes to India.'*" By W. P. ANDREW. Allen & Co., Leadenhall Street.

* The Sindian, Sept. 5, 1857.

IMPORTS.

Merchandise	Rs. 66,47,169	
Treasure	2,09,488	
		68,56,657
Which compared with the import value of the previous year		Rs. 62,98,134
Exhibits an increase of		5,58,523
Or 9 per cent.		

EXPORTS.

Merchandise	Rs. 73,46,406	
Treasure	98,816	
		73,45,222
Which compared with the export value of the previous year		60,44,403
Shows an increase of		13,00,819
Or 22 per cent.		

'" Contrasting the value of the trade of 1856-57 with its value on an average of the five preceding years, there is an increase in imports of Rs. 13,79,229, or 25 per cent., and in exports of Rs. 34,51, 014, or 88 per cent., equivalent, in the aggregate, to 52 per cent. The result of the past year's trade which the tables exhibit, cannot be viewed otherwise than as very satisfactory, when it is considered that the trade of the preceding year, 1855-56, with which it is compared, had, by the circumstances of war, been stimulated into unusual activity—to such a degree that the value of the exports in 1855-56 exceeded by 74 per cent. the value of the exports of the year preceding."

" The report proceeds to remark :"

'" There are few circumstances connected with India more remarkable than the rapidity with which a trade can be increased, notwithstanding the many obstacles, both physical and moral, which oppose its progress; yet a slight increase of demand, and consequently of price, oftentimes increases in a wonderful degree the export of some particular commodities. There are two periods by which, under different circumstances, though in effect the same, the export trade of Scinde is distinguished in a peculiar degree, demonstrating the above proposition. In 1852-53, without apparently the existence of any unusual demand for any particular produce in the home market, the exports from Scinde rose from Rs. 24,41,228 in 1851-52, to Rs. 37,63,376, or 54 per cent. in 1852-53. In looking for the cause of so extraordinary an increase in one year, it seems to be discovered in the hope held out to the traders by the proclamation of the fairs, which, had they met with the encouragement they unquestionably merited, would have enabled the traders to dispose of their produce at Kurrachee in exchange for British manufactures; but the Afghan, who showed so ready an appreciation of the advantage of markets within the province, was not rewarded, on arrival at the expected marts, by any display of British goods, so that the benefit he had expected to reap, by disposing of his goods at Kurrachee, was lost by the obligation forced upon him to proceed to Bombay, thereby increasing the value of his produce by a further journey to a distant market, and consequently diminishing the profits of his investments.

"The Report arrives at the somewhat remarkable fact, that 'whilst the trade of Scinde, despite the difficulties which encompass it, had advanced since the conquest 575 per cent., the trade of Bombay, notwithstanding the many improvements that have taken place in the interior of the country, and other advantages, has not increased within the same period more than 33 per cent., including her trade with Scinde.'" *

* Daily News, January 26th, 1858; and for further information, *vide* Appendix A.

CHAPTER V.

SCINDE RAILWAY.

IMMEDIATE OBJECTS.—CONTRACT WITH EAST INDIA COMPANY.—PROFITABLE CHARACTER OF LINE.—LOCAL AUTHORITIES' OPINION OF.—PUBLIC ADVANTAGES OF.—TRAFFIC RETURNS.—BRANCHES TO BOLAN PASS AND DEESA.

The Scinde Railway Company was established in 1855, to introduce railways into the province of Scinde,—the first section commencing at the port of Kurrachee, and proceeding to a point on the Indus in the vicinity of Hyderabad.

This line, about 110 miles in length, will place Kurrachee, the seaport of Scinde, in communication with the Indus, the great commercial artery of the countries on our north-west frontier, at a point where the river becomes free from the intricacies, dangers and delays of the navigation of the Delta.

The great political and commercial advantages which may be fairly expected from this undertaking were clearly set forth in the despatches of the Commissioner of Scinde and the reports of the Engineer officers in the service of the Honourable East India Company, who made a preliminary survey of the line.

The effect of the contract between the Honourable East India Company and the Scinde Railway Company which was signed in December, 1855, is that the East India Company guarantee a minimum rate of interest on the capital of 5 per cent. per annum for 99 years, and grant a lease of the land necessary for the railway and works for a similar period, free of charge. On the opening of the line, all net profits exceeding the rate of interest guaranteed are to be divided—one half of the surplus is to go to the shareholders, and the other half to the East India Company, in liquidation of the interest they have advanced. When this interest is repaid, the entire surplus profit goes to the shareholders. The East India Company reserve a right to regulate the trains and fares; and as soon as the dividend exceeds 10 per cent., to lower the fares, but not so as to reduce the profit below that rate. The East India Company also reserve power, after the first twenty-five or fifty years, to purchase the line at a price equal to the average market value of the shares for the three preceding years. On the other hand, the railway Company have the power, at any time after the line has been three months in work, to require the East India Company to take it off their hands at six months' notice, and repay them the capital expended.

Irrespective of the guarantee, this enterprise possesses, in the opinion of those personally acquainted with Scinde and its resources, a highly remunerative character:—

1st. From the country, presenting a series of firm and level plains, it is admirably adapted for the construction of a railway.

2nd. From the line being of moderate length and complete in itself, having an important town at either terminus (Kurrachee, the lower terminus, the present seat of Government, being the only sea-port for many hundred miles, and Hyderabad, the upper terminus, the former capital, being still the chief entrepôt for the inland trade of the province), thus of necessity forming the most important portion of any system of railways, or other form of transit, which shall follow the course of the Valley of the Indus or its tributaries.

3rd. From the *actual existence* of a paying goods traffic all the year round, which, in the opinion of the late Deputy Collector of Kurrachee, will have doubled its present value, and of a passenger traffic which will have increased tenfold, before a railway can be in operation.

The Line was preliminarily examined by that able and scientific officer, the late Lieutenant Chapman, of the Bombay Engineers, who reported it to present the greatest possible facilities for the construction of a railway, with the very best gradients (in fact nearly level), and at a low rate of cost. Colonel Turner, the Superintending Engineer in Scinde, Mr. Frere, the Commissioner of the Province, and Lord Elphinstone, the Governor of Bombay, all concur in desiring the early completion of the Line, which is now in the hands of the Scinde Railway Company's engineers. The requisite material for thirty miles of the permanent way has arrived at Kurrachee, and as much more is in course of shipment, and a contract for the construction of the line was concluded in December last, with the eminent contractors, Messrs. Bray, of Leeds.

The public advantages to be derived from this Railway may be thus recapitulated, viz.:—

By the construction of a Railway from Kurrachee to the Indus at or near Hyderabad—

1st. Greatly increased facilities will be afforded for the landing and conveyance of troops intended for any part of the Punjaub, and neighbouring territories.

2nd. A large sum will be saved to government in the transport of stores.

3rd. From avoiding the Delta, great improvements may be effected in the Indus Flotilla service, without any increased charges on the finances of the province.

4th. A very large sum would be annually saved to the country in freight by boats alone, besides the saving in loss and damage to goods, which in itself would be a very large item.

5th. Sources of trade would be opened which at present are not in action.

The Scinde railway would exert a powerful influence in promoting the development of the trade of the Indus valley. The annual losses, incident to the present system of navigation, are very large, from the accidents which take place in threading the narrow channels of the Delta. Major Preedy, the Collector of Lower Scinde, states, that "*if one or two boats only out of a batch of six or so were lost, it is considered a good venture.*"

The following is the return for boats which run the whole distance from Kurrachee to Sukkur :—

1851-2	1,284,920 maunds	=	45,890	tons.
1852-3	1,565,120 ,,	=	55,500	,,
1853-4	1,624,740 ,,	=	58,026	,,
1854-5	1,681,720 ,,	=	60,060	,,

The return of the number of boats passing any one station below Sukkur would be much higher than the above.

The number of laden steamers passing Hyderabad and

Kotree is 170 in the year, with a tonnage of 1,190,000 maunds, or 42,500 tons.

The Government receipts for goods and passengers carried in the river steamers have been—

	Gross.	Net.
1852-3, (the first year of the experiment,) „	Rs. 50,273	Rs. 43,291
1853-4, „ „	59,865	49,277
1854-5, „ „	67,981	60,554

The returns of camel traffic leaving Kurrachee are not complete,—but, assuming one-half of the amounts ascertainable as being intended for the Indus, the total is 112,000 maunds, or 4,000 tons.

The post-office outlay on the line is large.

From the recent orders transmitted to India, that the Government stores for the Punjaub and neighbouring territories should be sent from Bombay, up the line of the Indus, instead of as heretofore from Calcutta, up the Gangetic valley, a great increase of the above-shown traffic must ensue, and a revenue, at railway rates, derived, which would give a large return on the capital of the Company. The preceding figures convey but a moderate idea of the amount of tonnage which would come upon the railway.

In the first instance, the guaranteed capital of the Railway Company was limited to £500,000. In December, 1857, however, the Company received permission to double their capital on the original conditions, and have recently been requested by the local authorities to survey two branch lines—the one from Sukkur by Shikarpoor and Jacobabad to Dadur near the entrance of the Bolan Pass, the other southward from Hyderabad, by Omercote to Deesa, so as to effect a direct communication between Kurrachee and Bombay, by a junction with the intended extension of the Bombay and Baroda line to Deesa.

With reference to these branch lines, that distinguished public officer, Mr. Bartle Frere, the Commissioner in Scinde, in a despatch to the Governor of Bombay, dated 21st July, states, "that both the lines referred to appear of the very greatest importance, not only in a commercial, but in a military and political point of view. It seems almost superfluous to argue this point with regard to the line from Sukkur *viâ* Shikarpoor and Jacobabad in the direction of the Bolan Pass. Its necessity has been repeatedly insisted on by General Jacob, and it is obviously essential to secure rapid means of communication between the river and the important frontier towards the Bolan Pass. The country is a dead level, the canals and water courses have been bridged, the road has been carried in perfectly straight lines of from ten to twenty miles without turning or angle, and the portions subject to inundation have been raised." In the same despatch, the Commissioner, referring to the branch to Deesa, remarks, that "hardly less important is a line which would connect Scinde with Guzerat or Rajpootana. We are at this moment receiving a terrible lesson of the danger of depending in so extended an empire on single lines of communication. Emergent requisitions for reinforcements have been received here from the northern division of the army, and owing to the want of roads, it is at this moment doubtful whether the reinforcements we have sent will be able to reach Deesa."

CHAPTER VI.

THE INDUS STEAM FLOTILLA.

THE INDUS, ITS TRADE.—ITS BOATS AND ITS STEAMERS.—RAILWAYS IN CONNECTION WITH RIVER STEAMERS.—OPINIONS OF LOCAL AUTHORITIES.—OFFICIAL CORRESPONDENCE.—COMMISSION APPOINTED.—PUNJAUB REPORT, RIVER NAVIGATION.

From Kotree (port of Hyderabad) the northern terminus of the Scinde Railway to Moultan in the Punjaub there is a distance of 570 miles of permanently open navigation. The steamer *best adapted* for this portion of the Indus cannot get out and round by sea to Kurrachee, nor thread the narrow channels of the Delta. If, however, the troops and stores could be landed at Kurrachee and conveyed by railway to Kotree, a large saving would, according to the officer in charge of the Government Indus flotilla, accrue to the state on that service, while steam boats of improved construction could be employed for the inland navigation from Kotree to Moultan.

At present, large quantities of stores, particularly porter, obliged to be sent by country boats, are found to be worthless on reaching the Punjaub, the voyage of 800 miles from Kurrachee to Moultan lasting five months. During the season 1855, the cost of transport of government stores by country boats was about £150,000. By the railway, stores would be delivered in one day at Kotree on board steamers, which in less than a week might deliver them in the Punjaub.

So far back as 1846, as I have previously stated, I suggested that railroads should be *introduced* into Bengal, in connexion with river navigation, so that the new mode of transit should, instead of superseding, co-operate with the old —at all events in the first instance; and the same views and arguments are as applicable to the Indus as to the Ganges.

Indeed I have ever contemplated railways and improved river navigation in India in relation to each other; thinking it reasonable and desirable to aid the river navigation where it was defective, by the removal of natural obstacles, or by surmounting them by means of steam-vessels of improved construction, and co-operating with this improved river navigation by means of a railway, where the traffic was great and the rivers cease to be navigable, and where the absence of physical and other obstacles would render the construction of a railway comparatively of easy attainment.

This gradual mode of introducing the railway system of transit was strikingly adapted, in my opinion, to the Bengal Presidency, possessing, as it does, navigable rivers, and where the traffic, however vast in extent, being mostly of a bulky nature, was more adapted to water conveyance than to transit by railway, unless some great advantage had to be gained, and that more affecting safety and cheapness than speed. The Rajmahal line, for instance, would give 180 miles of railway instead of, for eight months in the year, 528 miles of dangerous navigation by the Sunderbunds, and for the remaining four months in the year, supersede t e tortuous and uncertain Nuddea rivers, which flow from the Ganges to the Hooghly.

Turning from the valley of the Ganges to that of the Indus and its tributaries, I have recommended precisely the same mode of introducing improved transit, substituting Hyderabad for Rajmahal, and Moultan for Allahabad. The rail from Kurrachee to Hyderabad will, as formerly explained, avoid the dangers and delays of the Delta, and debouche on a point of the river above which there is permanently open navigation for 570 miles, to Moultan.

The freight *via* the Indus by means of Government steamers has, I believe, on various occasions, and by various parties, been matter of doubtful propriety as to its continuance or otherwise on the part of Government. To dispel these doubts, it is sufficient to refer to the annexed statement.

In 1852-53	the gross receipts amounted to	Rs. 50.273
1853-54	„	59.869
1854-55	„	67.981

The net realizations during the same years :—

1st.	Amounted to	Rs. 43.291
2nd.	„	49.267
3rd.	„	60.554

These are very gratifying results, and go far to prove the vagueness of the doubts which many supposed existed in reference to the success of this traffic by Government vessels.

The steamers, however, at present on the Indus are ill adapted to the peculiar requirements of that river, and are quite inadequate to meet the pressing demands for passage and freight in ordinary times, to say nothing of the urgent need at the present moment for the means of transporting troops and stores along the line of the Indus. Goods frequently remain months at Kurrachee and Moultan from the want of the means of transport on the Indus; and notwithstanding that the home Government some time since ordered out from this country several additional steam-

ABSTRACT *of Freight Statement, showing the Receipts of Cash by the several Freight Agents on the River Indus, contrasted with the Charges attending the Collections, &c., from 1st May,* 1854, *to 30th April*, 1855.

PERIODS. From 1st May, 1854, to 30th April, 1855.	Freight on Mess Kit.			Freight on Merchandize.			Passage Money.			Total of Receipts in Co.'s Rupees.			Disbursements attending its collections, &c., from 1st May, 1854, to 30th April, 1855.	Amount in Co.'s Rs.			Total in Co.'s Rs.		
Kurrachee	7,406	4	7	28,885	10	2	8,738	11	10	45,030	10	7	Contingencies—Kurrachee .	3,154	4	0			
Kotree	125	14	9	336	14	0	2,593	6	9	3,056	3	6	" Kotree . .	234	11	3			
Sukkur	75	10	8	4,048	1	2	1,029	10	8	5,753	6	6	" Sukkur . .	406	10	5			
Mooltan	52	13	0	7,712	7	2	6,271	3	6	14,036	7	8	" Mooltan . .	1,226	2	10			
Miscellaneous	7	14	0	12	7	0	84	6	0	104	11	9	" Miscellaneous	5	5	7			
													Office allowances	2,400	0	0			
													Refunds on account of Freight and Passage Money . .				7,427	2	1
													Balance in favour of Receipts				60,554	5	11
Total Rs. . . .	7,668	9	0	40,995	8	3	19,317	6	9	67,981	8	0	Total				67,981	8	0

Balance in favour of Receipts from 1st May, 1854, to 30th April, 1855 .	Rs. 60,554	5	11
Contrasted with Receipts in favour of 1853-54	49,277	6	0
Increase at the end of 1854-55	11,276	15	11

(*Signed*) R. ETHERSEY, Captain, I. N., Commanding Indus Flotilla.

ers, of a superior description to the present flotilla, the residents in Scinde and the Punjaub have long been desirous that the impetus which private enterprise alone can impart, should be brought to bear on the navigation of the inland waters of the Indus, in connexion with the railway and direct steam communication between Kurrachee and England.

I am, however, assured, on the best authority, that "The steamers lately ordered out by the Court of Directors will do no more than replace those now on the river, which are old and worn out. They will add little to the available accommodation for goods.

"I have been," says the same authority, "repeatedly assured by the government agents for the river steamers, that they every month reject twice as much freight as the steamers are able to carry; and that this freight is applied for with a knowledge on the part of shippers, that the chance of its being taken is very small.

"Of course, if there were ample accommodation, the applications would be much more numerous.

"The Government river steamers on the Indus never take native second class passengers for hire. This would of course be a source of great profit to any private company, as the natives are most anxious to avail themselves of steamers whenever they can.

"I have known instances of goods AT KURRACHEE *intended for the Punjaub being sent back to Bombay, with a view of being forwarded by the Peninsula and Oriental Company's boats, via Galle and Calcutta, and so up the Ganges to the Punjaub, because there appeared no hope of tonnage being available for them in the Indus river steamers for several months to come."*

The navigation above Moultan is tedious and precarious, from the want of water, the tortuous course of some of the rivers and other causes, and unavailable except for native boats of light draught. The country, however, between Moultan, Lahore, and Umritsir, is singularly favourable for a railway, being almost level throughout, and having no rivers of any magnitude to cross.

In brief, then, it was my opinion that the line of rails from Kurrachee to Hyderabad, and another line of rails from Moultan to Lahore and Umritsir, co-operating with a fleet of river steamers, of improved construction, from Hyderabad to Moultan, would at once be the most judicious, the easiest, the least costly, the soonest constructed, and in every other point of view, the most advantageous mode of *introducing* the railway system into the Valley of the Indus and its tributaries.

The local authorities, especially Mr. Frere, the Commissioner in Scinde, Colonel Turner, Superintending Engineer of the Province, Sir John Lawrence, the Chief Commissioner of the Punjaub, Colonel Glasfurd, late Executive Engineer at Lahore, Major Hamilton, Commissioner at Moultan, and Mr. Edgeworth, the Commissioner of the trans-Sutlej States, corroborated the above views, which the writer had long entertained. The last-mentioned gentleman expressed himself as follows:—

"*But the main and only permanent improvement will be the formation of a railway from either Umritsir or Lahore to Moultan.*

"*With regard to the communication below Moultan, the main point is, increased accommodation for travellers and greater comfort in the boats, which are at present peculiarly ill-suited for the purpose.*

"The proposed Scinde Railway will do almost all that is required for the lower communication.

"For the conveyance of goods, the present steam accommodation is utterly insufficient."

Fully impressed with the importance of these views, and encouraged by the opinions in their favour expressed by the most eminent local authorities, on the part of the Scinde Company, I brought the question of the establishment of a steam flotilla between Hyderabad and Moultan before the Court of Directors of the East India Company, in conjunction with a proposal to survey the country northward from Moultan to Lahore and Umritsir, for the purposes of railway communication, and the following correspondence took place with the East India Company, with respect to the carrying out of these important measures.

SCINDE RAILWAY COMPANY,
GRESHAM HOUSE, OLD BROAD STREET,
14th March, 1856.

1. From the Commissioner in Scinde to the Governor and President in Council. Bombay, dated 12th Dec. 1855.

2. Extract of letter from Secretary of the Governor of Bombay to Commissioner in Scinde, dated 2nd July, 1855, par. 1 and 3.

3. Letter from the Agent to the Chairman, dated 26th Jan., 1856.

4. Extract from letter of Resident Engineer to Agent, dated 16th Jan., 1856.

SIR,

The Directors having received a communication under date the 26th January, from their Agent in India, submitting for the sanction of this Board, in compliance with a suggestion of the Government of Bombay, a proposal that surveys should be made by the Scinde Railway Company (enclosure 2), with a view to the extension of the line of railway towards Lahore and enclosing correspondence with the Government authorities relating thereto as noted in the margin; copies and extracts of the same, being annexed for the information of the Honourable Court.

2. I am requested on behalf of this Company, to state their readiness to undertake the necessary surveys of the line from Moultan to Lahore and Umritsir, under the direction of the Government Consulting Engineer; should it be the pleasure of the Court to have them proceeded

with, and that all the expenses occasioned by the surveys should be placed to a separate account, and be appropriated hereafter according to the arrangement that may be ultimately entered into.

5. Letter from Resident Engineer to the Commissioner in Scinde, dated 14th Dec., 1855.

3. Should the Honourable Court concur in the views expressed by the Commissioner in Scinde (enclosure 1), the Chief Commissioner of the Punjaub (enclosure 7), and the Government of Bombay (enclosure 2), as to the great importance of the extension of improved means of transit along the Valley of the Indus, this Board is of opinion, that instead of making a through communication by means of a railway between Kurrachee and Lahore, as appears to be recommended by the agent and resident-engineer of the Company, in their letters (enclosures 3 and 4), that the present is a favourable opportunity for introducing the economical and easily-established system of communication, combining steam transit by land with steam transit by water, so long advocated by their Chairman.

6. Extract from letter from the Commissioner in Scinde to the Chief Commissioner in the Punjaub, dated 21st Sept. 1855.

7. Extract from letter of Secretary of Chief Commissioner in the Punjaub to Commissioner in Scinde, of 23rd Oct., 1855, par. 2 and 4, with Extracts of letters from Chief Commissioner in the Punjaub to Government of India.

4. For instance, the lower portion of the line from Kurrachee to Hyderabad, by the railway already sanctioned, which will avoid the dangers and delays of the Delta, from Hyderabad to Moultan by steamers of improved construction, resuming the railway from Moultan to Lahore and Umritsir.

A reference to the letters (enclosures 6 and 7) from the Commissioner in Scinde, and the Chief Commissioner of the Punjaub, will show that these views are approved of by the local authorities.

I have the honor to be, &c., &c.,

(Signed) W. P. ANDREW,

Chairman.

SIR JAMES C. MELVILL, K.C.B.,

&c., &c., &c.

The East India Company having authorised the survey of the country between Moultan, Lahore and Umritsir, by the Scinde Railway Company, Mr. William Brunton, a superintending engineer of ability and experience, with a carefully-selected staff of six engineers, left England for India on the 4th of September, 1856, and have since reported on the survey of the line with elaborate plans, sections, and detailed estimates, and that eminent authority Sir John Lawrence has placed on record his approval of the ability and zeal which Mr. Brunton and his staff have displayed in the discharge of their duty.

From W. P. ANDREW, Esq., to SIR JAMES C. MELVILL, K. C. B., &c., &c., &c.

Gresham House, Old Broad Street,
5th January, 1857.

SIR,

With reference to my letter No. 74, dated 14th March last, copy of which is annexed, relating to the proposed survey of the country between Moultan, Lahore and Umritsir, and having reference to the establishment of a comprehensive system of steam transit by rail and river from Lahore and Umritsir to the sea, and the Court having authorised the said survey being made by the Scinde Railway Company, and the existing steam flotilla on the Indus being notoriously inadequate for the requirements of Government, irrespective of the necessities of the countries traversed by the Indus and its tributaries,—

2. I have now the honour to request that you would be good enough to submit for the consideration of the Honourable Court a proposal for the provision of steam vessels of improved construction for navigating the Indus for the 570 miles which intervene between Hyderabad, the

upper terminus of the Scinde Railway, and Moultan, the lower terminus of the proposed Punjaub Railway, now under survey.

3. The introduction of railways into the valley of the Indus, in connection with improved steam vessels on the river, appears to be the most economical and best mode of affording to the Punjaub and neighbouring countries access to Kurrachee, their natural port, and has already received the approval of the highest authorities in Scinde and the Punjaub.

4. The Court are aware that both Mr. Frere and Sir John Lawrence have placed their opinions on record, and the latter of these distinguished gentlemen in a recent dispatch to the Government of India, makes the following forcible remarks:—

"Indeed, these two essentials, viz., the railroad and the steamers, may be said with truth to be the crying wants of the Punjaub in the department of public works. These provided, the commerce and produce of these territories will be turned to their due course, viz., the Indus and its feeders, and to their natural outlet, viz., the port of Kurrachee."

"For the railroad, the face of the Doab offers an unusual equality of surface, while it possesses few, or none, of the requisite resources for metalling a road. For the rivers, it were preferable, instead of improving the navigable stream, to concentrate all efforts on the provision of powerful steamers of the smallest possible draught. The Chief Commissioner, while deprecating any general extension of the public works' department in the Punjaub for the present, would yet beg most earnestly to press these cardinal objects on the attention of the Government. He believes that, if carried out, they would effect more for the development of the resources of those territories than any other work, or number of works, that could be devised."

5. Major Hamilton, the Commissioner at Moultan, when recently in England, expressed in the strongest terms his opinion that the kind of improved transit by river and rail, as suggested in my letter before referred to, was peculiarly adapted to the requirements of the country on the banks of the Indus; and that eminent authority, Colonel Napier, the Chief Engineer of the Punjaub, has confirmed the accuracy of the views expressed by the distinguished local authorities just named, and also assured me that a railway from Moultan to Lahore and Umritsir, would have no difficulty of any kind to encounter, and would not interfere with the system of irrigating canals in the Punjaub.

6. Were any additional argument necessary, I might recall to the recollection of the Court their own despatch of the 4th of June last, upon the want of sufficient means of transport on the Indus, wherein it is stated, that "it is very desirable that the deficiency should be supplied by the enterprise of private associations, which might have the effect also of reducing the price of freightage which is much complained of."

7. Scinde and the Punjaub (including the States under control) cover an area of 130,000 square miles, with a population of nearly 25,000,000. The flower of the European and native army occupies these provinces, and numbers 70,000 men, more than 15,000 of whom are Europeans. The political importance of having improved means of communication along the valley of the Indus is every day becoming more apparent; indeed, for commercial and social, as well as state purposes, the improvement of the transit along this ancient line of communication has become a necessity.

8. Holding, as we do, the Indus from Cashmere to the sea,

we have a power which, if "well understood and wisely improved, puts us in possession of the key to the whole commerce of Central Asia, which cannot be pursued without adding to the prosperity and productiveness of our new territories (Scinde and the Punjaub)."* The resources of modern science judiciously applied to this line of communication would be of inestimable benefit to our own provinces, and the enterprising European merchants now resident at Kurrachee would soon afford a medium for extensive shipments from the Punjaub and provinces to the north-west of Delhi, and the distribution of our manufactures to the remote valleys of Afghanistan, as far as Herat, and in Balkh, Khiva and Bokhara.

9. To give effect to what appears to be the wishes of the authorities, as well as essentially necessary for the security and progress of the important provinces on our north-west frontier, I beg to state that a Company, under the same direction and management as the Scinde Railway Company, is prepared to raise the necessary capital of £250,000, upon the same terms and conditions as those granted for the formation of railways in India, for the purpose of providing steam vessels of the most improved construction, adapted to the peculiar requirements of the Indus, and to meet the rapidly increasing commerce of the countries through which it passes.

10. The above amount it is considered will be sufficient to furnish the requisite number of vessels for a daily service upwards and downwards between Hyderabad and Moultan, including the necessary depôts, wharves and landings, but the capital is only to be called up in such proportion as the requirements of Government and the wants of commerce may demand.

* Economist.

11. I may add that, before arriving at any determination as to the description of steam vessels to be employed in this service, the most eminent practical authorities, both in this country and in America, are being consulted, and the result of such enquiries will be submitted to the Honourable Court for their approval and sanction.

I have the honour to be,

SIR,

Your most obedient Servant,

(Signed) W. P. ANDREW.

SIR JAMES C. MELVILL, K.C.B.

&c., *&c.*, *&c.*

From SIR JAMES C. MELVILL, K.C.B., &c., to W. P. ANDREW, Esq., &c., &c., &c.

East India House,
4th March, 1857.

SIR.

I have received and laid before the Court of Directors of the East India Company, your letter dated the 5th January last, submitting a proposal for establishing steam communication on the river Indus, in connection with the Scinde and Punjaub Railway Companies.

The Court have also had before them a similar proposition from other parties. Before passing any decision upon either scheme, the Court desire to be furnished with a fuller indication of the plan, which you have submitted, than that afforded by your letter under reply; and I am desired to request that you will explain more particularly the mode by which it is contemplated to carry out the object in view, by stating the description of steam vessels to be used and the number to be put annually on the river, the number of miles they will run, and the range of their employment: also that you will furnish estimates of the first and prospective expense, and supply all the information in your power, in order that a fair comparison may be made of the advantages of the two plans which may be submitted to a competent Committee to enquire whether either of them deserve the encouragement and assistance of the Court.

I am, Sir,

Your most obedient, humble Servant.

(Signed) JAMES C. MELVILL.

W. P. ANDREW, Esq.,
&c. &c. &c.

From W. P. ANDREW, Esq., to SIR JAMES C. MELVILL, K.C.B., &c., &c., &c.

Scinde Railway Company,
Gresham House, Old Broad Street.
20th April, 1857.

SIR,

I have the honour to acknowledge receipt of your letter of the 4th March last, referring to a proposal submitted by me, for establishing steam communication on the river Indus, in connection with the Scinde and Punjaub Railways, and requesting me to explain more particularly the mode by which it is contemplated to carry out the object in view, by stating the description of steam vessels to be used, and the number to be put annually on the river, and the range of their employment: also, that I should furnish estimates of the first and prospective expense, and supply all the information in my power.

2. In reply I have the satisfaction to submit for the

consideration of the Honourable Court, an elaborate report on the subject under notice, by Mr. Yarrow, the Engineer of the Scinde Railway Company, drawn up by my instructions so as to place in a compendious form, the opinions of the most eminent and experienced ship builders (who have applied themselves to the construction of steam vessels of light draught, for navigating shallow rivers), as to the description of steamer, which in their opinion, would be best adapted to meet the requirements of the commerce and the peculiarities of the River Indus.

3. As to the description of steam-vessel to be used, I should prefer a vessel combining various points of construction, advocated by several of the builders referred to in Mr. Yarrow's report, which would secure ample accommodation for passengers and merchandise, drawing two feet of water, and of sufficient power to give an effective speed of ten miles an hour against the current of the Indus, which would enable the average passage upwards and downwards between Hyderabad and Moultan, the terminal points of the Scinde and Punjaub Railways to be accomplished in four days and a half.

4. The arrangement above suggested taken in conjunction with the Scinde Railway from Kurrachee to Kotree (the Port of Hyderabad), would reduce the time occupied, on the journey from Kurrachee to Moultan, and *vice versa*, to an average of five days, being less than a fifth of the time now occupied by the existing steam vessels employed on the Indus.

5. If I might venture to offer an opinion upon a scientific question, I would suggest * * * * *

6. It is proposed to construct fifteen steam vessels, so as to secure a daily service to and from the two points already indicated and upon the Scinde Railway Company,

receiving the sanction of the Honourable Court, for raising £250,000 for this purpose, * * * * * measures would be immediately adopted for the construction of the hulls and engines in this country, and the preparation of the necessary cabin and other fittings in India, and it is estimated that within two years from the date of the order for the construction, that five vessels would be ready for effective service in India, and five more each succeeding year, until the entire number should be completed, or more rapidly, should the requirements of Government or the exigencies of the commerce of the country demand it.

7. The distance proposed to be traversed by the steamers, that is from Hyderabad, the upper terminus of the Scinde Railway, and Moultan, the lower terminus of the Punjaub Railway, is 570 miles, which is the range contemplated for this mode of transit.

8. Providing five steamers for three successive years, the prospective expenditure would be as follows, viz.:—

1st year—		
Five Steamers with ten supplemental Barges	£72,000	
Workshops, Machinery, and River-Stations	20,000	
		£92,000
2nd year—		
Five Steamers with ten supplemental Barges	72,000	
3rd year—		
Five Steamers with ten supplemental Barges	72,000	
		£144,000
Contingencies		14,000
		£250,000

Entire Capital for 15 Steamers with 30 supplemental barges and necessary appliances.

9. For detailed information as to the capacity of the steam vessels, and their supplemental barges, and an estimate of the expected revenue and expenditure, I beg a reference to the accompanying Report of Mr. Yarrow.

10. The return of 20 per cent. may appear large, but the communications I have had on this subject with Mr. Frere, the Commissioner in Scinde, Major Hamilton, the Commissioner at Moultan, Colonel Napier, Chief Engineer of the Punjaub, Mr. Temple, late Secretary to the Chief Commissioner of the Punjaub, and other local authorities, lead me to conclude that the pecuniary result cannot but be of a highly favourable character.

11. It will be apparent to the Honourable Court, that much economy and many other advantages must accrue from the management of the proposed steam flotilla on the Indus being entrusted to the Scinde Railway Company, as that Company is already charged with the construction and working of the Line, which will connect the inland navigation of the Indus with the port of shipment.

12. In conclusion, it is the opinion of this Board, and all the authorities whom I have consulted, that the early establishment of an efficient steam flotilla is not only essential to the successful development of the Scinde and Punjaub Railways; but it is most urgently demanded for the proper discharge of the public service and the pressing necessities of the countries drained by the Indus and its tributaries, whose population and commerce are at present denied free access to Kurrachee, their natural port.

I have the honour to be, &c.

(Signed) W. P. ANDREW, *Chairman.*

SIR JAMES C. MELVILL, K.C.B., &c.

From Sir James C. Melvill, K.C.B., to W. P. Andrew, Esq., Chairman of the Scinde Railway Company, &c., &c., &c.

(EXTRACT)

East India House,
17*th June*, 1857.

Sir,

I am commanded to acquaint you that the Court of Directors of the East India Company, having considered the proposition submitted by the Directors of the Scinde Railway, for the navigation of the Indus between Kotree, the terminus of the Scinde Railway, and Moultan, the terminus of the proposed Punjaub Railway, have resolved to allow the Scinde Railway Company to issue shares, representing a capital of two hundred and fifty thousand pounds (£250,000) for that purpose * * * an agreement being entered into between the Company and the East India Company upon the same terms as those which are included in the Railway contract.

(Signed) JAMES C. MELVILL.

W. P. Andrew, Esq.
&c. &c. &c.

These terms were accepted and the Scinde Railway Company was empowered by an Act passed in the last session of Parliament, to raise capital for the construction of steam-vessels for navigating the Indus; and arrangements are already in progress for carrying out this important portion of the line of intercommunication throughout the valley of the Indus.

With the view of collecting information which might be applicable to the navigation of the Indus, in the autumn of last year the East India Company appointed a commission, composed of Major Craufurd, superintending engineer to the Government of Bombay, Captain Balfour, I.N., and a marine engineer of experience, to visit the Danube, the Rhine and other important European rivers, and a copy of their Report has recently been received by the Board of the Scinde Railway Company.

How much improvement is required in the present Indus flotilla, as well as in the native boats, the following extract from the Third Punjaub Report will show. Speaking of the native boats, the reporter says—"Their construction is primitive, though there is no want of timber, which can be, and is largely floated down the rivers from the Himalayan hill sides. A boat of this description costs 500 or 600 rupees (£50 or £60) will ordinarily hold 400 maunds or 14 tons, or 600 maunds or 21 tons, if heavily laden. The boats are flat-bottomed; they never draw less than 2½ feet of water, unless very lightly laden; if heavily laden, they will draw four or five feet. They manage to pass down the Five Rivers from the northern marts at all seasons. During the two months when the water is shallowest, namely, from 15th November to 15th January, their cargoes are kept lighter than usual; but even in these months they carry 200 maunds each, or more, and draw 2½ feet of water at least. If tolerably repaired, they will last several years. The freightage from Lahore to Kurrachee would be about 1 rupee or 2 shillings per maund, or 28 rupees (£2 16s.) per ton, and about half that amount from Moultan to Kurrachee. The voyage from Lahore to Kurrachee can, under fairly favourable circumstances, be performed in thirty-five days, but it might last for six weeks. The upward trip from Kurrachee to Lahore might last fifteen weeks. There is, of course, some risk of stoppage from sand banks, and occasionally danger from velocity of current."

"The present Indus flotilla steamers," continues the writer, "belong to the Bombay Government. They ply regularly from Kurrachee upwards to Moultan, but seldom beyond that place. On special occasions the steamers have, during the rainy season, proceeded as far as Kalabagh on the Indus, or Jhelum on the Jhelum, or Lahore on the Ravee, and Ferozepore on the Sutlej. But they do not appear to be generally suited for navigating the Punjaub rivers; their draught is too great for the shallow waters in the winter months. Their accommodation is not very large, and they are of course much occupied by passengers, troops, government stores, and treasure. Their freight, from Moultan to Kurrachee, is about ten or twelve annas per maund, that is, 60 or 80 per cent. in excess of the rates by native craft. The down-trip is performed in about twelve days, and the up-trip in twenty-five days. The character and merits of these vessels can be best described by the Government to which they pertain. So far as the Punjaub is concerned, it may be said that they are serviceable in a certain way; they are useful to the Government and to the European community, and render some assistance to traffic. But they are not sufficiently numerous, or capacious, or inexpensive, to materially affect the export trade of these territories."

The account of the traffic given in this important document is most satisfactory:—

"For some time past the civil officer resident at Mithunkote, just below the junction of the Five Rivers, where the several fleets of boats must unite, has kept up a registration of the native craft passing up and down the Indus. The last return received for the third quarter of 1855-6, showed 668 boats passing down, with cargo of 241,185 maunds or 8,613 tons; and 159 boats passing up, with cargo of 23,376 maunds or 835 tons,—in all 827 boats, with cargoes of 264,561 maunds or 9,447 tons. These numbers are in excess of any previously returned. A comparison of different quarters shows a progressive increase, and indeed this traffic is generally believed to be really increasing. At the present rate it may reach to nearly a million of maunds or 35,714 tons in a year. If the water-traffic be now so considerable, despite of impediments, how vast would it become with the facilities of science? In 1855, when the expectations regarding flax and linseed ran high, and when it was anticipated that Government would have to dispatch 250,000 maunds or 8,928 tons of produce to Kurrachee from several depôts in the upper Punjaub, there was every hope that water-carriage to this amount would be procurable."*

"At present, excepting those gentlemen who can well afford to pay for palkee dak, and wait for the half-monthly steamer, all travellers and consignments proceeding to or from Bombay or Europe, must toil through the tedious and hazardous river navigation before alluded to, in rude country boats, liable at any moment to be stranded or upset. The Bengalee or Hindostanee manjees are sufficiently unskilful, but they are men of science and dexterity compared to the Punjabees; yet, for want of a better and cheaper means of transit, most of the mercantile and other supplies, as well as passengers, destined for the Punjaub or cis-Sutlej States, take this route. The chances are risked to avoid the enormous expenses of a land car-

* Report on Administration of Punjaub from 1854 to 1856, pars. 121, 122, 123.

riage, comprising from twelve to fifteen hundred miles, via Calcutta; which, for goods, is equally as dangerous as the Indus and Sutlej passage, from the positive certainty of loss or damage occasioned by exposure to every vicissitude of the weather during four or five months; to say nothing of bad roads, and the usual careless indifference of hackery drivers and peons, or other pseudo guards."*

* "Calcutta Englishman." *Vide* "London to Lahore:" or the Euphrates, Scinde, and Punjaub Railways. Effingham Wilson, Royal Exchange.

CHAPTER VII.

THE PUNJAUB RAILWAY.

REPORT OF PUNJAUB GOVERNMENT.—REPORT OF MR. W. BRUNTON, SUPERINTENDING ENGINEER.—ROAD CENSUS.—TRAFFIC ON BRIDGE OF BOATS, RIVER RAVEE, AT LAHORE.—TABLE OF GRADIENTS.—OFFICIAL CORRESPONDENCE.—OPINION OF SIR JOHN LAWRENCE.—CONSTRUCTION OF LINE SANCTIONED.

HAVING thus shown how by the aid of the rail and the river, it is intended to open up the Valley of the Indus from the sea to Moultan, it remains only to describe the third section of the work, that by which the traffic is to be carried on from Moultan to Lahore. The necessity for the adoption of the railway system in the upper portion of the Indus Valley, had been fully recognised by the local authorities, and in consequence, in March 1856, the Scinde Railway Board requested permission of the India House to commence a survey of the country from Moultan to Lahore and Umritsir, with the object of completing the combined system of steam transit by land and water, so long advocated by their chairman. To facilitate operations, the Punjaub Railway Company was temporarily established as a separate company, though under the same management as the Scinde Railway Company, and the capital deemed requisite for the work raised without difficulty. In July, 1856, the permission to conduct the survey was given by the East India Company, and measures taken for its immediate commencement. Of the political and commercial value set on this third link in the chain of communication by the local authorities, the following extract from the elaborate report from the Punjaub Government in 1856 will be sufficient evidence.

"So far as the commercial and material interests of the Punjaub are concerned, there is a proposed line from the north-East to South-West, which is of greater consequence to the country than any public work, or any number of works that could be specified. A glance at the accompanying map will show that Northern India has two natural divisions, *first,* the Provinces of the Ganges and its tributaries; *second,* the Provinces of the Indus and its tributaries. In the first or easterly division, the stream of trade and wealth must ever flow down the valley of the Ganges to the natural outlet of Calcutta. In the second or westerly division, if the power of art and science be brought to the aid of nature, the commerce could follow the direction of the Punjaub rivers to the Indus, then down the valley of the Indus towards the rising port of Kurrachee, which is destined to be, to the North-West of India, what Calcutta is to the North-East. *A line drawn North to South, somewhere near Agra and Delhi, will form the probable boundary of the two natural sub-divisions. And if the same facilities were created Westward, which exist Eastward, then all the commerce west of the line would follow the Indus to Kurrachee, in the same manner as the commerce on the east follows the Ganges to Calcutta.* At present, however, the major part of the commerce of the extreme north-west travels eastward, merely from the want of a more direct route. But if the great route of the Indus were to be thoroughly opened, this commerce would go straight to Kurrachee. To this port there would then come the products from the North-Western India, and from the Central Asian countries beyond that frontier; and in exchange for these, the products of European countries. In this same direction, there would also arrive the vast quantities of Government stores and material for the military and public establishments in that quarter, and large numbers of European travellers would frequent this line (in preference to the Eastern route), on account of its comparative shortness and proximity to overland passage to Europe.

"For the opening up of this Western route, the importance of which, upon general considerations is so evident, it is proposed, in the first place, to establish communication by rail and steam from Kurrachee upwards to Moultan, just above the point where the Punjaub rivers join the Indus. For the first section of this line a railroad from Kurrachee to Hyderabad on the Indus, a distance of 123 miles, has been undertaken by the Scinde Railway Company. At first, the line may be continued thence up to Moultan, by steamers on the Indus, to be followed by a railway as soon as it can be constructed; there would then remain to be constructed a railroad from Moultan to Lahore and Umritsir, to join or cross (or rather continue) the great North-Western line between Calcutta and Peshawur. It is this last-named railroad, from Moultan to Lahore and Umritsir, which immediately concerns the Punjaub; and the Supreme Government have directed complete inquiries on the subject to be made. It will now be proper to state briefly what the advantages and facilities of the line are likely to be.

"The Northern terminus of the line will be Umritsir, which is not only the first mart in the Punjaub, but also one of the first commercial cities in Upper India. Its merchants have dealings, not only with all parts of India, but also with many parts of Europe on the one hand, and of Central Asia on the other. To this city there come the choicest Asiatic products, the wool of Thibet, the shawls of Cashmere, the dried fruit and spices of Afghanistan, the carpets of Turkey, the silk of Bokhara, the furs and skins of Tartary, the chintzes and leather of Russia. In return for these arrive the piece goods and iron of Europe, the fabrics of Bengal, the sugar of Hindostan and the Punjaub. To the same emporium are gathered all kinds of indigenous produce of the Punjaub. Of this trade, amounting, according to reliable returns, to three and-a-half million pounds sterling per annum, a large portion proceeds to and from Calcutta, by the Grand Trunk line, another portion to Bombay by difficult and laborious land routes, through Central India and the desert routes of Rajpootana; and a third portion (and at present the least portion) to Kurrachee, by water carriage on the Indus and its tributaries. *Of this traffic, then, nearly all would be diverted to the proposed railroad from Umritsir to Moultan, and thence to Kurrachee. From these parts, most things intended for export would not go to Calcutta, if there were facilities for going to Kurrachee; and of those things destined for Bombay, all would go by the rail to Kurrachee* via *Moultan, instead of the arduous route through Central India. In the same manner all the imports for Umritsir, and other parts of the country between Delhi to the North-Western Provinces Frontier, and the regions beyond it, which now come from Calcutta or from Bombay by land, would proceed to Kurrachee, and thence upwards by rail.*

" But besides the noble traffic above indicated, which is of general as well as local interest, there is already a traffic of some magnitude between the Punjaub and Kurrachee. *So strong is the tendency of trade towards the natural port and outlet, that large quantities of indigenous produce creep and labour in clumsy native craft down the Five Rivers.* In this manner, hundreds of tons of cereals, linseed, sugar, saltpetre and indigo pursue a tedious way over 400 miles of the five rivers to the sea-board. The water traffic is greatest on the Sutlej, next on the Jhelum, then on the Indus, and lastly on the Chenab and the Ravee. The united traffic of the rivers up and down (by the greater part, say four-fifths, being *down* traffic), as ascertained by registration of boats at the junction point, Mithunkote, on the Indus, is not less than 700,000 maunds, or 35,000 tons per annum. Now, if the rates of carriage by rail should be kept low, so as to attract commodities which can only afford to pay for *cheap* transit, then it may be certainly presumed, that of the above quantity *all that pertains to the Sutlej, the Ravee and the Chenab, and a part of that belonging to the Jhelum, will be diverted to the Umritsir and Moultan Railway; and if the railway up to Peshawur should have been established, then almost all the traffic of the Jhelum, and much of the Indus traffic, would proceed to Lahore, aud thence down the rail to Moultan.* The present means of navigation being wretched, and the rivers being difficult, the existing water traffic would preferentially take the railway, *provided always that the cost of transit be cheap,* It is, indeed, for the sake of this indigenous traffic that every well-wisher of the Punjaub people must be anxious to see the day when the rail shall be opened from Umritsir to Moultan. The traffic may be already considerable and promising, but *it is now as nothing* compared to *what it would become,* with the advantages of a rail. In the chapter on Land Revenue, the enormous and increasing production of cereals beyond the present consumption, the probable *surplus* produce amounting to a quarter, perhaps half a million of tons annually, the quantity of unreclaimed land, capable of production, the great productive power of the people, were demonstrated. Wheat of excellent quality is grown, and this is eminently a corn-producing province. Sugar-cane of first-rate quality is already grown. Indigo of similar quality can be produced; it is already exported to a considerable extent, though at present of inferior quality, owing to the defective mode of manufacture. It has been recently proved that good linseed in considerable quantities can be raised. If sufficient pains be taken, many hundred tons of fibre can be prepared. From some parts, good hemp could be exported. From many thousand square miles, the saline nature of the soil offers unusual facilities for the manufacture of saltpetre, which is even now largely made to meet a foreign demand; and from the same soil, carbonate of soda could be profitably made. The numerous flocks of sheep in the extensive pasturage of the central districts, and in the hills and valleys of the north, yield a wool that is already exported, and which might become an export of magnitude. There are various articles of manufacture fit for exportation, such as the shawls, stuffs, silks, and carpets of Umritsir, Lahore, Moultan, Noorpore and Loodhiana. It were vain to specify the amount which *might* be exported by the rail, but none acquainted with the Punjaub could doubt that the aggregate would be enormous. Lastly, independent of European travellers, who would be numerous, the number of native passengers would prove most profitable. Between the cities of Lahore and Umritsir, the transit of passengers has greatly increased since the completion of the new road; the average of travellers to and fro is not less than a thousand persons per diem; and whereas six years ago there were not twenty ekkas (small one-horse vehicles carrying two or three persons) in Lahore, there are now some 250 running daily between the two cities. It is believed, from this source alone a railway might, *even on its first opening*, realize £10,000 per annum on a section only thirty-five miles long. A similar passenger traffic would doubtless spring up between Lahore and Moultan; and it may be added, that the route *via* Kurrachee would be frequented by pilgrims to Mecca.

"Again, if the advantages, present and prospective, of this line, when constructed, are great, so also are the facilities for its construction remarkable. Though the country situated above its northern terminus is rich and highly cultivated, yet the particular tract through which it will run is for the most part poor. Between Moultan and Lahore, a distance of 240 miles, the country is a dead level, hard and waste. In the first place, then, there will be no cultivated or inhabited ground to be bought up. The price for the land will be almost nominal. There are no engineering difficulties whatever to be met with anywhere between Lahore and Moultan. The Doab, or country lying between the two rivers Sutlej and Ravee, is elevated in the centre, and the sides slope gently off towards the rivers. From the centre or *back-bone* of the tract, there naturally run drainage channels to the rivers; consequently, while a road traversing the Doab, near the banks of either river, must cross or be intersected by numerous little streams, a line constructed in the *centre* would meet *none of them*. But the railroad would run near the *central*, or dorsal ridge, parallel to the course of the new Baree Doab Canal, and consequently, the line will, perhaps, not meet with any stream whatever. There being no streams, nor depressions, nor elevations, there will, consequently, be no bridges, cuttings, or embankments, on at least four-fifths of the distance. As it approaches Moultan, the line would have to be carried across a few small irrigation canals, and to be partially raised. In short, it would be difficult to select, or even imagine, a champaign more suited for the cheap and easy construction of a railway than the country between Lahore and Moultan. Between Lahore and Umritsir, the country is fairly cultivated, and generally level. It offers no engineering obstacles. But there would be three or four small streams, and one canal to be bridged. As regards material, the iron would come from England; timber and wood of the best quality is obtainable from the Hills by water-carriage; fire-wood exists in the utmost abundance: kunkur would be generally procurable for at least half the distance; masonry would not be much needed; if it were, there are ample facilities for brick-making; the population near the line is sparse, but labour is largely procurable from other parts of this country for any great work.

"The absence of physical and engineering difficulties is indeed most fortunate. For economy and even *cheapness* of construction will be essential to enable the railway authorities to fix the transit line at *low* rates. The passenger-traffic and the more valuable commodities and products would be considerable, and might bear tolerably high rates. But for a mass of produce great in bulk, but comparatively less valuable, *lower rates* will be indispensable. For the goods' trains, speed will generally be of less consequence than cheapness of hire. It is upon this condition, namely, that of moderate hire, that the rail may be expected to supersede the native river boats. In a succeeding chapter the improvement of the river navigation will be urged. If this most desirable end should be accomplished, as well as the railway, the one will not interfere with the other; there will be such a great development of commerce and of national resources, that there will be ample scope for both rail and steam, and each will have its legitimate functions for the enhancement of wealth and civilization.

"Limited space has prevented details being embraced in the above sketch. The details, commercial and otherwise, are of great variety and interest, and will be treated of in a separate report; but if the arguments urged should (as it is fully believed they will) be supported by statistical facts and data, then it were superfluous to dilate on the importance of a scheme which will affect the trade of all North-Western India, will give birth to a new commerce yet undeveloped, will be carried out with unusual facility, will prove financially profitable in a high degree, will vitally concern the best material interests of twenty-one millions of industrious people, and will conduce more than any other circumstance that could be named to the future prosperity of the Punjaub."*

"No line more demands the support of the Government of India. It (the Railway from Umritsir to

* Report on Administration of Punjaub, from 1854 to 1856.

Moultan) would be the temporal artery of the Indian body. *From Meerut to the Soliman, the true outlet for Northern India is to be sought in Kurrachee.* As to Calcutta, even the grand advantage of the Ganges, with its perpetual fulness and the cheapness of its traffic, is overbalanced by the distance. Bombay is twice as far; for, in India, a mile of land carriage is equal in difficulty and expense to at least ten of water. It is the habitual disregard of this great fact which at the present moment retards the progress of those provinces. No improvement can be made in cultivation, and no increase acquired for the revenue; for the granary, bursting with wealth, is locked up. The produce can find no market, and until it has found one, it is useless to extend production. The means proposed do not, it is true, give these provinces a direct connection with Kurrachee. But they do surmount all the main difficulties in the way. Umritsir is already the grand *entrepôt* for the trade with Central Asia. The caravans which come down with spices and dried fruits, dyes and drugs, skins and carpets, chintzes and leather, through Peshawur, Dhera Ismael Khan, and the Bolan Pass, deposit their loads at Umritsir. Wools and borax from Thibet, shawls and carpets from Cashmere, sugar and grain from the Doabs, all pass through this bonded warehouse of Northern India. The instant the line is constructed, it becomes the great outlet for the north-west also. The indigo which now travels painfully to Calcutta, and the wheat which rots in the granaries for want of means of conveyance, will find its way to the head of the railway. Lahore itself, though it is the fashion to contemn its trade, is still the seat of a wealthy population, and the centre of political action for 19,000,000 of human beings. From Moultan to Hyderabad the road is open to steamers; and thence to Kurrachee the railway is in process of construction. The route, it is true, is imperfect, and the transhipment will be an addition to the cost of carriage. But it renders the steam communication between the Punjaub, Scinde, and the sea, complete. From thence a new route to Europe is open to all the residents of the north-west; and every officer and soldier destined for the north-west will soon reach it by the direct route.

"It is scarcely needful to point out that such a line must pay. Any line which connects a kingdom with the sea cannot fail to return a dividend. The Umritsir and Moultan line connects three, and its receipts must be proportionate. We are not, however, left to such conjectural arguments."*

The survey of this important line commenced in December, 1856, and although unavoidably interrupted by the outbreak in the Punjaub, and by the necessity imposed on the surveying staff of acting as soldiers as well as engineers, was completed in May, 1857, and the following letter from the Chairman, enclosing the report of the engineer, and requesting permission to raise the capital required without delay, was addressed to the East India Company:—

* "Friend of India." *Vide* "London to Lahore:" or the Euphrates, Scinde and Punjaub Railways. Effingham Wilson, Royal Exchange.

From W. P. ANDREW, Esq., to Sir JAMES C. MELVILL, K.C.B., &c., &c., &c.

SCINDE RAILWAY COMPANY,
GRESHAM HOUSE, OLD BROAD STREET,
20th October, 1857.

SIR,

With reference to the sanction of the Honourable Court of the 3rd July, 1856, to the survey of the country between Moultan, Lahore and Umritsir, I have the honour to transmit herewith for the information of the Court, copy of a Report from Mr. William Brunton, Superintending Engineer of the Punjaub survey, which accompanied elaborate plans and sections, together with a memorandum from Mr. Yarrow, the Consulting Engineer of the Company, to whom the documents above referred to have been submitted.

2. By a perusal of the report it will be manifest that the line of country presents most unusual facilities for the construction of a railway, offering no engineering impediment whatever, the gradients being equal to only one foot per mile in its entire length. The cuttings and embankments are merely nominal, and the total absence of all expensive bridges and culverts bring the cost of construction within the limits of levelling the face of the country to receive the permanent way, for providing for the natural drainage and irrigation, and for the ordinary appliances for working the line, such as station tanks, fencing, and rolling stock.

3. The line being nearly level, the working expenses will be consequently low, the consumption of fuel proportionably small, and from the almost entire absence of

curves, the wear and tear of the rolling stock will be considerably less than upon lines not possessing these advantages. Labour on the spot is abundant and cheap, and from the suspension of many public works, native contractors can be found competent to construct the line with efficiency and speed.

4. Aided by the Government surveys placed at the disposal of the Superintending Engineer, he has, with a comparatively small staff, been able to complete and forward to this Board, in an unprecedentedly short space of time, and under circumstances of great difficulty, a set of admirably executed plans and sections, which fully establish the advantages above referred to. Copies have been transmitted to the Chief Commissioner of the Punjaub, with a suggestion from the Agent of this Company, that as Lieut. Greathed, who was appointed by Government to report upon the line, is engaged on active service, the Chief Commissioner's report should be forwarded for the approval of the Bombay Government, and as railway communication is so urgently required in the country proposed to be traversed by this line, this Board respectfully submit that upon receipt of the Government approval no time should be lost in enabling them to take the requisite steps for raising the capital, and for carrying out the important object they have in view.

I have the honour to be, &c. &c.

(Signed) W. P. ANDREW,
Chairman.

Sir James C. Melvill, K.C.B.,
&c., &c., &c.

REPORT from WILLIAM BRUNTON, Esq., C.E., Superintending Engineer, to the CHAIRMAN and DIRECTORS of the Punjaub Railway Company.

LAHORE, 15*th June*, 1857.

GENTLEMEN,

I beg to forward plans, sections, and estimates for a line of railway uniting the towns of Umritsir, Lahore and Moultan.

My estimate is for a single line of railway of 5 feet 6 inches gauge, complete with every appliance to render it fully effective, both as regards the carriage of passengers and goods, and the public safety, with sufficient rolling stock, tools, and machinery to work the same, and every way in accordance with the recommendations of the Consulting Engineers of the Indian Railway Companies sanctioned by the Honourable Court, bearing date, London, March 7th, 1856.

In carrying out your instructions relative to this work, I have received great assistance from Captain Thompson, of the Revenue Survey, who has given me free access to his plans, which I must say from their extreme accuracy entitle the said officer to great credit.

The main reason, however, of my being able, in so short a time, to accomplish your views, is the extraordinary adaptation of the country to railway purposes. No tract I have ever seen even of much less area presented so few obstacles.

I have as far as possible chosen the highest ground between the rivers Ravee and Sutlej, in order to keep above the annual inundations, and where this has been impracticable, I have provided such drainage as from the information I have obtained will be sufficient to keep the works perfectly secure in case of floods. I shall personally inspect every portion of the ground during the next flood, in order to be satisfied that I have founded my calculations on correct data.

The working expenses of a line as laid down must of necessity be small. Being nearly level, the consumption of fuel will be proportionally low, and being almost entirely free from curves, the wear and tear of the rolling stock will be trifling in comparison with the lines not having the same advantage.

The pay also of natives is about 20 per cent. of that in England for labour of the same description.

I have estimated but not shown the position of a branch line from the Lahore station to the banks of the Ravee. My reason is that I wish to see the country over which it must pass inundated (which is the case every year) prior to fixing the most advantageous site for such branch. Whichever site I decide on, my estimate will be adequate for its construction.

I have consulted the wants of the Meean Meer cantonment, and have allotted a station at each end of their lines. The stations at Lahore, Umritsir and Moultan, I have placed more especially with a view to native passenger-traffic, which will be the main source of revenue from passengers: they are also in suitable positions for the delivery and reception of goods.

It is possible (I may say certain) that near each station between Lahore and Moultan, natives will form in time large villages. I should recommend you to make such arrangements with the Honourable East India Company as shall give you the control over the erection of any buildings within, say one mile, from each station; that the villages may be constructed with regularity, and proper sanitary measures taken, as you may be advised by your engineer for the time being.

Over the whole length of the line, timber for fuel is to be obtained in abundance.

At every ten miles along the line, wells will have to be sunk at an average depth of 80 feet, at which depth abundance of water can be obtained. This is a work which should be proceeded with immediately, so as to provide for the wants of the workmen.

The station-houses also should be erected without delay, as they would form head quarters for my residents, during the construction of the line.

I have formed the line entirely on embankment; I find it necessary, even where the surface of the ground would appear to warrant a cutting. The reason for this is, that in the rainy season any place below the natural surface becomes a pond, if level; and if at an inclination, a bed for a stream.

The quantity of land which will be occupied by the railway and station-plots, will be 1,700 acres, and liberty required to take side cuttings, exclusive of this amount. This quantity provides for a double line of railway.

I am not aware if the Honourable East India Company give the land required for the line, clear of all liability.* If the Company have to pay for crops, &c., £5,000 for same should be added to my estimate.

In my estimate you will perceive I have provided for grassing the slopes of embankments; this may seem an

* The East India Company provide the land free of charge. W.P.A.

unnecessary expense to parties unacquainted with the character of the rains in India, but it is absolutely necessary in order to keep the slopes perfect during the rainy season.

The fencing estimated for is post and rail; and I propose planting a fence also, in all places where it can be made to grow. The numerous herds of cattle that range over the whole Doab, render a fencing on every portion absolutely necessary, to secure the public safety.

The ballast I propose using principally is kunker (a limestone found in different parts of the Doab), where this is at such a distance from the line as to render its use too costly, I shall substitute hard burnt bricks broken to size; either of these materials will form excellent ballast.

At every mile along the line I propose putting occupation level crossings; this distance will, I believe, be satisfactory to all parties. I have taken the opinion of several gentlemen in authority over the different districts, and they state it will be ample. The canal engineers, in consequence of a crossing entailing such an expense in bridges, approaches, &c., &c., only put one every three miles; but this is at a distance, very detrimental to parties whose ground may be severed.

My estimates are made on fair local prices for each description of work, and on the price of all materials, &c., which must be imported, I have added an amount fully ample for charges in laying the same on the ground. I am convinced the railway can be completed for the sum named.

If a responsible English contractor will undertake it for such sum, you would not, in my opinion, do wrong in letting it; but from what I hear of the disagreements between contractors and railway companies in India, the said contractor, whoever he might be, should be tightly bound down, and should give good sureties in case of failure. There are plenty of native contractors here, men who have completed large works on different roads and canals, who would be glad to take from twenty to forty miles of line each, exclusive of the permanent way; and unless you can obtain excellent security for the proper construction of your works from some English contractor, I should recommend everything, except the permanent way, to be let in the above mode to native contractors, in which case I believe my estimate would be found to exceed the actual cost.

In ordering the chairs, 10,000 in number should be adapted for receiving check rails, which may be a flat bar; length not less than fifteen feet. Sleepers, of good quality, for permanent way, I can get here delivered on the ground for three rupees each.

All other articles belonging to the permanent way, with locomotives, iron work for carriages, and waggons, tools, and implements of every description, will have to be sent from England.

I recommend (in order that no delay may occur in our obtaining material) rails and all appliances for same, necessary for permanent way, be immediately ordered and sent to Kurrachee. From that place to Moultan they have to be sent by native boats, necessarily involving a loss of time. If this is done, and proper diligence used in getting them up the Indus, the subject of obtaining the necessary supplies of material needs no further comment. I believe there are plenty of native boats; it is a question of delay, in consequence of the time these take making a trip, the disadvantages arising from which, immediate prosecution will obviate.

The locomotives you send out should be adapted for burning wood. They should be light also, which tends to decrease the wear of permanent way. This involves engines of less power than those now generally made in England; but our line is so level that such powerful engines are not required. Forty locomotives will work the line. Twenty 6-wheel engines, leading and trailing wheels 3 feet 6 inches diameter, driving wheels 6 feet, 12-inch cylinders and 20-inch stroke, weight not exceeding 20 tons; and twenty 6-wheel engines, leading wheels 3 feet 6 inches diameter, driving and trailing wheels 5 feet diameter coupled, 14-inch cylinders, and 20-inch stroke, weight of engine not exceeding 22 tons, in both cases, exclusive of tender, which should carry 1,200 gallons, on 6 wheels, 3 feet 6 inches diameter; each engine and tender to be provided with a light frame or roof covered with painted canvas carried on uprights from the engine frame and tender respectively, the tender roof being higher than the engine roof, so as to work perfectly clear and to lap over each other 9 inches.

Every portion or part of each engine and tender in each set of twenty to be made from one template, so that any piece of an engine shall fit and be applicable to perform the same duty or any other of the set.

I should recommend you to have the wood work of all your carriages and waggons made here, the iron work being sent from England; and no delay should take place in making arrangements for such work, viz., for preparing shops and getting timber cut, so as to have it properly seasoned. I find the native workmen clever and intelligent, and with English foremen over them, can be made to turn out exceedingly good work.

The staff I should require during the construction of the line would be, six first-class engineers, residents, over certain districts, six second and six third-class, each first-class having two assistants; one first-class engineer, a good practical man, to take charge of the principal office and drawing department.

The number of inspectors required it is now impossible to state; it will depend on what works are being proceeded with at the same time. These men can be obtained in this country.

I can get here five men fully competent to fill the position of second class, having been engaged on public works and know the language. The third class should be good practical men, who understand the practice thoroughly, as well as some theory of railway works.

I cannot speak too highly of the willingness and energy displayed by the staff I brought out, who one and all have not flinched from their duties in the field, even when called on to perform the same much later in the season than customary. I beg to recommend that they be promoted to the duties of first class engineers, five being placed between here and Moultan, and one on the Umritsir line.

In case this is sanctioned by you, one first, one second, and six third-class engineers would be required from England during the construction, and sanction given to engage here the others, to make up the above-mentioned staff.

I am of opinion that I could complete this line of railway, ready for opening, in four years from this present date, if I have every facility for so doing afforded me.

I should recommend a good cotton press being erected at Lahore, close to the goods station. The native bales of ll descriptions are very badly put together, and can be reduced fully one half their bulk. This is a speculation, the carrying out of which, if not consistent for a railway company, would well pay any private individuals.

That the passenger and merchandise traffic are sufficient even now amply to repay the outlay, the statistical reports you already have from the Government officers fully prove, but in my opinion the increase of these sources of profit will be augmented to a degree that it is impossible to calculate, when there is an outlet for the products of the country. At present there is none, the natural result being, that only sufficient for the wants of the immediate vicinity is produced; and, added to its being a source of profit, the present position of India forcibly points to the absolute necessity of rapid communication with all parts of a country made up of so many discordant elements.

As your proposed lines of railway in connection with the river and railway communication to Kurrachee, will form the main artery through which the whole of the traffic from the Punjaub must naturally pass, I should, to complete the scheme, recommend that the cost of extending the line from Lahore to Peshawur be ascertained as quickly as possible.

I have the honour to be, Gentlemen,

Your obedient servant,

(Signed) WILLIAM BRUNTON,

Superintending Engineer, Punjaub Survey.

Lahore and Umritsir Road Census, taken at Shahleemar, between the 7th and 12th November, 1854.

Month and Date.	Travellers.	Coolies (Porters).	Carts Laden.	Bylees (Bullock Carriages).	Horses and Mules laden.	Horses and Mules unladen.	Asses laden.	Asses unladen.	Riders and Horses.	Empty Carts.	Ekas laden (Native Horse Carriages.)	Ekas empty.	Camels laden.	Camels unladen.	Riding Camels.	Elephants laden.	Elephants unladen.	Bullocks laden.	Goats and Sheep.	Buggies.	Mail cart and Bullock train.	Bullocks laden.	
Nov. 7th	1111	698	99	72	68	58	571	189	651	61	90	25	196	91	3	...	...	286	156	...	...	223	A Regiment on March.
— 8th	2605	1225	96	54	269	88	296	581	1297	89	134	25	198	115	2	...	...	52	672	25	6	545	
— 9th	1985	880	35	25	112	64	511	68	810	30	105	15	226	41	4	...	...	400	354	7	22	1206	
— 10th	1005	503	51	45	176	52	425	105	307	24	203	...	72	55	...	2	...	271	394	4	8	544	
— 11th	2900	1102	276	48	506	55	596	78	304	25	182	15	68	74	6	2	1	334	607	3	10	1600	
— 12th	2546	1122	576	22	510	146	608	94	143	55	208	10	703	188	...	3	2	503	815	3	8	2004	
Total.	10143	7560	1171	256	1521	3215	3007	1114	3215	284	922	90	1461	536	13	7	3	1936	2697	42	54	6123	
Daily Average.	$1630\frac{1}{2}$	1260	$195\frac{1}{6}$	$42\frac{4}{6}$	$253\frac{1}{2}$	$535\frac{1}{3}$	$501\frac{1}{7}$	$185\frac{4}{6}$	$535\frac{1}{5}$	$47\frac{1}{3}$	$153\frac{4}{6}$	15	$243\frac{1}{2}$	$89\frac{2}{6}$	$2\frac{1}{2}$	$1\frac{1}{6}$	$\frac{1}{2}$	$322\frac{4}{6}$	$448\frac{1}{2}$	7	9	$1020\frac{3}{6}$	

Traffic Return on the Bridge of Boats, River Ravee, at Lahore, for March, 1856.

Coolies, laden	24,372	7-bullock carts	408
Ditto, unladen	9,479	Bhilees	123
Poneys, laden	2,332	Ekas	180
Ditto, unladen	1,615	Buggies	16
Bullocks	7,957	Ditto	3
Donkeys	3,087	Buths	2
Camels, laden	4,957	Palkees	24
Ditto, unladen	597	Goats and Sheep	2,331
Horses, laden	198	Cows	652
Ditto, unladen	398	Buffaloes	237
2-bullock carts	1,867	Elephants	4
3 ditto ditto	371	Buffaloes	61
4 ditto ditto	1,451	Palkee Gharn	1
5 ditto ditto	118	Guns (great)	8
6 ditto ditto	5		

TABLES OF GRADIENTS

BETWEEN MOULTAN, LAHORE, AND UMRITSIR.

LAHORE TO MOULTAN.

Gradients.	Rising or Falling.	Length in Chains.	Height above Datum.		Remarks.
1 in 7920	Falling	61	304·00	303·49	Leave Lahore Sta.
1 in 877	„	52	303·49	299·50	
Level		8	299·50	299·50	
1 in 657	Rising	76	299·50	307·00	
1 in 782	Falling	83	307·00	302·00	
1 in 1900	Rising	72	302·00	302·50	
1 in 1540	Falling	175	302·50	295·00	Sta. No. 1 at 5m. 45c. fr. Lahore.
1 in 3592	„	273.75	295·00	290·00	
Level		120	290·00	290·00	
1 in 2640	„	79.75	290·00	288·00	
1 in 1440	„	120	288·00	282·50	
Level		140	282·50	282·50	Sta. No. 2 at 15m. 47c. fr. Lahore.
1 in 2640	„	100	282·50	280·00	
1 in 1320	„	100	280·00	275·00	
Level		201	275·00	275·00	
1 in 4148	„	440	275·00	268·00	
1 in 2970	„	540	268·00	256·00	
1 in 3520	„	240	256·00	251·50	
1 in 2263	„	240	251·50	244·50	
1 in 6600	„	100	244·50	243·50	
1 in 5808	„	220	243·50	246·00	
1 in 1320	„	160	246·00	238·00	
1 in 1650	„	100	238·00	234·00	
Level		110	234·00	234·00	
1 in 742	Rising	90	234·00	242·00	
Level		29.75	242 00	242·00	
1 in 570	Falling	110	242·00	299·27	
1 in 9354	„	180	229·27	228·00	Sta. No. 3 at 52m. 47c. fr. Lahore.
1 in 2200	„	100	228·00	225 00	
1 in 5280	Rising	80	225·00	226·50	
1 in 3520	Falling	80	266 50	224·50	
1 in 2209	„	80	224·50	222·11	
1 in 1616	„	55	222·11	219·66	
1 in 588	„	84.75	219·66	210·68	
1 in 3149	„	219.75	210·66	206·07	Sta. No. 4 at 59m. 47c. fr. Lahore.
1 in 2918	„	180	206·07	202·00	
1 in 4903	„	260	202·00	198·50	
1 in 1508	„	80	198 50	195·00	
1 in 6600	„	80	195·00	194·20	
1 in 4400	„	80	194·20	193·00	

Gradients.	Rising or Falling.	Length in Chains.	Height above Datum.		REMARKS.
1 in 1992	Falling	160	193·00	187·70	Sta. No. 5 at 71m. 70c. fr. Lahore.
1 in 6600	,,	40	187·70	187·3	
1 in 5280	Rising	119	187·30	188·80	
1 in 13200	Falling	59·75	188·80	188·50	
1 in 6600	,,	100	188·50	187·50	
1 in 1294	,,	100·75	187·50	182·40	
1 in 26400	Rising	40	182·40	182·50	Sta. No. 6 at 77m. 45c. fr. Lahore.
1 in 2253	Falling	140	182·50	178·40	
1 in 5775	Rising	139·75	178·40	180·00	
1 in 1600	Falling	80	180·00	176·70	
1 in 713	,,	40	176·70	173·00	
1 in 6600	,,	100	173·00	172·00	
1 in 1015	Rising	20	172·00	173·30	
1 in 5866	Falling	320	173·30	169·70	
1 in 2200	,,	240	169·70	162·50	
1 in 52800	Rising	80	162·50	162·60	
1 in 4620	Falling	420	162 60	156·50	
1 in 3947	,,	320	156·50	151·25	Sta. No. 7 at 97m. 50c. fr. Lahore.
1 in 2956	,,	280	151·25	145·00	
1 in 20307	Rising	80	145·00	145·26	
1 in 1378	Falling	160	145 26	137 60	
1 in 23100	Rising	140	137·60	138·00	
1 in 5280	Falling	200	138·00	135·50	Sta, No, 8 at 112m. 5c. fr. Lahore
1 in 1280	,,	60	135·50	129 64	
1 in 1218	Rising	60	129·64	129 90	
1 in 3771	Falling	80	129·90	127·60	
1 in 11000	,,	100	127·60	127·00	
1 in 4950	Rising	60	127·00	127·80	
1 in 4400	Falling	120	127·80	126·00	
1 in 13200	Rising	200	126·00	127·00	
1 in 6734	Falling	100	127·00	126·00	
1 in 1590	Rising	120	126·00	131·00	
1 in 2640	Falling	40	131·00	130·00	
1 in 754	,,	40	130·00	126·50	
1 in 1602	,,	340	126·50	112·50	
Level		120	112·50	112·50	
1 in 2329	,,	100	112·50	109·10	
1 in 1740	,,	240	109·10	100·00	
1 in 3696	,,	140	100·00	97·50	Sta, No. 9 at 125m. 3c. fr. Lahore.
1 in 2700	,,	180	97·50	93·10	
1 in 2357	,,	100	93·10	90·30	
1 in 14850	,,	180	90·30	89·50	
1 in 3882	,,	100	89·50	87·80	
1 in 943	,,	140	87·80	80·80	
Level		440	80 80	80·80	
1 in 682	,,	60	80·80	75·00	Sta. No. 10 at 150m. 65c. fr. Lahore.
1 in 2062	,,	200	75·00	68·60	
1 in 776	,,	60	68·60	63·50	
1 in 3017	,,	160	63·50	60·00	
1 in 880	,,	40	60·00	57 00	
1 in 3696	,,	280	57·00	52·00	
Level		240	52·00	52·00	

Gradients.	Rising or Falling.	Length in Chains.	Height above Datum.		Remarks.
1 in 5940	Falling	180	52·00	50·00	
1 in 1885	,,	60	50·00	47·90	
1 in 1722	,,	120	47·90	43·30	
1 in 3882	Rising	200	*143·30	146·70	* 100 ft. added to Datum Line.
1 in 1031	Falling	100	146·70	140·30	
1 in 5525	,,	360	140·30	136·00	
1 in 3630	,,	220	136 00	132·00	
1 in 609	,,	120	132·00	119·00	
1 in 3089	,,	220	119·00	114·30	
1 in 13200	,,	260	114·30	113·00	
1 in 4400	,,	100	113·00	111·50	
1 in 1760	,,	40	111·50	110·00	
Level		80	110·00	110·00	
1 in 1523	Rising	60	110·00	112·60	
1 in 1660	Falling	140	112·60	111·10	
1 in 39600	,,	60	111·10	111·00	
1 in 2299	,,	100	111·00	108·13	
1 in 2108	,,	100	108·13	102·37	
1 in 4400	Rising	100	102·37	106·50	
1 in 1945	Falling	140	106·50	101·75	
1 in 4693	Rising	160	101·75	103·00	Sta. No. 11 at 199m. 19c. fr. Lahore.
1 in 4659	,,	120	103·00	104·70	
1 in 1158	Falling	100	104·70	99 00	
1 in 5280	Rising	120	99·00	100·50	
1 in 1760	,,	60	100·50	102·75	
1 in 8297	Falling	220	102·75	101·00	
Level		60	101·00	101·00	Sta. at Moultan 207m. 60c. fr. Lahore, Datum 101·00
1 in 1848	,,	140	101·00	96·00	
Level		520	96·00	96·00	River Cheenaub.

Distance from Moultan to Lahore, 216 miles 60 chains.

LAHORE TO UMRITSIR.

Gradients.	Rising or Falling.	Length in Chains.	Height above Datum.		Remarks.
1 in 7920	Falling	121	304.00	303·00	304·00 datum at Lahore.
1 in 470	Rising	58	303·00	311·00	
Level		10	311·00	311·00	
1 in 808	Falling	50	311·00	307·00	
1 in 3118	Rising	189	307·00	311·00	Meean Meer Sta. 3m. 10c. fr. Lahore.
1 in 2404	,,	256	311·00	318·00	
1 in 2640	,,	318	318·00	326·00	
1 in 6820	,,	311	326·00	329·00	Attaree 10m. 27c, fr. Lahore.
Level		273	329·00	329·00	
1 in 4059	,,	246	329·00	333·00	
1 in 1409	,,	298	333·00	347·00	
1 in 3267	,,	198	347·00	351·00	
1 in 7689	,,	232	351·00	353·00	Umritsir Station.

Distance between Lahore and Umritsir, 32 miles.

Total length of Line, 248 miles 60 chains. *(Signed)* T. A. Yarrow,

(Consulting Engineer to the Scinde Railway Company.)

From W. P. Andrew, Esq., to Sir James C. Melvill, K.C.B., &c., &c.

Gresham House Old Broad Street,
24th October, 1857.

Sir,

With reference to my letter, No. 193, of the 20th instant, reporting the completion of the survey of the country between Moultan, Lahore and Umritsir, I have now the honour to inform the Honourable Court that this Board has received copies of correspondence from their agent in India, relative to the examination of the country from Lahore to Attock, and Peshawur by the engineering staff lately engaged in the Punjaub survey, with a view to its adaptation to railway purposes.

2. On the 10th June last, the agent of the Company, in a letter to the Commissioner in Scinde, after having shown that the present state of India calls marked attention to the necessity for facilitating to the utmost the means of communication between distant parts, reports for the information of the Commissioner, the surveys from Moultan to Umritsir being completed, his intention of submitting to the Punjaub Government a proposal to extend those surveys to Attock.

3. On the 11th June the Commissioner in Scinde, in transmitting copy of the letter above referred to, to the Governor in Council of Bombay, expressed his entire concurrence in the views of Mr. Warren, and strongly recommended that the required sanction of the surveys proposed by him should be given; and on the 29th June the Chief Commissioner of the Punjaub expressed the

pleasure it would afford him to obtain sanction for the contemplated surveys, and that he had on that day addressed Government in hopes of its speedy sanction.

4. In the report from the superintending engineer of the Punjaub survey, which I had the honour to transmit on the 20th instant for the information of the Court, with reference to the proposed survey from Lahore to Peshawur, Mr. Brunton expresses himself as follows :—

"The present position of India forcibly points to the absolute necessity of rapid communication with all parts of a country made up of so many discordant elements."

"As your proposed lines of railway in connection with the river and railway communication to Kurrachee will form the main artery through which the whole of the traffic from the Punjaub must naturally pass, I should, to complete the scheme, recommend, that the cost of extending the line from Lahore to Peshawur be ascertained as quickly as possible."

5. The Board entirely concurs in the views expressed by their agent and superintending engineer, as to the propriety of taking advantage of the services of the Punjaub staff for the above surveys now at Lahore, and unoccupied, especially as they could be prosecuted with greater economy and dispatch than at any future period; and should it be the pleasure of the Honourable Court to have them proceeded with, all the expenses incurred should be placed to a separate account, and be appropriated hereafter according to the arrangement that may be ultimately entered into.

6. I beg leave to enclose a memorandum from Mr. Yarrow, the consulting engineer of the Company, to whom the subject has been referred.

7. I need not remind the Honourable Court that almost ever since the annexation of the Punjaub, the Marquis of Dalhousie, and many other eminent authorities, have attached the utmost importance both on political and commercial grounds, to the bringing of Peshawur at the mouth of the Khyber Pass into railway communication with the seat of the local Government at Lahore.

I have the honour to be, &c., &c.,

(Signed) W. P. ANDREW,

Chairman.

Sir JAMES C. MELVILL, K.C.B.,
&c. &c. &c.

From A. BRANDRETH, Esq., Officiating Secretary to the Chief Commissioner, Punjaub, to J. NEVILLE WARREN, Esq., Agent to the Scinde Railway Company.

PUBLIC WORKS, LAHORE,
29th June, 1857.

SIR,

With reference to the request contained in your letter No. 161, of the 15th instant, I am directed by the Chief Commissioner to inform you, that it would give him much pleasure to obtain sanction for the survey contemplated by you, and that he has this day addressed Government in hopes of its speedy sanction.* Lahore to Attock.

I have the honour to be, &c., &c.,

(Signed) A. BRANDRETH,

Officiating Secretary.

J. NEVILLE WARREN, Esq.,
&c. &c. &c.

* Since the above was written, the survey of the country from Lahore to Peshawur has been recommended by the Government of India, and authorised by the East India Company, and its execution entrusted to the Engineering Staff of the Scinde Railway Company.

From W. P. ANDREW, Esq., to Sir JAMES C. MELVILL, K.C.B., &c., &c., &c.

SCINDE RAILWAY COMPANY,
GRESHAM HOUSE, OLD BROAD STREET,
26th October, 1857.

SIR,—In continuation of my letter (No. 193) of the 20th instant, which I had the honour of addressing to the Honourable Court, with Report of the Superintending Engineer of the Punjaub Survey, and other documents, I am now instructed to state, that if the information submitted to the Court be considered sufficient to induce them to sanction the necessary steps being taken, with a view to the early prosecution of (the Punjaub Railway) a work of vital importance and urgent necessity, this Board would be prepared to raise the necessary capital of £2,500,000, on the same terms and conditions as those which are included in the existing contract between the Honourable East India Company and this Company, so soon as the state of the money market will admit of their doing so.

By entering into the above preliminary agreement, much valuable time would be saved, as this Board could then take advantage of the first favourable opportunity for raising the requisite funds, and no delay would thus be allowed to occur in the prosecution of a design, which was declared in a recent Report of the Punjaub Government, to be "of greater consequence to the country than "any public work, or any number of works, that could be "specified,"—"which will affect the trade of all North-

"western India—will be carried out with unusual facility—will prove financially profitable in a high degree—will virtually concern the best material interests of twenty-one millions of industrious people—and will conduce more than any other circumstance that could be named, to the future prosperity of the Punjaub."

I have the honour to be, &c., &c.,

(Signed) W. P. ANDREW, *Chairman.*

From Sir JAMES C. MELVILL, K.C.B., &c., &c., to W. P. ANDREW, Esq., &c., &c.

(EXTRACT.)

EAST INDIA HOUSE,
17th November, 1857.

SIR,—I have received and laid before the Court of Directors of the East India Company, your letter (No. 193), dated 20th ultimo, forwarding reports of surveys of the country from Moultan to Lahore and Umritsir, executed by the Engineers of the Scinde Railway Company, and I am commanded to state, that upon the receipt of the Report of the Government Engineer, together with the views of the Government of India thereon, the subject will receive the Court's attention.

I am, &c., &c.,

(Signed) J. C. MELVILL.

The next mail from India brought an additional confirmation of these views in the following official communication from that eminent statesman, Sir John Lawrence, to the Supreme Government, which was at once forwarded by the chairman to the India House.

SCINDE RAILWAY COMPANY,
GRESHAM, HOUSE, OLD BROAD STREET,
Jan. 14, 1858.

SIR,

In continuance of my letter (No.212) dated 14th of December last, requesting permission for this company to take the necessary steps for raising the capital for the construction of the railway from Moultan to Lahore and Umritsir, I have now the honour to transmit herewith copy of a letter just received through the agent of the company, addressed by the officiating secretary to the Chief Commissioner of the Punjaub to the secretary of the Government of India, Public Works Department, which cannot but be highly satisfactory to the court, as the letter in question embodies the views of that distinguished statesman, Sir John Lawrence, as to the importance and urgency of the work.

I have the honour to be,

&c., &c., &c.,

(Signed) W. P. ANDREW, *Chairman.*

Sir J. C. MELVILL, K.C.B., &c.

From Lieut. E. H. Paske, Officiating Secretary to Chief Commissioner of the Punjaub, to Colonel W. E. Baker, Secretary to the Government of India, Public Works Department, Fort William.

Lahore, *October* 21, 1857.

Sir,

In compliance with the invitation conveyed in your letter (No. 224) dated 19th January, 1856, the Chief Commissioner laid fully before the Supreme Government, in Mr. Temple's letter to your address, No. 278, dated 26th August, 1856, his views in regard to the desirableness of a railway connecting Umritsir with Moultan, and I have now the honour to submit, by the Chief Commissioner's directions, copies of the documents noted in the margin,* which show that the scheme has passed from the stage of speculation to that of action, and that the approval and sanction of the authorities in England are now alone required to admit of the work of construction being at once and vigorously proceeded with.

* 1. Letter to the address of my predecessor from Mr. J. Neville Warren, agent for the Scinde Railway Company, dated 11th February, 1857, No. 51, inclosing prospectus of Punjaub Railway Company.

2. My predecessor's reply, No. 546, dated 3d March, 1857.

3. Letter addressed by William Brunton, Esq., to the directors of the above company, dated 16th June, 1857, reporting on the survey for a line of railway between Umritsir and Moultan, effected under his supervision as their chief engineer.

4. Estimate of probable cost of constructing the above railway, with rolling stock, &c.

2. The plans, maps, and sections of the above railway, which accompanied Mr. Brunton's report, were despatched from Lahore on the 27th August last, and reached Moultan the subsequent day. Inquiry will be made regarding their arrival at Kurrachee and transmission onwards, the result of which will be communicated. The Chief Commissioner regrets that, by some mistake in his office, these documents were not sent to the Bombay Government, as was intended. At that time a great pressure existed in every department, and the Chief Commissioner himself had just started for Jullander to ascertain the feeling of the Jammoo troops, and push them on as fast as possible to Delhi.

3. As a company has been formed for carrying out the above project, the directors of which have placed themselves in communication with the authorities in London, matters are now in the best position for ensuring a successful prosecution of the undertaking. But the Chief Commissioner has nevertheless deemed it his duty to keep the Supreme Government informed, as far as is in his power, of the progress which is being made on the spot, and to offer such suggestions or remarks as may appear to him likely to be useful at the present time.

4. In the 19th paragraph of Mr. Temple's letter, above referred to, it was assumed that two millions sterling would probably be required for the completion of a double line of rail from Umritsir to Moultan. From the accompanying documents it will be seen that the company proposed to lay down a single line only, for reasons which, though not therein stated, have doubtless been

considered valid by competent parties, after fully considering all that can be said in favour of either course. The maximum cost, as estimated by Mr. Brunton, is £1,676,295, and the Chief Commissioner has reason to believe that the actual outlay is not expected to reach this amount if the work be carried out judiciously and with economy.

5. Mr. Brunton's report and the plans which accompany it abundantly corroborate the opinions expressed in Mr. Temple's letter in regard to the unusually favourable character of the country to be traversed for the laying down of a railroad. The slope of the surface is so slight as to be hardly deserving of consideration, while it is nearly uniform throughout; no elevation or hollows of importance occur in any portion of it. No stream or rivulets, save of the most insignificant character, have anywhere to be crossed, as the line keeps to the water shed throughout until it approaches Moultan, which is situated in the alluvial plain or kadir adjoining the Chenab, and even in that portion no engineering difficulties of importance occur. Some of the small inundation canals will have to be crossed, and some of the outlets of the Baree Doab Canal; but none of these will involve works of a costly character.

6. The Baree Doab Canal and proposed railway, it will be observed, run nearly parallel to one another through the greater portion of the length of the latter. Each will in many ways be productive of advantage to the other, and both will lead in the most effective manner to civilise and supply with inhabitants a wild tract which is at present, for the most part, the resort exclusively of nomadic races

of graziers and camel breeders. The natural adaptation of the line for the laying down of a railway is sufficiently indicated by the fact that it is nearly identical with that independently selected for the course of the canal; and it is stated by Mr. Brunton that a portion of it, as laid down by him, exhibits a continuous straight line of greater length than can be found, he believes, in any European railway.

7. The returns to be expected from the railway even at an early stage of its existence, as shown in the 21st paragraph of Mr. Temple's letter, were calculated at 9 per cent. gross income upon an outlay of two millions. The Chief Commissioner is not aware that the grounds on which these calculations were based have been in any way impugned, or that anything has occurred to show that they were erroneous; on the contrary, all the statistical data collected by parties interested in the question, as given in the several publications of Mr. Andrew, the chairman of this and other companies, tend in his opinion very strongly to indicate that a vast and increasing traffic may be calculated upon with confidence, while the rapidity with which the trade of Kurrachee has increased, the returns showing an aggregate value of exports and imports in 1854 of £1,233,000 against £122,010 in 1843, attests the tendency of the traffic of these parts to expand in proportion as it is facilitated and encouraged. If then so considerable a return was anticipated, on valid grounds, from an outlay of two millions, it seems not unreasonable to expect that with an outlay reduced by one-fifth or one-sixth, the net return will amount to 6 per cent. at the least.

8. It may be further remarked that the completion of

the proposed line of railway has become the more important and essential in consequence of the establishment of a company to whom a remunerative rate of interest on their capital has been guaranteed for the completion of a line of railway from Kurrachee to Kotree, with a powerful flotilla of steamers from thence to Moultan. The success of these undertakings, in a financial point of view, must mainly depend upon the amount of goods and number of passengers passing to and from the Punjaub and other places beyond it, to which the proposed railway must afford an immense stimulus; when to this is added the exceeding importance to Government of being enabled to convey troops and military stores to the capital of the Punjaub and stations beyond it with ease and rapidity, there can, the Chief Commissioner believes, be but one opinion as to the vast advantages to be anticipated from the carrying out of the undertaking now under consideration.

9. The experience of some of the railways heretofore opened in India, appears to show that very considerable modifications in the form and arrangement of both the carriages employed and the railway stations erected on lines in England, are indispensable to adapt them to this country. It is, therefore, in the opinion of the Chief Commissioner, most desirable that prominent attention be directed at once to this point; and he is glad, therefore, to observe that Mr. Brunton urges the building of the carriages in this country, importing the ironwork only, a measure of the expediency of which he has no doubt. No plans have as yet been drawn for railway stations, as it is thought that this would be premature at the present

stage. But the Chief Commissioner has seen a sketch, showing roughly the ground plan of the buildings Mr. Brunton recommends, which appear appropriate; and from Mr. Brunton's character, and the Indian experience now acquired by him and his assistants, it may be confidently anticipated that if a discretion be allowed him in these matters, all necessary points will be attended to.

10. The Chief Commissioner would further suggest that the station-houses be so arranged as to render them easily defensible. Recent events have forcibly shown that this is a consideration which cannot be safely overlooked in any part of India, and this is more especially the case in a wild tract, such as that which will be traversed by a great part of the proposed line, the tribes inhabiting which are to some extent at the present time in a state of rebellion. He thinks, also, that the fences which are to be placed along either side of the road should be of such materials and construction as to afford as little temptation as possible to the people of the country to remove them, or no ordinary vigilance will suffice for their protection. The planting of a hedge, as suggested by Mr. Brunton, would probably be found the best plan of all, and many thorny plants suitable for the purpose are indigenous to the country.

11. It is not necessary to refer in this place to the professional portions of Mr. Brunton's report. But in regard to his proposition that the Directors of the company should have a control over the erection of any buildings within a mile of each station, in order that all new villages may be constructed with regularity and a due regard to sanitary considerations, the Chief Commissioner would remark that

this can apply to those portions only of the line, the country adjoining which is at present waste; and in such localities he will be quite prepared to direct district officers not to allow buildings to be erected within a reasonable limit without the concurrence and advice of the officers of the company, which will probably be the most appropriate mode of meeting Mr. Brunton's views. The question also mooted by him, whether or not the land required for the railway is to be given by Government and the owners compensated by it for any property standing thereon, which may be destroyed, will doubtless be determined according to precedents supplied by existing railways in India, so that it is not necessary to enlarge upon it here.

12. There is another point adverted to by Mr. Brunton, on which the Chief Commissioner is desirous of offering an opinion, viz., the party by whom the work shall be executed, the Chief Commissioner doubts the expediency of entrusting it to contractors in England, who are new to the country, its languages, and its population. If European contractors can be met with on the spot, possessed of capital and resources, they will probably be preferable to all others. But such persons are rare, especially in the Punjaub, while substantial native contractors are ready to come forward to any required extent; and these men having an intimate acquaintance with all the resources of the country—many of them having already acquired, as contractors in the canal and other engineering departments, experience in works analogous to those of the railway—must obviously possess immense advantages over persons arriving fresh from Europe with no previously acquired Indian experience.

It would indeed be quite indispensable for European contractors to employ this very class of men; so that by inviting such contractors we should be but creating a body of go-betweens, who would simply have to perform functions which could be equally well or better performed by the engineers themselves, seeing that these have now acquired considerable local experience. The Chief Commissioner has reason to believe that Mr. Brunton himself is pretty much of this opinion; and, indeed, as his estimates are based on existing local rates, it may be doubted whether they will afford a sufficient margin to remunerate a European contractor, in addition to the profits of the actual executors of the work.

13. It is understood that Mr. Brunton and his assistants are about to proceed shortly to Scinde with a view to surveying a new line in contemplation in that province, as nothing further can be done in this quarter until sanction shall have been accorded by the authorities in England, and definitive orders shall have reached India. The delay resulting from this cause it is presumed cannot be avoided. But as every necessary inquiry has now been made and communicated to the directors, the surveys completed, and the remarkable adaptation of the proposed line for railway purposes established beyond all room for doubt, the Chief Commissioner earnestly hopes that the requisite orders may be speedily issued and (seeing that Mr. Brunton considers four years at least to be necessary, under the most favourable circumstances for the completion of the railway)—that this work, from which almost incalculable benefits may be anticipated for the Punjaub, may be commenced upon at the earliest practicable period.

14. In conclusion I am directed to observe that the Chief Commissioner considers it due to Mr. Brunton and his assistants to give his testimony to the very satisfactory manner in which the work has been conducted thus far. On the professional merits of the survey it will be for others to decide; but as respects all that is of an administrative character, Mr. Brunton appears to the Chief Commissioner to have evinced throughout much judgment and firmness, as well as a very conciliatory spirit. There has been no clashing with the local authorities or with the people. The work entrusted to him has been carried on steadily, effectively, and unobstrusively, even throughout a period of most alarming excitement; and the conduct of all parties connected with the undertaking has, in the Chief Commissioner's opinion, been deserving of much commendation.

I have, &c.,

(Signed) E. H. PASKE,

Officiating Secretary to Chief Commissioner.

Thus fortified by the opinion of every person most capable of judging on the matter, on the 27th of January last, the East India Company sanctioned the raising of £1,500,000 for the commencement of the railway, under the same conditions as the previous portions of the Scinde Capital.

CHAPTER VIII.

PROVINCES OF INDUS.

IDENTITY OF INTERESTS OF PUNJAUB AND N.W. PROVINCES WITH SCINDE.—AREA.—POPULATION.—OFFICIAL CENSUS DECEMBER, 1854.—COMPARATIVE DENSITY OF POPULATION IN DIFFERENT PARTS OF INDIA.

THE union of the Punjaub with the Meerut and Delhi territory for political and military purposes, has been so plainly marked out by recent events, that their political connection under one distinct government appears inevitable, and the fortunes of these extensive and important regions are inseparably connected with that of Scinde. Both Mr. Frere and Sir John Lawrence have done good service to the British Crown, not only by their energy and administrative ability, but by advocating more direct communication with England, and the introduction into their respective provinces of the railway, the telegraph, and other improvements.

"The two provinces (Scinde and the Punjaub)" says a late writer, "have been inseparably connected by the hand which made them. They have been connected also, by the fortunes of the great empire to which both belong. They are *the provinces of the Indus*, as Bengal and Behar are *the provinces of the Ganges*. They constitute one section of the empire, and are separated from every other part of it by rivers, mountains, the sea, or broad belts of sandy desert. Their commercial interests are inseparably united. Both must ultimately depend upon the traffic of the mighty river, which is the artery fed by the five veins of the Punjaub.

"Both depend for their communication with the external world upon one and the same port. The Punjaub has no outlet towards the north, but an imperfect outlet towards the west, and a long, difficult, and expensive, though open outlet towards the east. This river system, which is already equal in magnitude, and may be equal in value to that of the Ganges, should be under one government, and improved on one system, devised by a single mind. Would the Government place Bengal under one authority, and the Hooghly, from Cutwa downwards, under the commissioner of Pegu? Yet that is exactly what we have done with our north-west possessions. Our Danube has its mouth occupied, not by enemies, it is true, but by allies, owing allegiance to a different authority.

"Again, the physical, political, and social characteristics of the two countries are identically the same. Physically, the districts of Moultan, Dhera Ghazee Khan, and Khangurh might be districts of Scinde. The soil is the same, the products are the same, the people are the same. Politically, both have the same disadvantages, and the same military necessities. Both have a turbulent frontier to be guarded, which is identical in character from one end to the other, and which should be arranged on one principle, and be obedient to one head. The vast chain of military forts which stretch along the Scindian and Punjabee frontiers, depend upon each other, and should alike for military effectiveness and economy depend upon one head. Both have populations whom it is necessary to disarm and overawe, and in both an enormous military force requires an energetic central administration. The system, too, of the Punjaub, would suit the province of Scinde better than that of Bombay. It is less regular, and better adapted to the fierce passions and uncontrolled habits of a wild Mohammedan people. The revenue settlement, too, is more in consonance with the ancient ideas of the population. The administration would be infinitely cheaper; for, with a slight re-distribution of force in the Punjaub, much of the military expenditure of Scinde might be removed;—while, after two years of expense, the customs' receipts of Kurrachee, as the foreign entrepôt of Central Asia and the Punjaub, would totally remove the deficit. Of course, with the improvement, the pressure on the more fertile province would be removed, and the strong counter argument with which we commenced our article becomes of none effect. Scinde and the Punjaub, then, we submit, should be united."

"It (the union) would strengthen, not root up, the system already successful; and on every other ground it is indispensable. The presidency would be the second of the great divisions of British India. The immense triangle, broadest between Kurrachee and Peshawur, and tapering almost to a point below Moultan, would cover an area of 130,000 square miles.* This vast area is occupied by a population of nearly twenty-five millions, thus:—

Punjaub, by census	13,000,000
States under control, including Cis-Sutlej chiefs, and Cashmere	8,000,000
Scinde (probably)	2,000,000
States under Scinde (at a guess) . . .	1,000,000
Populations of Presidency . . .	24,000,000

* Great Britain covers 53,000 square miles.

"The revenue, unimproved, would be two-and-a-half millions. The surplus is far more than adequate to the necessities of Scinde, and Lord Dalhousie would thus have redeemed the consequences of the act of Sir C. Napier. Amid this population, all warlike, is stationed a great irregular force, which must be directly subject to the civil authority, and is apt to be jealous of a mere commissioner. The flower of the European and native army is there also, and occasionally even with these the weight of high official dignity is imperatively required. Our most dangerous foreign relations, with Central Asia and Dost Mahomed, with the Beloochees and Daoodpootras, and with the innumerable warrior chieftains of the highlands, must be conducted at Lahore. Whoever may be the final authority, every word of the Commissioner reverberates among the hills, every blunder is bitterly resented in Cabul." *

On the night of the 31st December, 1854, a careful and minutely-detailed census was taken of all persons who slept in any house of every city, town, village, hamlet, and detached tenement throughout the Punjaub territories, between sunset on that day and sunrise on the following 1st January, 1855. The natives themselves are described as entering warmly into the spirit of the thing, without the slightest indication of alarm or suspicion; and at Umritsir they even "stood waiting with a light at their doors for the arrival of the enumerators, and the streets and alleys were half illuminated." It appears, from the result of that night's operations, that the Punjaub territories contain 81,625 square miles, 28,879 villages, and a population of 12,717,821 souls, in a proportion of 155 to the square mile, though varying from 62 to 334; and that they yield a land revenue of £1,701,021. exclusive of

* "Friend of India."

excise and miscellaneous receipts, which raise the total amount to something over two millions sterling.

But in addition to actual British possessions, there are numerous *quasi*-independent native principalities, subject to the political superintendence of the Chief Commissioner of the Punjaub. These are the Cis-Sutlej Principalities, the Simla Hill States, the Trans-Sutlej Principalities, Bhawulpoor, and the kingdom of Cashmeer, with the Jummoo raj. These various states comprise an area of 102,884 square miles, with a population of 6,750,606 souls, in the proportion of 65 to the square mile, though varying from 36 to 257; and yield a revenue of £1,405,653 to their own rulers. With regard to the density of the population in the Punjaub territories, the following tables contrast the most thickly and the most thinly-peopled districts with corresponding districts in other parts of India.

There are 26,210 villages, with an average population of 440; 2,124 small towns, containing from 1,000 to 5,000 inhabitants; 76 from 5,000 to 10,000; 32 from 10,000 to 50,000; and three cities with more than that number. The most populous city is Umritsir, with its 122,184 inhabitants; next, Lahore, with 94,143; and third in order, Peshawur, with 53,294. Loodianah contains a population of 47,191 souls; Jullundur, 28,422; Buttiala, 26,208; Moultan, 22,493; Dehra Ghazee Khan, 21,097; Sealkote, 19,249; Wuzeerabad, 16,846; Dehra Ismael Khan, 15,899; Rawul Pindee, 15,813; Ferozepoor, 12,032; and Jhelum, 6,060.

Thickly-Peopled Districts.

PUNJAUB. Per Square Mile.		N. W. PROVINCES. Per Square Mile.		BENGAL. Per Square Mile.		MADRAS. Per Square Mile.		BOMBAY. Per Square Mile.	
Umballa	420	Benares	856	Burdwan	833	Tanjore	469	Kaira	310
Jullundur	513	Jounpoor	737	Hooghly	759	Malabar	250	Surat	302
Umritsir	436	Ghazepoor	732	Kondah	614	Trichinopoly	243	Broach	220
Goordaspoor	470	Azimgurh	657	Kungpoor	619	Arcot	225	Belgaum	189
Sealkote	475	Delhi	552	Patna	656	Chingleput	214	Dharwar	196
		Agra	537						

Thinly-Peopled Districts.

PUNJAUB. Per Square Mile.		N. W. PROVINCES. Per Square Mile.		BENGAL. Per Square Mile.		MADRAS. Per Square Mile.		BOMBAY. Per Square Mile.	
Shahpoor	74	Banda	247	Monghyr	223	Cananore	149	Tannah	150
Jhung	44	Mirzapoor	214	Backergunge	193	Madun	129	Poonah	125
Goozaira	74	Hameerpoor	245	Bancoorah	101	Vellore	123	Sholapoor	135
Moultan	73	Hissar	100	Sylhet	45	Guntoor	119	Ahmednuggur	100
Leia	50			Bhagulpore	28	Cuddapah	109	Kandeish	83
Kohat	35					Bellary	101		

CHAPTER IX.

PROVINCES OF INDUS.

MAJOR HAMILTON'S ESTIMATE OF IMPORTS AND EXPORTS, VIA MOOLTAN.—TRAFFIC ON THE INDUS AT MITHUNKOTE. —AMOUNT OF MILITARY FORCE.—SUPPLY OF EUROPEAN GOODS FOR TROOPS.

The provinces on the Indus and its tributaries are cut off from India by the Great Desert, and cannot naturally communicate with the sea by any other route than by the valley of the Indus. Of course, goods do find their way to the Punjaub, through Calcutta and Bombay, but they have to follow round-about and unnatural routes; and if they can be supplied through the direct and natural channel, the benefit to the provinces so supplied will be felt even at Calcutta and Bombay, far more than the loss of any traffic which may leave those ports, to pursue a more direct and cheaper route.

Some of the products of the Punjaub, North-west Provinces, and Scinde, which, under the improved facilities of communication suggested, are calculated to feed and maintain steam communication, are treated of in subsequent chapters.

Regarding the existing trade on the Indus, I am indebted to that able officer, Major G. W. Hamilton, Commissioner at Moultan, for the following interesting letter:—

"I am sorry to say that I have not any details of the quantity of imports and exports of the Punjaub, *via*

Moultan. Full returns of the trade were made out before I left the Punjaub and forwarded to the higher authorities, and it is possible that copies of these may be in the India House. Some of the returns were also published in the *Lahore Chronicle*.

"As well as I can recollect, the chief exports from the Punjaub to Scinde were—saltpetre, wool, cotton, indigo, oil-seeds, silk goods, shawls, hill-produce, bees'-wax, borax, &c.

"The imports were—cotton goods, cotton twist, sheet iron, bar iron, rod iron, metals, hardware, groceries, wine, beer, &c.

"I cannot state the quantities from memory, but I know that, for the three years embraced by the returns, there was a steady increase in exports and imports.

"The exports being in general bulky articles, were usually sent down the river by boats, the freight by the steamers being too expensive to allow of the transport of such goods by that mode of conveyance. The cargoes of the steamers generally consisted of some saltpetre and the more valuable kinds of goods.

"The freight afforded by steamers proceeding up the river was, however, quite inadequate to the demand. Every vessel was as full as she could hold; and had quadruple the number of vessels been employed, they would have obtained full cargoes. Goods were often detained for months at Kurrachee for want of a means of conveyance; and the agents were eventually obliged to forward them to the Punjaub by land on camels. This difficulty was chiefly felt by the European community in the Punjaub; and were the means of transport by the river more extensive,

I am sure that nearly all articles of sea-borne produce used by Europeans in the Punjaub, would be conveyed by the Indus instead of the line of the Ganges and Jumna. Nor would this trade be confined to the Punjaub; it would also extend to the north-west provinces. Indeed, before I left Moultan, goods from Bombay for Delhi had been sent by steamers by the Moultan route.

"There is at present a considerable trade between Moultan and Lahore, Umritsir, &c., and between Moultan and Ferozepore. From Lahore and Umritsir, the imports to Moultan are silk goods, grain, oil-seeds, &c.; the exports from Moultan to these places are madder, and various articles of English, Afghan, and other produce. From Ferozepore the imports are chiefly grain, and the products of the Gangetic provinces.

"Moultan is also a chief entrepôt of the trade with southern Afghanistan and Persia. The Afghan caravans arrive at Moultan in October and November, bringing fruits, madder, asafœtida, raw silk, goat wool, camel-hair goods, furs, &c. A few of the caravans proceed in advance to Delhi and the Gangetic provinces, but the greater portion of the traders remain at Moultan and dispose of their goods through native agents, who forward the articles to Hindostan. The Afghan traders make up their investments at Moultan during the cold season, and the return caravans from Hindostan arrive there in April, when they all return to Afghanistan. Besides the trade by the Indus and its confluents, there is also a considerable traffic along the valleys of the rivers between Lahore, Umritsir, Moultan and Scinde. On all the lines of road I have mentioned the goods are carried on camels, at the rate of about twelve miles per diem.

"If there were an improved communication by steamers between Moultan and Kurrachee and a railroad between Moultan and Lahore, I feel certain that this line would attract all the traffic on the different lines above mentioned. The Europeans in the Punjaub would prefer getting their supplies of English and China goods by this route. The Afghan merchants would be able to forward their goods to Hindostan without delay—a matter of great importance, as many of the articles are of a perishable nature. I omitted to mention the exports from India to Afghanistan. They are mostly cotton goods, hardware, indigo, sugar, cotton and groceries. Few of these are articles of European produce, which are still little known in the Punjaub. But I feel assured that were such articles procurable at moderate prices at Moultan, they would be eagerly purchased by the Afghan merchants for the markets of Afghanistan and Central Asia. The articles most likely to be in demand are cotton piece goods (chintzes and blue calico are preferred), cotton twist, coarse woollens, hardware, cutlery, paper, &c.

"At all seasons there are plenty of sea-borne travellers between Moultan and Lahore, and between Moultan and Scinde in less numbers. Moultan is a celebrated place of pilgrimage for the Scindians, who resort thither in great numbers in the spring. There is also a famous shrine near Deri-Gahzee-Khan, west of Moultan, and every year, at a particular season, several thousand natives from the eastern Punjaub visit that place. The Hindoos of the western Punjaub also visit in great numbers Umritsir, Hurdwur, and other sacred places in Hindostan.

G. H. HAMILTON.

April 21, 1856.

From a return received from the local Government, during the third quarter of the official year 1855-56 there passed down the Indus at Mithunkote 668 native cargo boats, having an aggregate burthen of 241,185 maunds, or 8,613 tons. The upward traffic was, indeed, very disproportionate as there were only 159 boats carrying 23,376 maunds, or 835 tons. But the very fact that the balance is so enormously in favour of the downward trade, shows the want of steamers to battle with the stream. For the sake of those who require detailed information regarding the traffic on the Indus, we give the items in the return before us—omitting fractional parts of maunds.

Downward traffic on the Indus at Mithunkote for the third quarter of the financial year 1855-56 :—

Wheat, maunds -	29,519	Almonds, maunds -	150
Barley, „ - -	12,640	Raisins, „ - -	455
Gram, „ - -	7,297	Salt, „ - -	981
Rice, „ - -	4,914	Saltpetre, „ - -	8,293
Dall, „ - -	4,759	Iron, „ - -	61
Wool „ - -	16,129	Mustard seed, - -	5,581
Cotton, „ - -	12,832	Till, „ - -	39,129
Goor, „ - -	15,298	Tobacco, „ - -	150
Shukur, „ - -	1,867	Spices, Cloves, Cardamums, &c. - -	30,221
Cheenee, „ - -	6,575	Hemp, „ - -	135
Indigo, „ - -	676	Opium, „ - -	6
Munjeet, „ - -	2,063	Bales of cloth Cotton	489
Ghee, „ - -	032	Horns, (number of)	8,535
Oil, „ - -	1,071		
Dried dates, - -	001		
		Total - - - - - - - - -	2,41,185

UPWARD TRAFFIC.

			Oil, &c.
Wheat, maunds -	108	Oil, - - - - - -	12
Rice, „ - -	306	Dried dates - - -	2,543
Wool, „ - -	4	Brimstone, - - -	201
Munjeet „ - -	60	Sujee, maunds -	250
Cocoa-nuts, (number)	82,700	Iron, „ - -	3,858
Ghee, maunds, - -	55	Pewter, „ - -	708
Lime, „ - -	3,837	Bales of cloth, cotton, maunds -	210
Tobacco, „ - -	21		
Spices, „ - -	11,412	Hides, „ - -	3,980
		TOTAL - - - - - - -	23,376

GRAND TOTAL, - - - - - - - maunds 2,64,562
(equal to 94,486 tons).

Previous to the recent disturbances in northern India, the military force of these provinces, going no further east than Umballa, numbered upwards of 70,000 men, more than 15,000 of whom were Europeans. This was independent of officers, which, allowing for absentees, could not fall short of 2,000, without taking into account their wives and chidren, besides the covenanted and uncovenanted civil servants and their families, which must have made the total European population of these provinces little short of 20,000.

The large supplies of overland goods which such an army must annually consume, would, doubtless, form a considerable item in the receipts of the proposed undertaking. We have no means of forming an estimate of the probable consumption of such goods; but some idea of their extent may be obtained from a statement of Colonel Jacob (now

Brigadier-general), the Political Superintendent of the Upper Scinde frontier; that about fifty camel loads, or 24,000lbs., is about the average annual supply of European goods required by the regiments (the renowned Scinde Horse) he commands; and which, were the proposed steam communication established, could be forwarded to him with much greater ease and celerity.

If, then, this be the annual consumption of overland borne goods by two native regiments, 1,600 strong, what must have been the consumption of an army of 70,000, of which above 15,000 were Europeans, besides civilians, women, and children—and what must be the wants of the European force that must henceforth be cantoned between Delhi and Peshawur?

CHAPTER X.

INDIA AND CENTRAL ASIA.

TRANSIT OF EUROPEAN GOODS TO CENTRAL ASIA.—CASHMERE.—THIBET.—PERSIA.—TURKESTAN.—BALKH.—KHIVA.—BOKHARA.—CASPIAN SEA.—RUSSIA.—VOLGA.—PERSIAN GULF.—THE LEVANT.—BALFRUSH.—BUSTUM.—LOHANEE MERCHANTS.—MERV.—IMPORTS AND EXPORTS.—TRADE OF INDIA WITH CENTRAL ASIA.—DHERA ISMAEL KHAN.—CARAVANS.—COST OF TRANSIT.—IMPORTS AND EXPORTS.—DIRECT COMMUNICATION BETWEEN ENGLAND AND KURRACHEE.—VALUE OF INDIAN TRADE.—TRANSIT DUTIES ABOLISHED ON INDUS AND ITS AFFLUENTS.

A proper system of transit, once established through Scinde and the Punjaub, a few enterprising European merchants at Kurrachee would soon afford a medium for extensive shipments from the Punjaub and provinces to the north-west of Delhi, and the distribution of our manufactures to the remote parts of central Asia finding customers along the valleys of Afghanistan as far as Herat, and in Balkh, Khiva and Bokhara.

I will now point for a moment to the extensive provinces of Central Asia, which are now our near neighbours, and explain briefly how those important and comparatively far-advanced countries have been supplied with merchandize, and have disposed of produce since the course of the Indus was comparatively closed to commerce by the exactions of the native princes. To follow the description the reader must refer to a large map of Asia. First, he will find to the north-east of our frontier, in the immediate vicinity, the celebrated valley of Cashmere, inhabited by a people renowned for their great skill and ingenuity. Beyond that lies Thibet, famous for its fine goat wool, and the manufacture of yarn for the shawls woven in Cashmere. To the west and south-west we find the Afghan territory, with the large towns of Cabul, Ghizni, Kandahar, and Herat the *Gate of India;* in the same direction, the northern provinces of Persia. In a north-westerly direction we find the extensive and fertile countries of Turkestan and Bokhara, with the large central towns of Balkh, Khiva, and Bokhara; and, at a great distance westerly, we find the Caspian Sea.

The commerce of this vast territory is now carried on by so circuitous and expensive a route, that it will be easy to restore it to the ancient and natural channel of the Indus, and by that means how much it is likely to be increased, now that it is freed by the supremacy of England from the political obstructions and exorbitant demands of the turbulent and semi-barbarous states on its banks may be readily conceived.

"In former times," says a late writer, "the Indus was the great highway of commerce between India and Central Asia; but upon the dismemberment of the empire of the Great Mogul, the river fell under the power of a multitude of petty chiefs, whose exactions gradually extinguished the traffic. One consequence of this revolution was, that Cabul, Bokhara, and Persia, instead of being supplied from India with manufactured goods, as had previously been the case, received most of their supplies from Russia, which, from the facilities of conveyance afforded by the Volga, running into the Caspian Sea, was enabled to come into the markets of the East upon eligible terms. These advantages possessed by Russia have, it is understood, been latterly augmented by the establishment of steam-vessels upon the Volga and the Caspian; and the Russian are now supplanting the English manufactures in the Punjaub, and even threatening to do so in the north-west provinces of Bengal."

"The imports into Central Asia consist of European manufactures of every description:—Calicoes, long cloths, chintzes, muslins, and other kinds of cotton goods, broad cloths, velvets, nankeens, gold-thread, copper, and brass wares of all descriptions, cutlery, and jewellery, and, in fact, of almost every article which compose British exports, and including considerable quantities of refined sugar. At present (besides the valley of the Indus), there are three routes by which these imports are received:—1st. By the Persian Gulf, through Persia; 2nd. By the caravans from Smyrna and the ports in the Levant; and 3rd. chiefly, and by far in the largest proportion, through Russia. Let us trace the route from the latter, as being the chief source. Goods either manufactured in, or imported into Russia from England, France, and Germany, many of them purchased at the great German fairs, after paying very high transit duties, are shipped at some point on the Volga, and conveyed by steam-boats down that river to the head of the Caspian Sea. They are then conveyed the whole length of that sea by other steam-boats established thereon to Balfrush, where they are again landed. From that point they are conveyed by the eastern caravans by the high road through Sari to Bustum. At this point one road diverges in a north-easterly direction to Bokhara, Khiva, and Balkh. Another road continues onward in an easterly course to

Herat thence to Candahar, and so on to Ghizni and Cabul; from whence Peshawur, Attock, Lahore and all the country of the Punjaub and Cashmere have partly been supplied."*

According to the writer previously quoted, "The imports of Cabul are indigo, cotton, sugar, calicoes, muslins and shawls; and the exports are horses, the madder of Ghizni and Candahar, and fresh and dried fruits. The chief carriers of the trade are the Lohanee merchants,† a pastoral race of Afghans, who occupy the country eastward

* "The Economist."

† Lohanee Merchants. — The following is an extract from a recent letter from Mr. H. B. E. Frere, Commissioner in Scinde, to the author: — "These men are the great carriers of the Afghan trade. They have their homes about Guzni, where they spend the summer. Since the trade, via Tatta and the Indus, was extinguished in the latter end of the last century, these people have supplied themselves with seaborne goods, via Calcutta. They descend the passes before they are blocked up by snow, between Guzni and the Indus, in vast caravans of eight or ten thousand souls —the whole tribe moving bodily—men, women, children and cattle—their goods being on camels and ponies. Arrived in the Derajat, they leave the aged men, women and children in black felt tents, with their flocks and herds in the rich pastures bordering on the Indus, while the able-bodied men push across the Punjaub with their goods for sale either in that province or on the banks of the Ganges. The leading merchants precede the main body on dromedaries, taking with them a few samples, letters of credit, &c. &c., make their purchases at Delhi, Agra, Allahabad, Cawnpoor, Mirzapoor, and even Calcutta, and return with them express—collect their families and flocks, and force their way up the passes. Their numbers generally enable them to compound with the tribes of the mountains for a reasonable amount of blackmail, but they have sometimes to fight their way. I have heard of the wife of an eminent merchant of this tribe, whose husband had been detained longer than he expected at Delhi, offering the "Kaffila-

from Ghizni to the Indus. The Lohanee caravan usually reaches Cabul about the beginning of June; and after the merchants have disposed of their goods they prosecute their journey onward to Bokhara. The imports which Bokhara receives from India are the same as those received by Cabul. About 2000 camel-loads of goods reach Cabul from India yearly, and about half this quantity is transmitted to Turkestan.

"The imports into Bokhara from Russia are—white cloths, muslins, chintzes, broad-cloths, velvets, brocade, nankeen, gold-thread, cochineal, refined sugar, honey, furs, locks, iron, iron pots, wire, copper and brass, leather, paper, needles, inferior cutlery and jewellery, hardware, and a variety of other small articles. English broad-cloth is much prized in Bokhara, but none reaches that country, except through Russia or Persia; from which countries, although its transmission is subject to heavy imposts, it can be

bashee" (head of the caravan) demurrage at the rate of 10,000 rupees a day, to defer the upward march of the caravan, and enable her husband to rejoin, as she knew that if left behind he would be unable to follow them through the passes, except at great risk to his life and the property he might have with him.

"*Last year, the first of this tribe came down to Kurrachee*, and told me that they would soon all come that way; that they had no idea of its comparative shortness and other facilities. When I met them, they had shipped the wool they had brought down from Guzni on board river boats at Dhera Ismael Khan, and were taking their unladen camels down to Kurrachee, expecting there to find return loads, with which they would go back to Afghanistan.

"The fact that the merchants who carry on this trade *have* turned their attention to Kurrachee as a substitute for Calcutta, seems to me a point of much importance."

(*Signed*) H. B. E. Frere.

W. P. Andrew, Esq.

brought at a cheaper rate than from India, in consequence of the expense of the land-carriage through Afghanistan, which, however, the opening of the Indus would in a great measure supersede.

"Besides the Russian and Indian trade, Bokhara carries on a considerable traffic with China, by way of Cashgar and Yarkund. The imports to Bokhara, from China, are—China ware, musk, bullion, and tea. Of the latter article there are nine hundred and fifty horse-loads, or two hundred thousand pounds, transmitted annually, although the difficulties of the roads, and the long land-carriage through Thibet, necessarily much enhance the price. A horse-load of two hundred and fifty pounds costs sixty tillas in Yarkund, and sells for one hundred tillas in Bokhara. It is entirely green tea which is carried to Turkestan, and the best comes from a place in China called Turkht, and is packed in small boxes of Banca tin, from whence it is called Banca tea. The sugar-candy of China is also imported into Turkestan, but being a comparatively cumbrous article, it cannot be carried by the same route as the tea, but is conveyed from China to Bombay, from thence up the Persian Gulf, and on by land to Teheran: from thence a large quantity is carried across the Caspian to the Bay of Balkhan, from whence it is carried to Khiva,* and a small quantity is also

* "Khiva, of the site of which Major Abbott gives a new determination, placing it in latitude 41° 20″, and longitude 60°, is the modern capital of the kingdom of Khaurasm, the ancient Chorasmin. On the north-west this is separated from the district of Orenburg by a belt of steppe inhabited by Kirghese Cossacks, or as Captain Abbott chooses to call them, *Kuss-auks*, whose Chief is a nominal tributary of the Russian government—an allegiance, probably, secured mainly by the market which his people find at Samara for the skins that their flocks produce. On the west, Khaurasm is bounded by the Caspian Sea,

carried by way of Meshed. It is obvious, that if the Indus were available for commerce, it would afford a much easier route for the produce of China to Khiva and Bokhara, than either the route through Thibet, or the route through Persia; and many of the commodities which find their way into Central Asia through circuitous routes, would necessarily take the route of the Indus, so soon as that channel of communication was properly opened up.

"The principal exports of Bokhara are silk, wool, and lamb-skins. The silk is chiefly produced on the banks of the Oxus, where the mulberry grows in the most luxuriant manner, and nearly all the inhabitants are engaged in rearing the silk-worm during the summer months. The lamb-skins of Bokhara are renowned throughout the East, and are only procurable at Karahool, a small district lying between Bokhara and the Oxus. These skins are chiefly carried to Persia; but the risks of the transport are great, in consequence of the unsettled condition of the tribes between the two countries. From these causes it is not possible to negotiate a bill between Meshed and Bokhara, and the cost of transport is very high.

on the south west by Persia and Herat, on the south-east by Bokhara, and on the north-east by Kokann. Taken roughly, its area extends about 800 miles from north to south, and 600 from east to west, and it entirely separates Russia from Bokhara, and consequently commands the line of traffic between those two places."

Merv, the principal town of the district of Yoollataun, is an extremely important position, as the trade between Bokhara and Persia, and also that between Khiva and Afghanistan passes through it, and contemptible as its present appearance is, it might, with judicious care, rapidly rise into wealth and consequence.

"The manufactures of Russia find ready access into Persia by the Caspian; but Tabreez and Teheran also receive Russian goods by way of Tiflis and the Caucasus. Latterly a route has been opened for English goods into the northern parts of Persia by way of Trebizonde, from which much benefit has accrued—the southern districts being supplied with English goods from Bushire, on the Persian Gulf. To the north-west of Bushire the Karoon, a large and navigable river, ascends into the heart of Persia, and under suitable arrangements, goods might be carried by this route to within a comparatively short distance of Ispahan."

Goods brought to Attok, on the Indus, by steamer and rail, may be placed in the Cabul, Ghizni, Candahar, Herat, Balkh and Bokhara markets, at a much less cost than by the expensive caravan route from Novogorod and the Volga.

There is a great trade in silk between Bokhara and the Punjaub; and the export of raw silk from Kurrachee, last year, amounted to £31,641.

The trade of India, with central Asia, amounts to about one million sterling. One portion of this seeks egress and ingress on the borders of Scinde, and the remainder passes through the Punjaub. By the former route the trade is carried on by means of the Indus, and by camels, horses, mules, and more recently by carts; by the latter route it is carried on by multitudes of camels, mules and ponies which are used in the transit instead of wheel carriages. A string of camels, numbering five thousand, occasionally comes from Bokhara to Dhera Ismael Khan, on the Indus. The merchants travel armed, and are accompanied by their families, and the caravan constitutes as it were a moveable bazaar.

Silks and wools, groceries and spices, furs from Russia, and gold with the Bokhara stamp, although extracted from the Ural Mountains, dyes, books, cloths and metals are the wares they carry. Arrived at Dhera Ismael Khan, the families and baggage are deposited, and the merchants severally start, with their trains and merchandise, for the south. About 20,000 camels are employed in this trade, exclusive of ponies and mules. A large number of armed retainers accompany the caravans, besides 8,000 servants. The import trade carried on in this truly primitive fashion, *cost for transit from 6d. to 1s. 6d. per ton per mile,* and "amounted on the average of the five years, ending 1849 to—

Article.	Country of Produce.	Value.
Raw silk	Bokhara, Khorasan	Rs. 2,80,000
Wools	Hills north of Cabul, Ghuzni	12,000
Notions	Afghanistan, Herat and Bokhara, Persia and Khorasan	85,000
Dried fruits	Cabul, Jellalabad and Kandahar	91,000
Red dye	Kandahar	1,20,000
Iron	Mines west of Bunoo	33,500
Alum	Kalabagh	22,000
Raw fruits	Afghanistan, except pomegranates from Kandahar	22,000
Horse cloths	Dhera Ismael Khan	12,000
Gold	Bokhara	3,00,000
Horses	Afghanistan and Persia	1,50,000
Light articles		30,000
Total		11,57,500
Add specie payments		6,00,000
Grand total		Rs. 17,57,000

"The word which we have translated by the American equivalent 'notions,' includes, gum-arabic, rose leaves, asafœtida, *yellow amber*, medicines, sulphur, liquorice, antimony, dyes, and a variety of groceries, spices, and all that is pleasant—and unpleasant—to taste and smell. The phrase 'light articles' covers a variety as miscellaneous as the stock-in-trade of a marine store dealer, or a shop in the Calcutta China bazaar. It includes Persian silks, Russia leather, Russia chintzes, pet animals, great coats, Ispahan and Damascus blades, fans, punkahs, ermine and sable furs;"* in fact anything and everything not absolutely necessary. "Silk, it will be perceived, is, with one exception, the most important item. Of the whole quantity imported, one-half is consigned to a single house at Umritsir, and a moiety of the remainder to a second. The latter, moreover, the house of Tukht Mull, imports half the wool. The raw fruits are confined chiefly to Jewan Singh of the same place, and we may remark generally, that although the trade is widely scattered, the greater portion alike of merchandise and profits remains in exceedingly few hands. The traders are generally 'Kabulees,' 'Lohanees,' and 'Purachas,' the two latter being natives of Daman and Attock. The Purachas are remarkable for their branch establishments. They maintain them throughout the Punjaub at Umritsir, Moultan, and Hooshearpore, in Behar, in Moorshedabad, and at Radhanagore. The only caravans apparently which reach Calcutta are those which convey the articles under the head 'notions.'"*

The export trade during the same period amounted on the average to—

* "Friend of India."

	Place.	Value.
"Shawls	Cashmere	Rs. 6,50,000
Loaf sugar	Jullundur	50,000
Rough sugar (goor)	Baree and Rechna Doab	8,000
Indigo	Moultan and Upper India	1,57,000
Coarse native cloth	Punjaub	3,54,000
Piece goods	Manchester	3,80,000
Notions	Europe	45,000
	Total	Rs. 16,44,000

"The 'notions' again include hardware, glass, cutlery, camphor, cloves, cinnamon, sandal wood, verdigris, quicksilver, tea, and everything with which Sheffield can tempt the taste of semi-barbarian tribes."* The amounts of exports and imports through the Punjaub, was only £340,000; but it has increased since the estimates were made, and there is little doubt but that it, taken in conjunction with that traversing the province of Scinde, approaches nearly a million sterling. The appearance of bullion amongst the imports, shows that the balance of trade is in favour of India, and the trade being in every item susceptible of considerable extension is well worth the attention of Manchester and Yorkshire. English chintzes and broad-cloths are greatly esteemed in central Asia; and broad-cloth of light texture, such as *ladies' cloth*, at moderate rates, would meet with a ready and extensive sale.

"We have already mentioned the many products which Central Asia has to give in exchange! but there is one very important one which appears to have been almost entirely overlooked, and which is capable of great extension—we mean sheeps' wool. All the countries bordering on the

* "Friend of India."

Indus, and especially those to the west, contain very extensive pastoral districts, where wool is produced in great abundance. The rapid increase in the supply of wool to this country from that territory during the last few years even under all the disadvantages which have existed, and the great cost of transit and re-shipment from the ports on the coast to Bombay and thence to England, is the best proof of what may fairly be expected with the facilities now for the first time about to be offered. Little as India is noticed as a source for the supply of wool, the quantity now imported is as large as our whole Australian colonies produced as lately as 1836. In 1833, the quantity of sheeps' wool imported from India was but 3,721 lbs; in 1841 it had risen to about 3,008,000 lbs."

"But it is quite essential to its success that direct communication between this country and Kurrachee should be established as early as possible, and there can be no doubt that private interest and competition will soon lead to such arrangements. According to the most recent accounts from India, it appears that some American trading ships have already availed themselves of the new facilities afforded by the improvement of Kurrachee as a port. A direct communication between the Indus and this country will be of even more importance as respects the importation of the raw productions of Asia, than the export of the more expensive and less bulky articles of British manufacture."*

Our trade with India, important as it is, is only to be regarded as in its infancy. In 1834 it was scarcely £4,000,000 in value, while it now amounts to nearly £27,000,000. †

* The "Economist."

† *Vide* note, page 9.

To develop properly the trade of Upper India and the Punjaub, besides the establishment of a direct communication between this country and Kurrachee, they must, of necessity, have a connexion with their natural port.

The Indus debouching into the plains, separates the Himalaya range from the Hindoo Koosh, and after receiving the Punjaub rivers and other tributaries, flows through many mouths into the Arabian Sea.

The Indus and its affluents being now subject to us, it becomes our duty to re-open to the world this ancient highway of nations. The resources of modern science judiciously applied to this line of communication would at once not only be of inestimable benefit to our own provinces, but would loosen the political hold which Russia possesses over Central Asia by her commercial relations with that country.

It remains for private enterprise to occupy this magnificent field for commerce and civilization.

The transit duties being abolished and all fiscal restrictions removed, and the energetic and turbulent races of the valley of the Indus having been reduced to peaceful cultivators of the soil, the life and property of the trader, before the recent outbreak, were as safe as in this country, and the advent of the steam engine, that herald of commerce, enlightenment and peace, is alone wanting to enable enterprise to take possession of a field which has been hitherto to the British merchant almost hermetically sealed, and "with the facilities which will be afforded to the traders of Cabul, and those who supply the extensive markets of Khiva and Bokhara; and, lastly, with the impetus that will be given to the coasting trade of the Persian Gulf, by the establishment of Kurrachee as a great emporium of British commerce, it is not difficult to foresee that in a few years it must become one of the most extensive and lucrative markets in our Eastern possessions." *

The importance of completing trunk lines is apparent. The railway from Lahore and Umritsir to Moultan, once in operation, the rivers of the Punjaub, covered with the smaller boats of the country, will act as feeders of the railway, which will become the highway of an extended commerce; while the river steamers from Moultan to Hydrabad, and the railway from Hydrabad to Kurrachee, will give a continuous steam communication to the natural port of the valley of the Indus. †

* "The Economist." † For further information *vide* Appendix B.

CHAPTER XI.

PRODUCTIONS OF VALLEY OF INDUS.

COAL.

There is every reason for believing that, in accomplishing the objects contemplated by the united undertakings of the Scinde and Punjaub railways and the Indus Steam Flotilla, a very large profit will result, especially since the important discovery of a bed of coal, believed to be adapted to steam purposes, within thirty miles to the westward of the northern terminus of the railway. The spot lies about twenty-eight miles from Kotree, the port of Hydrabad, five miles from the foot of the Erie hills on the east side of them, and about seventeen miles from the nearest point of the Bahrun river. The discovery was due to accident, though the existence of coal strata along the edge of the valley of the Indus has long been known. The Kardar of the district had recommended a portion of the Verow plain to be enclosed for cultivation, and the Collector, Major Preedy, desired him to sink a well for water. At the depth of forty feet, this seam of coal, eight feet thick, was found, and lower down another seam of 1½ feet thick. The result of an analysis of the specimens sent to England, was highly satisfactory, though they were too small to admit of being tested practically. This last, however, has been made on the spot, with the most gratifying results. The following account of the trial is given by a correspondent of a Scinde paper of recent date.

"The recently discovered Scinde coal was this morning tried on board the Honourable Company's steamer *Nimrod*, and I am glad to say with the most gratifying results. It is now proved to be a coal perfectly well adapted for steam purposes. The *Nimrod* is a steamer of 60 horse power, and her boilers being tubular, her furnaces are well adapted for burning coal. The following gentlemen were present at the trial, viz., Captain Daniell, I.N., Lieut. Searle, I.N., Captain Groube, 13th N. I., Messrs. Morris and Hughes, Chief Engineers, and the Deputy Collector, Captain Phillips. The fires were lighted at a quarter past 6 A.M., without any wood whatever to assist in igniting the coal, it being Captain Daniell's wish fairly to test the quality of the coal itself. Nothing was therefore used, but a small quantity of greased tow.

" Some difficulty was at first experienced in getting the coal to light, but when this did take place, the furnaces, three in number, burnt up with a clear bright white flame, and apparently of great power.

"At twenty minutes past eight, steam was up, and the steamer then weighed anchor, and proceeded at a rapid rate up stream, presenting the gratifying spectacle of the first steamer seen on the Indus, steaming with coal—the produce of the Province. The wind was blowing strongly up stream, and the pressure of steam obtained on the square inch was from 6½ to 7lbs. This is a fair average pressure. On returning down stream, with the wind a-head, the draught was much increased, and the steam guage showed a pressure of nearly 9lbs to the square inch, the steam consequently blowing off, as 8lbs. is the highest working pressure. This speaks much in favour of the power of the coal. The vessel was under weigh one hour, and ran eight miles, four up stream and four down. The coal consumed was one ton and four cwt., viz., fifteen cwt. in getting up steam, and nine cwt. when under weigh. The coal appeared to burn almost entirely away, so that hardly any ash was left, but much of it was in such a pulverised state, that it fell through the furnace bars and mixed with the ashes at the bottom; it was therefore difficult to determine the quantity of ash left.

"On the whole the experiment was deemed most satisfactory by the officers of the Flotilla, who appeared to be greatly interested in its success. The only drawback appeared to be, that as already stated much of the coal was in very small pieces, and consequently either fell through the bars without burning, or burnt with too much rapidity. This is caused by the coal having been brought in from the pit on camels; if brought in carts it would doubtless arrive in much larger particles.

"The coal appears to be free of sulphur, and is much improved by being sprinkled with water previously to use.

"In ordinary practice the coal would probably be at first ignited in the furnaces with wood, and so much time would not be occupied in getting up steam. However, as with cold boilers, one hour and thirty minutes is the usual time with wood, two hours and five minutes with coal, quite unassisted with wood, cannot be deemed unsatisfactory.

"The whole affair is promising, and the time may not be far distant when the Scinde Coal Pits may supply the whole of Western India with this valuable fuel."*

Mr. Inman, a gentleman formerly engaged in Bengal in connection with the coal mines there, but now directed to examine and report upon the coal deposit in the Veron

* "Sindian," May, 1857.

Plain, has stated as his opinion, that there is a large coal formation in that district, and what is not to be found in any other part of India,—coal, iron, and lime—all three together.

It is obvious that these discoveries are calculated to exercise a powerful influence in developing the resources not only of the valley of the Indus, but of the whole of north-western India.

"In the valleys and mountain ranges east and north-east of the great Lahore and Peshawur road, it was reported to me, by natives of those regions, that metallic ores were in abundance—such as iron, copper, lead, silver, and gold in the sands of some streams. The Armenian timber-merchant, Mr. Arratoon, informed me, in December, 1854, that he had discovered the existence of immense coal strata, during his annual excursions to these mountains, for the purpose of cutting timber from the deodar forests I have mentioned. He stated having forwarded specimens of this coal to Mr. H. Cope, at Lahore, where it was pronounced to be of the finest quality. Some of the deposits were laid bare by the action of mountain torrents, which sometimes cut away the rock and soil to a great depth."*

* "Calcutta Englishman." "London to Lahore:" or the Euphrates, Scinde, and Punjaub Railways. Effingham Wilson, Royal Exchange.

CHAPTER XII.

PRODUCTIONS OF VALLEY OF INDUS.

TIMBER FOR BUILDING AND RAILWAY PURPOSES IN PUNJAUB AND NEIGHBOURING TERRITORY.*

THERE are five different kinds of timber which have been more or less applied to building purposes in the Punjaub, viz., "Deodar," "Dear," or "Kailoo," which is the "Pinus Excelsus," "Cheel," "Kile," and "Ray." The two first mentioned, although generally very much confounded, are in fact of different species, the Deodar being a Cedar, whilst the Kailoo is of the Pine species; the grain and colour also differ materially, that of the "Deodar" being a dark yellowish brown, whereas the "Dear" is much lighter; both have a strong smell of turpentine, but the "Deodar" is particularly pungent.

Very little "Deodar" is procurable at Lahore: It is the second named "Dear," called at Simlah "Kailoo," which has been used to so great an extent in all buildings.

"Cheel," which, like the "Dear," is of the pine species, is also much esteemed for building, particularly in trusses for roofs and such like; for which purpose, on account of its larger grain, it is often preferred to the "Dear;" but for doors, window-frames, barrack furniture, boxes for shot

* For the information in this chapter, I am mainly indebted to a memorandum by an engineer officer long resident in the Punjaub.

and shell, the "Dear" always holds the first place. Either will answer very well for flooring, for which purpose the "Cheel" would, probably, be preferred on account of its cheapness.

The comparative prices of the two at Lahore are in the proportion of three to two in favour of the "Cheel," of which three puckee tussoos can be got for a rupee—the selling price of "Dear" being two tussoos puckee. Timber is always sold by the tussoo, which is a measurement of a "guz" (33 inches) long, a "guz" broad, and a tusso (one twenty-fourth "guz") thick.

Cheel wood suffers somewhat from moisture and in this the "Dear" has the advantage; the latter has, also, the reputation of being impervious to white ants; but I should be careful how far I received and acted upon this opinion, as I do not, myself, think it is likely to prove correct.

I have named two other species of timber, the "Kile" and the "Ray;" these appear in my list more to be warned against than for any other reason; they have, however, both had their share of patronage, and the "Ray" was used to some extent in building the barracks at Anarkully; it has there proved itself totally unserviceable; the "Kile" is little or no better. Putting out of the question the general dislike of the natives to the cutting of timber, I see no reason why any number of logs should not be brought down for the use of Scinde, by either of the Punjaub rivers, except the Indus, which is, I fancy, too rapid for the purpose. The forests, which supplied the Sutlej, are, I hear, pretty nearly exhausted; otherwise from the timber agency having been established on it, I should have been inclined to suggest it as in all probability supplying the best timber.

Plenty of trees are to be found near the rise of the Beas, but the difficulty of bringing it out is great. It would, probably, take two seasons to accomplish it, and this would tend to make it expensive.

The timber, used at Lahore, comes down the Ravee from a sort of depôt at Soojahanpore.

It costs 8 annas per tusso here, bought by contract, but can be obtained at a much more reasonable rate at Soojahanpore—from three to four tussoos per rupee probably. The only objection which can be made to the Ravee is the expense which would occur in carriage from the very great number of windings.

The Chénaub viewed as a means of transit for timber has the disadvantage of running, for a great distance, through a foreign country; but the same objection does not apply to the Jhelum, which is, I believe, the straightest of all the rivers, and would, probably, prove the least difficult. There is, I hear, plenty of timber to be obtained at its sources, but I cannot venture to give any opinion as to the exact cost, either of bringing it to the river, or, the freight down to Scinde.

With the exception of the Teak, which is not applicable to building purposes, I do not think there is any jungle wood in Malabar equal to the fir tree of these hills.

"The bullies (fir posts) for piling are also only 8 rupees or less per scorce, each from 4½ to 7 inches diameter, and 13 or 14 feet long. South-west, lower down about sixty or seventy miles, the Jhelum and Ravee both fall into the Chenab, and by this river is rafted all the deodar timber (Cedrus Deodara), the principal wood used in the Punjaub, and even down to Moultan, Hyderabad, and Kurrachee It is obtained from the splendid forests on the great Peer

Punjaub mountains in the Chumba, and other petty rajas' territories bordering on Jummoo and Cashmere. Submerged in water, this wood will last an incredible time; there is an instance, in the latter country, where it has so stood for 500 years. At Wuzzeerabad the price of deodar logs is, up to 25 feet length, 3 tussoos per rupee; beyond 25 feet, 2½ tussoos;—this was the contract rate to an Armenian timber merchant, Mr. Arratoon, but for shorter lengths 4 or 4½ tussoos may be got from natives, or by a properly regulated system of obtaining the wood direct. The tussoo is a Punjabee measure, 3 cubic feet being equivalent to 3 tussoos, or 1 tussoo is very nearly equal to ·857 of a cubic foot. Sawyers' work at Wuzzeerabad is from 90 to 96 superficial feet per rupee; carpenters, masons, and blacksmiths in the Punjaub are at 4 annas per day. Commanders and owners of vessels at Kurrachee, and even Bombay, are extremely anxious to get this wood for decks or other interior work, on account of its lightness and durability." *

* "Calcutta Englishman."

CHAPTER XIII.

PRODUCTIONS OF VALLEY OF INDUS.

FIBROUS SUBSTANCES.—COTTON.—WOOL.—SILK.—LINSEED AND FLAX.

THE demand for flax, hemp, silk, hair and especially cotton, is now becoming so great that the market cannot be supplied with a sufficiency of these raw materials to keep our large manufactories in full operation, and India is looked to as the country whence these supplies must be derived. That she can furnish these supplies, if only assisted by the development of her internal communications, there is no doubt; whilst it is equally clear that it is our interest, as the great manufacturing nation of the world, to make ourselves independent of foreign countries for the supply of raw materials, and especially to provide against the sudden diminution or failure of the cotton crop of America.

COTTON.—Speaking of the character of the cotton crop of the Punjaub, a correspondent of an Indian paper says:—"In April last (1855), I brought to England a small quantity of cotton (the raw material) grown from *acclimated* American cotton seed in a district on the banks of the river Jhelum; this specimen I had shown to several cotton spinners in Manchester. They pronounced it to be the finest specimen of cotton they had seen grown in India, even directly from American seed, and to be worth from 6¼d. to 6¾d. per lb.

"Along the banks of our Punjaub rivers lie tracts of land admirably situated for the growth of cotton. It only requires steady encouragement on the part of the local Government, trouble and perseverance on the part of the district officer, to cover those lands with cotton of the finest quality.

"The cotton that could thus be grown might, with ease and at trifling cost, be conveyed in country boats (until we have, as we ought to have, steamers on those rivers) down the Indus to Kurrachee, and there shipped for England.

"Kurrachee is a port of great importance; but, like many things of great importance, not heeded or taken advantage of. *The one article, cotton, if properly cultivated in the Punjaub and in Scinde, would afford export freight for a vast number of ships visiting Kurrachee, while Government stores for the Punjaub, private property and merchandize would afford endless import freight, to say nothing of the great number of passengers who would avail themselves of that route.*"

According to a Scinde paper—"Any one located on the banks of the river Indus might observe fleets of boats coming down the river in the winter months, all laden with cotton." The cotton brought to Scinde and shipped at Sukkur comes across the Jaysulmere Desert from Rajpootana, and is either consumed in Scinde or exported to Afghanistan.

"The Cotton Wool of Cutch, which adjoins the province of Scinde, whose last year's exports to Bombay amounted to upwards of one-sixth the produce of the Bombay Presidency, will probably eventually be imported into Kurrachee as being the nearest market.

"Two hydraulic presses, adapted for the compression of any description of produce, have lately been imported from

England, so that we have now the means of packing at Kurrachee, which will afford increased facilities to direct exportation." *

WOOL.—The western presidency yields her millions of tons annually of this article of commerce and she is indebted for it chiefly to the countries which are in greater proximity to Kurrachee than to Bombay. "Why, therefore (says a Kurrachee paper), should we not avail ourselves of the advantages of our position, and establish a direct commercial communication with England?

"There existed one drawback to this before, which was the circumstance of no European vessels calling here likely to receive cargo. The example set us by the Court of Directors, in making Scinde the highway for troops for the far north-west, should, however, remove this difficulty. The Punjaubee, Afghan, and Patan merchants would, we are certain, be glad to avail themselves of the opportunity of shipping their wool at Kurrachee, and thereby avoid a sea trip to Bombay; but the first step towards overcoming the present apathy, must be the establishment of a screw company,† or perhaps, more appropriately, a *working* company, of people who will undertake and guarantee the screwing of the wool; and our ships, which bring us annually cargoes of human beings, for the service of their country in India, may receive in return cargoes of wool and other raw produce, for the use and the benefit of our brethren at home."

* Memoranda on the External Trade of Scinde for 1856-57.—*Vide* Appendix A.

† This has been accomplished, in some degree, by private enterprise, and screws for cotton and wool have been provided for Moultan and Kurrachee by the liberality of the East India Company.

The export of wool from Kurrachee five years ago, was to the value of £75,716; it now amounts to £311,590, an increase equivalent to 312 per cent.*

* Messrs. Jehangheer Nusseer-Wanjee and Co. beg to draw the attention of the mercantile community to the following letter;—the wool can be seen at their Godowns.

To Messrs. Jehangeer Nusseer-Wanjee and Co., Kurrachee.

LAHORE, *November 27th*, 1857.

Dear Sir,

I beg to acknowledge the receipt of your letter of the 27th ultimo; and in reply to state that you had better examine and see one or two bags of the wool I sent you. I got it after three years' labour 300 miles beyond Chinese Tartary, brought over snowy passes of 20,000 feet high, conveyed by goats alone. Such wool Khorasan, Kurrachee, or England, never saw; the fibres are of extraordinary length, and very fine—let me assure you it is far superior either to the Australian or Merino Wool; the sheep which yields this wool is nearly as large as a donkey, and its wool hanging to the ground. I was offered at Umritsir at 40 rupees per maund; but I want to introduce it into the English market.

Shipping, with troops from England, are daily expected at the Kurrachee harbour; therefore, the ship captains, supercargoes, or merchants and consignees, will gladly seize the opportunity of buying my wool up for exportation to England; when once known there, I expect there will be large orders for this description of wool—length of fibre is sought after.

Yours faithfully,

M. ARRATOON.

P.S.—I enclose a regular invoice of the wool, in all 29 twenty-nine bags; weighing Bengal maunds sixty-five; and twenty-five seers.

The fine White Wool is	25	bags.	58 mds.	30 srs.
Black do.	2	do.	3 mds.	22 srs.
Grey do.	2	do.	3 mds.	13 srs.
	—		—	—
Total bags	29		Mds. 65	Seers 25
			or in lbs. 5254	

So that only 4 bags are grey and black, and the rest fine white.

SILK.—We extract the following on the silk trade as worthy of notice, from the selections from the Records of the Bombay Government:—The importation of raw silk from the north-west to Shikarpoor is one of the most important branches of the import trade from that direction. The article appears to be of a superior description; and as I am not aware of its being known in the Bombay market, I have collected the following particulars.

The following are the descriptions of the raw silk, with the prices of each in the Shikarpoor bazaar, import duty paid (at Rs. 1 6 0 per maund):—

1. *Kohanee*, from Bokhara (produced in Toorkistan), price Shikarpoor Rupees 10 per Assar.*

2. *Toonee*, from Herat, price Rs. 13 12 0 per Assar.

3. *Shal bafee*, from Herat, price Rs. 15 10 0 per Assar.

4. *Nuwabee*, from Bokhara, price Rs. 14 12 0 per Assar.

5. *Gheilanee*, from Kirmare and Yezd, price Rs. 9 per Assar.

6. *Kaloochar*, frem Herat, price Rs. 9 per Assar.

The value of annual imports may be about Rs. 50,000 and the route is through the great Pass of the Bolan. The traders are principally Afghans, who visit Shikarpoor with the annual Kafilas from October to March (though much of the article is purchased by the Hindoo agents of the Shikarpoor Soucars, who are to be found in all the important cities and marts of the north

* Silk, raw and prepared, is weighed at the rate of 90¼ Shikarpoor Rupees to 1 Assar; 90¼ Shikarpoor Rupees equal in weight 88¼ new company's. The present exchange between the two currencies is 94¾ company's per 100 Shikarpoor, or 5¼ per cent in favour of the former.

west), according to the late Sir A. Burnes and other travellers.*

Nos. 1, 2, 5, and 6 of the raw silks above enumerated are prepared for weaving, and dyed at Shikarpoor; the *Shal bafee* and *Nuwabee* (Nos. 3 and 4) are manufactured at Roree, on the opposite bank of the Indus, into a coarse silk fabric, known as *Duryaee,* value at Roree, seven annas per Guz. The silk threads prepared at Shikarpoor, and hereafter enumerated, principally find a market at Khyrpoor, Sukkur, Roree, Larkhana, Gundava, Bagh (in Kutchee), and towards Lower Scinde as far as Sehwan and Tatta, where they are manufactured into Loongees of various descriptions, Goolbuduns, and other fabrics used in the country. The raw material, or prepared thread, does not appear to enter into the export trade of Shikarpoor with any of the neighbouring countries.

The following is a list of prepared silk threads from the raw *Kokanee* :—

1. *Pistakee,* yellow Gooljuleel (Mellilat) dye, price, Rs. 20 per Assar.

2. *Chumunee,* light green mixture of indigo with the above, price Rs. 20 per Assar.

3. *Subz,* dark green, ditto, ditto, price, Rs. 20 per Assar.

4. *Soormaee,* indigo, price, Rs. 20 per Assar.

5. *Koombaee,* orange Koomba (safflower dye), price, Rs. 28 per Assar.

6. *Jillaee,* deep yellow (not known), Kumbera dye, price, Rs. 16 per Assar.

7. *Kirmdz,* cochineal dye, crimson, price, Rs. 21 12 0 per Assar.

8. *Acho,* white, undyed, price, Rs. 20 per Assar.

* Sir A. Burnes' Report on the Route of Shikarpoor.

List of prepared threads from the raw *Toonee* :—

1. *Pistakee*	}	Same dyes used as the above price, Rs. 24 per A.
2. *Chumunee*		
3. *Subz*		
4. *Ashmanee* (light blue indigo) . .		
5. *Acho* (white)		

6. Three shades of cochineal, price, Rs. 26 12 0 per Assar.

The raw silks, *Ghielanee* and *Kaloochar* are not in very general use, *Kokanee* and *Toonee* being the principal importations, and the most in use.

The expense of transmitting goods from Shikarpoor to the sea by water carriage may be easily ascertained, as certain rates have been established by the British Government for freight by packet boats—thus, from Sukkur to Kurrachee bunder Co.'s Rs. 1 per maund dead weight, or Rs. 1 per cubic foot for light goods. The expense of transport from Shikarpoor to Sukkur by the Scinde Canal is about 4 annas per maund, or 2 annas per camel carrying 6 maunds.

The export town duties to be paid at Shikarpoor, and the export duties again at Kurrachee, on raw silk, would be thus :—

1. All duties on purchasing in the bazaar, and clearing the town of Shikarpoor, as far as the Scinde Canal, Shikarpoor Rs. 16 14 0 per maund.

2. Export duty at Kurrachee, about Rs. 5 per cent. *ad valorem.*

A calculation from the above may be pretty accurately formed at the price at which the article would come into the Bombay market; and as it will hereafter be to the interests of the native governments to modify many of the imposts which may at present be considered vexatious and oppressive upon trade, silk, and other commodities from the north-west may, with the advantage of improved carriage from Shikarpoor to the Presidency, enter considerably into the market of Bombay by the route of the Indus.

There is no doubt that when irrigation and the means of transit are fairly established, there will be no difficulty as to the growth of mulberries, that the silk trade will prove an important item in the resources of Scinde. There *is* a good time coming for this province; and it is coming quickly.

"In the past year it has been seen that the exports of raw silk from Scinde have increased from Rs. 3,761 to Rs. 3,16,413, or 90 fold, derived from a new and unexpected source, Bokhara; having once taken the direction of the Indus, this trade will not probably depart from it; and having once established itself, may, if properly fostered, be increased to an incredible degree." *

LINSEED AND FLAX.—"One consequence of the war with Russia will be, to make us, to a great extent, independent of many of her staple exports. In the case of oil seeds, the trade with Calcutta has been so greatly developed, as to render seeds one of the most important features in our trade with that port; and our East Indian possessions bid fair, at no distant period, to supply the entire consumption of this country." †

"By the judicious, public-spirited, and energetic exertions of Sir John Lawrence, and many other civil servants attached to the Punjaub, the extensive culture of flax, linseed, and other valuable agricultural produce, is warmly

* Memoranda on the External Trade of Scinde for 1856-57.—*Vide* Appendix A.

† Messrs. Laing and Campbell's Annual Circular for 1856.

encouraged in the rich districts watered by the Sutlej, Beas, Ravee, and Chenab rivers. These products are principally designed for exportation, as scarcely any are consumed by the inhabitants; but the foreign demand is yearly increasing. To create a spirit of emulation, Government in 1853 and 1854 undertook the purchase of all the new crops raised; and in 1855, an association of capitalists, I am informed, bought them up." *

Major Hollings, Deputy Commissioner of Shahpore, in the Punjaub, observes:—"My attention has been directed to the cultivation of linseed and the preparation of flax —subjects which have been taken up by the Financial Commissioner, Mr. McLeod, with a view to the exportation of these products to the markets in England. The position of the Punjaub is peculiarly favorable for the development of commerce, and there are in it soils and climates suitable for the production of every kind of fruit and vegetable. When the mineral resources are better known, it will be found that the Punjaub contains unlimited supplies of those valuable manures which chemistry has lately introduced to agriculture."

"When intelligence reached us," says the *Bombay Times*, "that war had been declared by our Queen against the Emperor of Russia, Mr. Frere, the Commissioner of Scinde, and his friends here, began to consider how they could assist our manufacturers and their territory by supplying us with raw material usually heretofore received from Russia. If we were only able to take their goods during hostilities, it might be a profitless transaction for Scinde to supply part of the vacuum caused by war; but one use of

* "London to Lahore:" or the Euphrates, Scinde and Punjaub Railways. Effingham Wilson, Royal Exchange.

this quarrel is to compel a thorough search of our own resources, and one loss to Russia from its existence will be the employment of other lands to grow those staples that it has hitherto supplied. Two productions of Russia which we buy in large quantities may be profitably grown in Northern India. Wheat is the first, and probably the more important of these articles. Flax is the second staple of Russia referred to in the preceding sentences, and which the friends of Scinde expect it to supply. Egypt is a somewhat similar country, and the flax of the Egyptians must have been of high quality thousands of years since; for their fine linen was, at that distance of time, in high reputation. We have, therefore, no reason to doubt the capabilities of Scinde to produce fine flax. The value of the staple in a great measure depends upon its quality. Very few articles present an equally long range of quotations. It has been sold at £30, and it has brought £140 per ton. The average price in this country is higher, however, than that of cotton; and therefore no great difficulty will arise regarding the freight, although the construction of railways, or the improvement of the Indus, is still an important essential to a great flax trade from northern India."

Some 5,000 maunds of linseed were, sometime since, sold in Lahore at two rupees a maund. This is a price which amply repays the cultivator, and the demand is likely to continue. The seed was intended for Kurrachee and Bombay, to be exported to England, where prices were then ranging about equal to seven rupees a maund.

An Indian paper gives the following statement, from a correspondent, regarding the sale of the seed sent down to Scinde to be disposed of:—

"We have now the pleasure to wait on you with the

result of the first sale of Punjaub linseed, which took place yesterday, when 1,200 bags were submitted for competition in lots of 25 bags each, and sold at prices varying from Rs. 4 to 4 13-16th per maund of 80 lbs.

"After this a lot of 40 maunds of Scinde linseed was put up, which realized Rs. 4 8-6th per maund, and another batch of 84 packages, in six different lots, which realized Rs. 4 8-6th to 4 12-6th per maund.

"Shortly afterwards a batch of 700 bags of Punjaub linseed, now on its way from Moultan, was sold to arrive at Rs. 4 10-16th per maund. After which the whole of the remaining quantity of the Punjaub linseed, estimated at 7,000 or 8,000 maunds, was offered for sale to arrive. The bidders at first showed some hesitation in offering for the quantity in consequence of the uncertainty as to the time of delivery, when it was agreed that the whole quantity that may arrive before the end of October becomes the property of the purchaser. With this stipulation, the lot was knocked down at 48-16th per maund." *

In the Punjaub, the encouragement of the cultivation of flax has been earnestly taken up by the local Government, the result of whose efforts are fully detailed in the following extract from the valuable Report from which we have previously quoted.

"The chief efforts of the last two years have been directed towards the cultivation of flax and linseed; that is, the cultivation of the plant which yields the fibre from its stem, and also the seed termed linseed. Under any circumstances the plant, if grown at all, will yield linseed, which, though less used in the country, is valuable for exportation. But in order that the plant may yield fibre, it must be carefully cultivated, so that the stem may be

* The "Bombay Telegraph and Courier," October, 1856.

long. In this case, however, it will produce a less amount of seed, because it does not ramify; whereas, when the stem is short, there generally is ramification and a better out-turn of seed. In 1854 the Government, at the instance of the Agri-Horticultural Society, invited the people to cultivate the plant largely, offered rewards, and offered to buy up whatever seed or fibre might be produced, if the producer should be unable to dispose of the produce otherwise. Instructions regarding the proper mode of culture were circulated. European seed was also procured in such quantities as were obtainable at the time; but this was chiefly sown, either under the Society's auspices or in the immediate vicinity of Lahore. In the interior of the districts the farmer depended on the seeds of the country. The plant is sowed in the autumn and reaped in the spring. During the year 1854-55, a very large area, not less than 60,000 acres, was covered with the plant. The out-turn of seed was very considerable, perhaps not less than 5,400 tons; but owing to defects of culture, of irrigation, and of soil, the stems proved nearly all short, and consequently the out-turn of fibre was nominal. Near Lahore, however, the seed having been superior, and the culture having been carefully supervised, a small amount of good fibre was produced, and was successfully prepared for use and exportation. The mass of linseed produced in the interior of the country did not, however, fall upon the hands of Government, though fair market prices were offered according to promise. For, contrary to expectation, merchants from Hindostan, Moultan and elsewhere, purchased nearly the whole. The remainder was bought by Government, transported down the Indus to Kurrachee, and was there sold at rates which more than covered the original cost price and cost of transit. In 1855 about

250,000 acres were sown, but the season being dry, were unpropitious. About 2,300 tons of linseed have been produced and will be bought up by the merchants. No mercantile fibre was obtained. Such, briefly, was the history of the Government flax and linseed experiment of 1854 and 1855. It was not unsuccessful pecuniarily. The Government outlay was much smaller than had been anticipated, and did not exceed rupees 50,000, or £5,000; but it was fully covered by proceeds. The experiment may also serve as a basis for some sound conclusions. It appears that in the Punjaub, linseed can be produced even on second-rate lands without any great effort or cost, and may be either sold on the spot or exported with advantage, so that the culture would be fairly remunerative to the growers. But the production of fibre is a much more difficult matter: care, intelligence, cost, trouble, good soil fairly irrigated, are all required. There must be, *first*, good stems; and *secondly*, skilful preparation of the fibre: both objects are, probably, beyond the ordinary power of a Punjabee farmer. And then, if he were successful, it might happen that the same soil and culture would have produced superior crops, more valuable even than flax. The thing can, however, be done, especially with the advantage of European seed. There are several districts which offer natural facilities, and in which it is probable that farmers may be found who, with suitable encouragement, both will and can grow flax; and thus, eventually, a new product may be produced into a province where such staples are much needed."*

* Report on Administration of Punjaub from 1854 to 1856, par. 194.

CHAPTER XIV.

PRODUCTIONS OF VALLEY OF INDUS.

WHEAT.

"Till within the last two years, (1854 and 1855) we had but a few isolated cases of this article being imported from India, and, from various causes, these importations gave no encouragement to importers to continue them. Several thousand quarters imported in 1854, however, have induced further shipments; and about 60,000 qrs. were shipped at Calcutta for England during the last year, from January to the 22nd of November. The article being little known, the importers found it difficult to sell for arrival on satisfactory terms till November last, when sales on c. f. and i. terms commenced to be made; and since then to the present time upwards of 40,000 qrs. have been sold. The highest price paid for good qualities of soft wheats was 70*s*. c. f. and i., on terms considered equal to 80*s*. delivered; and this was when the price of good white English wheat was 85*s*. per qr. The lowest price since the decline in the corn market has been 62*s*., c. f. and i., for hard wheat. We are informed that some few thousand quarters are now on the way from Bombay (no doubt Punjaub wheat, which is the best grown in India); and, from the samples shown, we estimate the value of the hard at about the same as Spanish hard, and the soft the same as good soft English. Some quantity of the Calcutta wheat has lately arrived, and most of it in excellent condition, and its present value on the spot is 68*s*. to 72*s*. per quarter of 504 lbs." *

During the Russian war, an Indian paper mentioned the curious fact that a trade in "bread stuffs" was springing up between the Western Presidency and the Levant. Large freights had been offered for the conveyance of grain from Bombay to Constantinople.

The *Times*, also, showed that that war was producing strange effects on the corn trade. The closure of the Russian corn-exporting ports in the Black Sea, combined with the unusual demand created by the presence of the allied army, had led to a wonderful development of agriculture in countries hitherto only known, at least in modern times, for their unproductiveness. Thus, the shores of the Bosphorus, the plains of the Troad, and the desert places of Syria, were all turned into corn fields. But it is certainly more than was generally expected, to find India within the influence of this centre of attraction.

"It often happens that an article of commerce, once violently as it were introduced into the market under the pressure of circumstances, continues to keep good its place after the pressure has been withdrawn. It was so with Indian indigo, and it may be so with Indian wheat. Certain it is, that a market for cereals is the crying want of India. Make India a corn, as well as cotton-exporting country, and the greatness of England and the prosperity of India are secured."

It is understood that several inquiries have reached Scinde from home, as to the feasibility of exporting wheat from that province to England. It is believed that

* Messrs. Laing and Campbell's Annual Circular for 1856.

with improved means of transport there would be little or no difficulty in the matter. There is excellent wheat grown in the neighbourhood of Sehwan. The specimens of Scinde wheat which I have seen, prove it to be a sound, heavy grain, of an unusually large size. And, in comparison with average English prices, it is so cheap, that, after the cost of carriage and freight, its exportation would yield a handsome profit.

Let those who feel interested in the welfare of Scinde and the development of her resources, direct their attention to this matter. An enhanced price for the grain-produce of the country, would give the cultivators heart to raise superior crops, and render England independent of all foreign corn markets. The sum saved by this country being able to feed her people from her own resources may be understood from the fact, that the price of food in England during the Russian war was higher than during any previous year for thirty years. The highest average price of wheat in any year, from 1828 to 1854, was in 1839, and that was several shillings per quarter lower than the people were paying during 1854 and 1855. Even the famine year of 1847 fell much below the average of 1854 and 1855; and the amount of capital which was thus abstracted from commerce may be estimated at a sum equivalent at least to the whole cost of the Russian war. So that, in point of fact, while the commercial classes had to pay their quota directly to the cost of the war, they were indirectly paying to the owners of the soil a sum more than equal to the immense burden imposed by our naval and military expenditure. The high price of food was not referable to deficient harvests—for the English harvest of 1854 was the most bountiful ever known, and that of 1855 is alleged by the best authorities to have been a full average one. The war operated precisely as the corn law operated, and, in reality, was equivalent to a reimposition of the monopoly of our own landowners. The soil, with the most abundant produce, did not suffice to feed the population; and the late war, by closing against us some of the largest corn markets in the world, maintained a famine rate of food prices, as well as the enormous fiscal drain of capital to meet the direct expenditure by the Government. Estimating the annual consumption of wheat alone at 20,000,000 quarters, what is the probable excess of price which was paid for the two years, 1854 and 1855, on that quantity, over and above what it would have cost had the war not closed against us the chief ports of supply? The average of the entire year 1854 was 72*s*. 5*d*. the quarter, and the average of the following year was, it is believed, higher. The six weeks' average, ending the 20th October, 1855, was 76*s*. 11*d*. for the whole country; and subsequently the average for all wheat sold was 80*s*. 3*d*. Not less than 20*s*. or 25*s*. per quarter may be taken as the excess of price caused by the war on every quarter of wheat consumed for a period of eighteen months. And if to this be added the proportionate rise in all other kinds of agricultural produce, the extra absorption of capital in food alone cannot have been much less than equivalent to all the loans and taxes raised directly for war purposes.*

With an immense wheat country at its back, Kurrachee

* I am indebted to a writer in an Indian paper for the figures in the above paragraph.

can at present export but little wheat. Scinde has almost boundless means for the production of wheat, and could, with railways, without difficulty, and at a moderate price, supply the entire consumption of Great Britain and Ireland. From many causes now in operation the price of the quartern loaf may any day become again a serious matter for consideration to all housekeepers, and a terror to the poor. The opening of such a source of supply is like the finding of concealed treasure. At present, the capabilities of production are useless from the want of means of transport. Colonel Turner, Superintending Engineer in Scinde, observes that—"In travelling through the country after the inundation of 1851, I found at a place called Naree, a few miles above Sehwan, stocks of Government grain of three successive years:—the excessive inundation of that year had swamped it, and it was utterly spoiled, fit only for manure. At first I imagined the Kardar must be to blame, but on enquiry, I learned that there had been repeated attempts to sell it by auction, but that no one would buy it, *because the cost of conveying it to a market would render it an unprofitable speculation.*"

Major Preedy on this head remarks, "that as the proposed Railway was to be constructed entirely in his collectorate, he considered it his duty to bear testimony to the great commercial advantages likely to be gained by it, in the transport of large quantities of grain of all descriptions, which are produced in such luxuriance in Upper and Middle Scinde. The quantity of grain which might be exported from Kurrachee, was immense when Sir C. Napier was here—in the year of the Irish famine, he offered to have ready 11,000 tons of grain at Kurrachee for transmission, and such a quantity might and could have been spared without interfering with the consumption of the country. The cost of carriage now was so great as actually to prohibit grain as an export. The price of wheat and grain was at Shikarpoor and Hyderabad, just one half its price in Kurrachee, the navigation of the Indus rendering attempts to bring grain down as an export very hazardous. Major Preedy instanced a case where *out of seven boats laden with grain which started from Kotree, but one arrived in Kurrachee, the other six being lost; if one or two boats only out of a batch of six or so were lost, it was generally considered a good venture.* He looked, therefore, upon the grain transport alone to give a large return—a return far exceeding what Lieut. Chapman had allowed towards the profits of a railroad in Scinde."

"During the activity of the Russian war, a large quantity of Scinde wheat was exported to England *via* Bombay. Peace probably rendered further speculation in the article unremunerative." *

In the Report of the Administration of the Punjaub already freely quoted from, in the chapter on Land Revenue, the enormous and increasing production of cereals beyond the present consumption, the probable *surplus* produce amounting to a quarter, perhaps half a million of tons annually, the quantity of unreclaimed land capable of production, the great productive power of the people, are demonstrated. Wheat of excellent quality is grown—the Punjaub is eminently a corn-producing country.

* Memoranda on the External Trade of Scinde for 1856-57.—*Vide* Appendix A.

The oscillation in price for a period of five years may be seen in the following table :—

AVERAGE PRICES IN THE PUNJAUB.

For ten years,* up to 1850-51.	Wheat. Rs. 2 per maund of 82-lbs.	Indian Corn. Rs. $1\frac{11}{16}$ per maund.
1851-52 . .	Rs. 1 per maund .	Rs. $0\frac{14}{16}$ per maud.
1852-53 . .	Rs. $1\frac{3}{16}$ ditto . .	Rs. $1\frac{1}{16}$ ditto.
1853-54 . .	Rs. $1\frac{3}{16}$ ditto . .	Rs. $1\frac{2}{16}$ ditto.
1854-55 . .	Rs. 1 ditto . . .	Rs. $0\frac{13}{16}$ ditto.
1855-56 . .	Rs. $1\frac{1}{16}$ ditto . .	Rs $0\frac{14}{16}$ ditto. †

" The price has always been one maund, more or less, or 82 lbs. for the Rupee, during the last five years, that is, *nearly as cheap again* as it used to be before Annexation. Furthermore, not only are the prices much lower than they used to be in the Punjaub, but also lower than they are in other parts of Upper India. During the past five years, the average price of gram, in the North-Western provinces, has been 33 seers to the Rupee, and in the Punjaub, 37 seers."

" The Punjaub cannot export to the West or to the North, as those regions are poor; nor can it export to the East, as in that direction there is already abundance. It can

* Seven prior to Annexation.

† The great cheapness, which has generally prevailed during the last year, (1855-56,) which was dry and unfavourable, leads to the conclusion that granaries were full, and markets glutted with the grain of former years.

only export to the South, to Kurrachee, the port destined by Nature to be the outlet for these territories. Thence the produce can be shipped for Bombay or for distant countries and colonies. Already it is found that Scinde and Punjaub wheat can be profitably exported to the Mauritius. Already some 5,357 tons or 150,000 maunds per annum of Punjaub produce find their way with difficulty down the Indus, and this will, it may be hoped, become the nucleus of a mighty traffic. That the Punjaub must be producing more than it can consume is easily calculated. The cultivated area has been returned at 12,751,151 acres. Some three-fourths of this area are certainly grown with articles of daily food, namely, wheat, barley, and Indian corn, maize and rice. At an ordinary average of production per acre, namely 6¼ maunds, some 80,164,616 maunds or 2,863,022 tons may be produced annually. There are thirteen millions of souls; at an ordinary consumption per annum of about 4½ maunds or 360 lbs. to each person, they would consume 59,000,000 maunds or 2,107,143 tons in a year, which, deducted from the aggregate produce, leaves a surplus of 777,481 tons, which surplus, though attained by a rough calculation, will give some idea of the actual state of the case. What is to become of this surplus? If possible, it should not be allowed to fill our granaries and glut our markets, causing derangement of prices and embarrassment to the agriculturists, yet it cannot be exported to Kurrachee, unless the communication shall be improved by steam or rail, or by both. That this can be effected, there is happily reason to suppose, as will be seen in one of the following sections (IV.) In this place, therefore, it is sufficient to urge that the measure is of the very last importance to the agricultural interest and to the future prosperity of the Punjaub, and that until something of the kind be effected, there must always be some anxiety regarding our land revenue. Let means of export, the grand desideratum, be once supplied, everything will follow. There are known to be nearly six millions of *culturable* acres yet to be brought under the plough. There is a population, prolific to increase, hardy and industrious to labour. There are vast supplies of water in the rivers and facilities for excavating canals. Then money will be abundant, prices will recover their standard, and the land revenue will flourish." *

* Report on Administration of Punjaub, from 1854 to 1856, pars.—45 and 46.

CHAPTER XV.

PRODUCTIONS OF VALLEY OF INDUS.

SALT.

Salt, of the purest quality, is formed naturally on the coasts of Scinde, and the Indian system of taxing salt is not extended to that province. The immense trade which might be carried on in this article was pointed out eight or ten years ago, by Lieut. (now Major) Burke, of the Bombay Engineers, who published a small pamphlet, giving an account of the vast and practically-inexhaustible deposit whence the supply might be derived. But no notice was taken of the fact by mercantile men till January 1855, when the captain of a vessel going round to Calcutta in ballast took a cargo. The venture was so successful that it has since been repeated. The duty paid on import of Scinde salt into Calcutta for the portion of the year up to August 1855, was Rs. 30,000.

A Company was formed at Kurrachee, some years since, for the purpose of exporting Scinde salt to Calcutta. Its operations have not been very extensive, but so far they appear to have been successful. From information supplied by the Bombay Government, we learn that about half a lakh of maunds of Kurrachee salt have been exported to Calcutta by the Company since December 1854, and that, "though previously unknown there, it has commanded prices beyond the prices obtained for Bombay salt, which, next to Liverpool and foreign Europe salt, had heretofore stood in the highest favour in the Calcutta market." But according to the Scinde Commissioner:—"There is one cause which retards the development of this trade, that is, the apparent ignorance, in the mercantile circles in England, that we have such an article as salt in the province, though some pains had been taken last year to give the fact publicity through the medium of the Prospectus of the Salt Company."

Mr. Dalzell gives, as the results of the Salt Company's experience, that the cost of digging and shipping the salt on board coasting vessels, of fifty to sixty tons burden, has been about Rs. 3 10 4 (about *7s.* 3½*d.*) per hundred maunds, or including freight in such coasting vessels to Kurrachee, about 12*s.* 6*d.* per hundred maunds. After being landed and housed at Kurrachee, it has been shipped for Calcutta at the rate of 30*s.* per hundred maunds,—the price at Calcutta being from £4 10*s.* to £8 per hundred maunds.

This salt is likely to have a very beneficial influence on the commerce of Kurrachee, as removing much of the risk of loss should a vessel fail in getting other cargo at Kurrachee, and be obliged to go round to Calcutta in search of freight; by carrying a cargo of salt she will always be able to earn something.

The Court of Directors has already given orders that Kurrachee shall be at once connected with the Indian system of electric telegraphs; and when that connexion is complete, the commander of a vessel at Kurrachee will be able to communicate in a few hours with Calcutta, Madras and Bombay, ascertain the rates of freight and prices of salt, &c., at each port, and regulate his movements accordingly.

"We have much pleasure," says a Scinde paper, "in responding to the invitation of our Contemporary of the *Bombay Times*—whose observations on our article on

Scinde Salt, which appeared in our issue on the 13th ultimo, will be found elsewhere in our columns—to enlighten him, for he appears to be sadly in the dark, as to the source whence our supplies of Salt are obtained and at what cost; for he has got hold of a very erroneous idea of the rate at which it will be shipped at this Port.

"The supplies of Salt are derived from the great natural deposits in the delta of our Classic Stream. Hitherto they have been drawn from the deposits situated on the Seir Gunda Creek, which lies about half way between the Gora and Koree mouths of the Indus, about 100 miles South East of Kurrachee.

"Native Craft, not exceeding the burthen of 50 tons, can ascend this Creek about 30 miles, at which distance from its mouth lie extensive natural Salt deposits, extending over an area of miles on either side; and approaching to within half a mile, the place of shipment.

"The expense of digging and bringing this Salt to Kurrachee by boat, is one anna and seven pies a maund. Here it is stowed in Godowns, and shipped at the rate of Rs. 15 per 100 maunds of 82 lbs. or Rs. 4-1 anna a ton, without a fraction of further charge,—and as the Salt stores are within 50 yards of the anchorage ground, an ordinary sized ship can be laden in ten days; which, as far as our expenses go, has seldom, if ever we should think, been accomplished in Bombay, for these reasons; that the Salt has to be brought from a distance of some miles, at the moment it is required —that delays occur in weighing it at the pans,—and, that at some pans, the distance which intervenes between the Salt heaps and the place of lading, is often-time considerable.

"Our Contemporary says that Salt can be manufactured

in Bombay at Rs. 2 a ton and shipped, he "should suppose, for less than three." If our Contemporary will point out to us a single instance in which Salt, of even ordinary quality, has been shipped to Calcutta for less than three Rs. a ton, we promise to make a present of a ship load.

"Salt, we admit, may be procurable at Bombay for Rs. 2 a ton; but what description of Salt? Mixed with 50 per cent of foreign matter; we have often seen such an article, and therefore speak from experience; but a pure, unadulterated Salt, such as we have in Scinde, Bombay is incapable of producing; and if it did produce it, could not afford to sell it at the price of the natural produce of this Province.

"Although Scinde Salt has been only lately introduced into Calcutta, and, consequently, is still only partially known there, it has hitherto realised much higher prices than Bombay Salt; and we feel almost certain, that, when its qualities become better known, it will command the market in a still higher degree than it does at present; one valuable property it possesses is, that it is less deliquescent than manufactured Salt.

"We subjoin an analysis of it, and of English Salt, and shall be happy to afford our Contemporary any further information on the subject which he may desire; but, let him never repeat that 'nowhere in the world can Salt be loaded more economically than at Bombay.'"*

* Opinion of Dr. GIRAUD in a letter addressed to the Secretary to the Medical Board, Bombay.

GRANT MEDICAL COLLEGE, BOMBAY,
12th November, 1847.

Para. 16.—"With reference to your letter No. 1475 of 1847, accompanied by specimens of salt from the western bank of the Koree mouth of the Indus, I have the honour to inform you that I have

Kurrachee throws down the gauntlet in maintenance of her right to be considered the cheaper market; let us see who will have the hardihood to pick it up.

The salt trade of the Punjaub is of the utmost importance, producing nearly twenty lakhs of rupees of clear revenue to the Government. The supply is inexhaustible, arising from a complete range of salt hills, running from the Indus to the Jhelum, of the mines of which the Government has a monopoly. This salt, from its medicinal as well as general properties, is in general use throughout the

carefully analysed the salt, and find it to be of remarkable purity, being absolutely free from bromides, iodides, and salt of iron; containing only a very small proportion of chloride of magnesium, with mere traces of sulphate of lime, as shown below, where its composition is compared with some well known salt."

(Signed) H. GIRAUD,
Professor of Chemistry, G. M. College.

Opinion of the Medical Board, addressed to Government.

MEDICAL BOARD OFFICE,
12*th November*, 1847.

Para. 17.—"I am directed by the Medical Board to acknowledge the receipt of your letter No. 4065, of the 28th ultimo, and in reply to forward for the information of the Honourable the Governor in council, the accompanying report of an analysis made of the salt from the banks of the Indus by Assistant Surgeon Giraud, Professor of Chemistry, which shows it to be the purest natural chloride of sodium, or common salt, that the Board are acquainted with."

(Signed) J. SCOTT,
Secretary Medical Board.

Analysis.

	Chloride of Sodium.	Chloride of Magnesium	Sulphate of Magnesia.	Sulphate of Lime.
Salt from the Indus . .	99·7352	0·2647	0·	a trace.
Cheshire Salt	98·2500	0·750	0·	1·55
Lymington Salt	93·7000	1.1000	3·500	1·50

country, and most extensively exported until it meets the salt of the Sambhur lake and the other salt-producing portions of our territories. The present supply, says the author of the Report from which we have before quoted, "is produced from some five mines in the salt range of hills running from the Jhelum to the Indus; of this salt the Government has a monopoly. The article is excavated at the Government expense, and sold on the spot to the merchants at two rupees, or four shillings, per maund of 80 lbs. In the Kohat district, beyond the Indus, there are also some four mines from which the salt is excavated by Government, but sold at the almost nominal price of from two to four annas, or from 3*d*. to 6*d*. per maund of 80 lbs., out of consideration to the mountaineers of that region. But in order that this lightly-taxed salt may not compete with the article from the mines of the cis-Indus salt-range, a preventive line is established along the left bank of the Indus. There is no preventive line along the northern border of the Punjaub, as no salt produced in those Himalayan regions could compete with the Punjaub salt. The Rajpootana salts of the north-western provinces, which pay duty on the Delhi line, do not at present enter the Punjaub by the upper route, though a proposal for admission of one of these salts (the Sambhur) has just been sanctioned. In order that the salt from Rajpootana may not enter the Punjaub by the lower and direct route, and thereby evade the Delhi line, a preventive line has been established along the Sutlej, near Moultan.

"Formerly, the Sikh Government had a similar monopoly of the cis-Indus salt mines, but they farmed their revenue out and otherwise mis-managed it. The out-turn of the mines was not worth more than eight lakhs of rupees, or £80,000, of which not more than half, or five lakhs, found its way to the coffers of the State. After annexation of the Punjaub in 1849, the average demand for salt at the mines was calculated at 600,000 maunds per annum, which, at rupees two, or four shillings per maund, would yield twelve lakhs of rupees or £120,000 per annum. But the demand continued to rise year after year, till in 1854-55 the demand amounted to 10,47,028 maunds or 10½ lakhs, and the revenue to rupees 20,94,056 or 21 lakhs, or £210,000. During the past year (1855-56) there has, indeed, been a slight falling off, the salt amounting to maunds 9,65,860 or 9½ lakhs, and the revenue to rupees 19,31,720 or 19⅓ lakhs, or £193,000. This slight deficiency may be accounted for partly by the prevalence of drought during the last season, and partly by the existence of an impression among the merchants that there would be an alteration of duty,—an impression which has now been removed. It is probable that the increase has not yet reached its final limit, and that as population increases, a still larger revenue may be confidently expected from this source.

"The above increase is indicative of prosperity, at least among the lower classes. The consumption of Punjaub salt has nearly doubled since the establishment of British rule. The increase of population, the pacification of the province, the great diminution of the land tax, the abolition of import and export duties, have caused an enhanced consumption of salt among the agriculturists and lower orders. Considerable quantities are also exported towards the eastward, and to the north as far as Jummoo and Cashmere, but there is no likelihood of exportation to the west or the south. It is gratifying to reflect, that where the Sikh

Government obtained only five lakhs of rupees the British Government obtain twenty lakhs, and this, too, without any appreciable increase to the burdens of the people. Formerly, the average price of salt at Lahore used to be 1 rupee (2*s.*) for 36 or 40 lbs. It is now much the same, viz., 1 rupee for 32, 34, and 36 lbs, or rupees 2—4 or 4*s.* 6*d.* per maund of 80 lbs., the 4 annas (6*d.*) being the merchant's reimbursement and profit over the Government price of 2 rupees.

"It is clear, then, that the excess of our revenue over that of our predecessors is owing, not to increased taxation, but to increased consumption. That the present price is light and can be readily paid by the consumer, is clear, when it is considered that a poor person would consume, perhaps, half a seer or one pound of salt at the utmost in a month, which might be worth about half an anna in Indian money and three farthings in English money. The poorest man earns three rupees or six shillings per mensem (many day labourers receive much more), and having a very few wants, which are most cheaply supplied, he can certainly afford to give two or three pence in the month to purchase for himself and family an article which is at once a necessity and a luxury. The best proof, however, is in the eating; there never was so much salt eaten in the Punjaub as there is now. In fine, it may be said that the Punjaub salt is largely consumed; that it is productive to the revenue; that it is not perceptibly dearer now than in former days; and that its present price is so light as not to be seriously felt by even the poorest consumer."*

Besides these mines, according to Burnes, there is

* Report on Administration of Punjaub from 1854 to 1856, pars. 57, 58, 59.

another deposit of salt on the verge of the mountains towards Mundee, though not of so superior a description as that of the Salt-range. "In the same vicinity," continues that traveller, "if I can rely on my information, some veins of coal have been discovered, and there are also extensive mines of iron. The ore, after being powdered, is pulverised by grindstones, and then smelted. Matchlocks and swords are formed of this metal, and the warlike weapons of Lahore are famous among Indian nations. The precious metals are more scarce; yet gold is found among the sands of the Acesines, as it issues from the mountains. The Salt-range, as well as the other high lands, yield alum and sulphur. Nitre is gathered in quantities from extensive plains; and 'toree,' or nulkbush, which gives the best charcoal, completes the enumeration of what is necessary for the manufacture of gunpowder."*

A recent correspondent of an Indian paper writing from the spot, remarks that, "from Wuzzeerabad to Shahpoor, and the coal and salt mines of the salt range in its vicinity, is roughly estimated at 70 or 80 miles; the celebrated Punjaub salt being here quarried and used in preference to any other, wherever it can be obtained at a moderate price. Were its price double that of the common salt in Calcutta, none of the latter would be used. Why this article is so esteemed in India, must be attributed to its purity and the supposed presence of some magnesia and oxide of iron; doubtless, owing to these foreign bodies it is, that the salt is said to have tonic or alterative properties.

"It is quarried in great solid blocks, and conveyed by camels throughout the country, and even beyond the

* Burnes' Bokhara, &c., vol. ii., p. 400.

Hindoo Koosh mountains. No refining process is required—the lumps merely require to be washed, dried, and pounded or ground into powder, when it appears white as the driven snow. I have no hesitation in asserting, that this article would alone form an important branch of railway traffic, and prove also profitable to Government." *

* "London to Lahore:" or the Euphrates, Scinde and Punjaub Railways. Effingham Wilson, Royal Exchange.

CHAPTER XVI.

COLONIZATION IN INDIA AND AUSTRALIA COMPARED.

HIMALAYAN AND INTER-HIMALAYAN REGIONS.—OFFSPRING OF EUROPEANS.—EAST INDIANS.—PRODUCTIONS AND CAPABILITIES.—TEA CULTIVATION.—AUSTRALIAN IMMIGRATION, ADVANTAGES AND DISADVANTAGES OF.—INDIAN IMMIGRATION, ADVANTAGES AND DISADVANTAGES OF.—SIMLA.—KANGRA.—INDIAN AND COLONIAL IMMIGRATION CONTRASTED.—MILITARY COLONIES IN INDIA.*

In the preceding chapters, the political and commercial importance of introducing improved means of transit into the extensive territories drained by the Indus and its affluents was explained and illustrated. Some information was also given as to the population and products of those regions, and it is now proposed to conclude with a few observations on a kindred subject—the colonization by Englishmen of the fertile valleys and slopes of the lesser Himalayas which abut upon and bound to the north, the Punjaub and Upper India.

Although we have occupied and ruled India with our armies for more than a hundred years, we have made no attempt as a people, to go and possess the land, and dwell and plant homesteads as elsewhere. A European, until comparatively recent date, was not even allowed to settle in

* In the preparation of this chapter I have aided my personal knowledge of the Himalayas and Upper India, by recent information contained in Indian papers, particularly the "Lahore Chronicle."

India. Having gained India by the sword, we have ruled by the sword, and held her with a mailed hand, and have hitherto only been in military possession—encamped in the country. Now, however, the dawn of a better era is at hand, the late rebellion has aroused us with a voice of thunder to the performance of duties too long delayed, or only partially and reluctantly performed.

The telegraph and the rail will speedily give us such a grasp of India as will render invasion from without hopeless, and prolonged rebellion within impossible; but those symbols of knowledge and power will do more, they will not only impart that necessary element to progress—security—but they will directly promote in the most powerful manner, commerce and general enlightenment.*

* "Never since its discovery has the electric telegraph played so important and daring a *rôle* as it now does in India. Without it the Commander-in-Chief would lose the effect of half his force. It has served him better than his right arm. By it he is enabled to direct the march of his battalions, the movements of his artillery and cavalry, to receive news of their successes, to survey, as it were, at any one time the whole position of his army and of its auxiliaries, to communicate with the Governor-General and with his subordinate generals, to sift the truth from the falsehood of native information, to learn what posts are likely to be threatened, where the enemy are in force, to spare his staff and his messengers, and yet to send messages with clearness and despatch. So much for its importance. As to the daring action of the telegraph, which includes, of course, those who direct it, I need only observe that in this war, for the first time, a telegraphic wire has been carried along under fire and through the midst of a hostile country. *Pari passu*, from post to post it has moved on with our artillery, and scarcely has the Commander-in-Chief established his head-quarters at any spot where he intended to stay for a few days when the post and the wire were established also. The telegraph was brought into communication with the Governor-general at Allahabad, with Outram at the Alumbagh, with Calcutta, Madras, Bombay, and the most remote districts over which the

I am strongly impressed with the belief that when the means of intercommunication are improved in India, that Manchester and other great manufacturing towns will be induced to send English agents into the interior of the country to purchase the raw materials, especially cotton, on the spot where they are produced, instead of receiving as

system is distributed. It is mainly to the zeal, energy, and ability of a young officer of the Bengal Engineers, Lieutenant Patrick Stewart, that these advantages are due. He is assisted, it is true, by a few men, but he it is who devises and superintends the execution and the extension of the line from place to place. At one time his men are chased for miles by the enemy's cavalry—at another time they are attacked by the Sowars, and they and the wires are cut into pieces—again, their electric batteries are smashed by the fire of a gun, or their cart knocked to pieces by a round shot, but still they work on—creep over arid plains, across watercourses, span rivers, and pierce jungles, till one after another rude poles raise aloft their slender burden, and the quick needle vibrates with its silent tongue amid the thunder of the artillery. While Sir Colin Campbell was at Cawnpore he could learn from Sir James Outram the results of an attack before the enemy had disappeared from the field. As he advanced towards Lucknow, the line was carried with or soon after him; a tent was pitched near his, a hole was dug in the ground and filled with water, and down dropped the wire from the pole stuck up in haste, dived into the water otter-like, the simple magnet was arranged, the battery set in play, and at once the steel moved responsive to every touch. Owing to the extreme dryness of the atmosphere and the power of the sun—which at this season bakes the earth like a brick, the insulation of the current is nearly complete. The wire is thick, and is not protected by non-conducting coatings of any kind; it is twisted round the top of a rude pole, 15 or 16 feet high, and, under ordinary states of the atmosphere, it is found to answer perfectly. We had not been very long in the Dilkoosha ere we saw, in dim perspective, the line of posts advancing towards us, and soon the wire was slipped into one of the drawing-room windows, and now it is at full work, surrounded by all the shattered splendour of the palace, inquiring after the Ghoorkas, asking for more of something or other, exchanging ideas between at present the goods at the port of shipment through the slow, expensive, and inefficient system of barter of the native traders, and that other persons of intelligence may be induced to settle in a country possessing every variety of climate, and producing indigenously every product necessary or agreeable to man. India, unlike our colonies, is a densely peopled country, and labour is abundant and cheap, an able-bodied labourer is paid 3d. per diem, and it is computed that three able-bodied men do as much in the field as one good labourer in this country.

In India there is no field for the bone and muscle of the English peasant, what is wanted is the capital, the enterprise, the skill of England to direct the many millions of willing hands hanging listlessly in idleness to explore the resources of a country known to be rich in mineral treasures, and possessing a soil capable of returning three harvests in the year to the most rude and inefficient husbandry.

Much discussion has recently taken place in Parliament and elsewhere regarding the European colonization of India; and a Committee of the House of Commons has

Sir Colin and Lord Canning, or flurrying along a newspaper message to yourself, amid the whistle of the bullet, the roar of the round shot, and all the feverish scenes of war."—"Times' Special Correspondent," before Lucknow, 9th March, 1858.

"What a glorious thing it would have been, had the Euphrates Valley Railway and the Scinde and Punjaub Railway been accomplished facts at the time of the present insurrection. How it would have 'astonished the Natives' to have seen a gallant British Army landed at Lahore, within a month of the outbreak taking place! and yet such a thing would have been possible, supposing the Electric Telegraph to have been also completed so as to establish an electric messenger between the Indus and the Thames."—"Lahore Chronicle."

been appointed to investigate the subject—this is significant, but much more attention is at this moment concentrated on the impending changes in the form of the Home Government of India; but the consideration of the future of India ought not to be dwarfed to mere questions of the machinery of the administration. It has been well remarked that "There ought to be another movement, the result of which may create an influence in that possession of the Crown only second to that which may be expected to result from good government, and that is, the throwing open of India to British enterprise—in short, the beginning of the colonisation of that country. We have occupied India, we have ruled it, well or ill, as the case may be, but we have never thoroughly endeavoured to inoculate it with our commercial spirit. We have never sought to apply to it the principle which has actuated us in our dealings with our colonies; we have never sought to colonise. Arguments, weighty enough in their way, have been used against the adoption of this principle, and which go to show the impossibility of establishing a large European population in India, owing to difficulties connected with climate and habits. But with a view to working out a system of colonisation, such as can alone be adopted in India, it is not indispensable to have a large European population. It is not European labour that is wanted in Hindostan in order to develop its vast resources, but it is the European, and, above all, the English mind that is required for that purpose. It is knowledge, capability of teaching the native cultivator of the soil how best to avail himself of its productiveness; it is the application of European science and skill to the art of production that is needed to bring the growth of cotton, indigo, sugar, and tea of India into relative proportion with its acres and its capabilities. You dot the whole of that country with European administrators, magistrates, judges, residents, and soldiers. Why for every Englishman in the service of the Government should there not be three or four representatives of the English capitalist, in the shape of scientific agriculturists and commercial agents? There is nothing to prevent the training and transmission from this country at an early age of a class of men of this description, who would be able to meet the climatic difficulties of life in India quite as well as civil servants and military men; and, if due attention be paid to quality, there need be no necessity for numbers in such a system of colonisation. Something of this kind was done in our West Indian possessions, where a comparatively few European supervisors of African labour created colonies which in their day sent home millionaires who used to rival the nabobs of the golden time of the pagoda-tree. It is not, therefore, so very rash an assertion to say that, by means of an intelligent and well-directed European colonisation, a new era may be inaugurated in India which would gradually ameliorate the condition of the native population, act favourably upon the existing tenure of land, and operate on our establishment in India by those moral and commercial influences which will tend more surely and more readily to amalgamate her with our empire than the presence of a million of soldiers, or the most perfect machinery of government which the art of man can devise."

The plains of India are unfit for European settlers, further than as masters of labourers; but in the capacity of coffee, indigo, and, above all, cotton planters, zemindars, manufacturers, clerks, master artificers, contractors, tradesmen, there is room for an enormous increase of numbers, and every encouragement ought to be given to their settling in the country.

The Himalayan and Inter-Himalayan regions are wonderfully adapted for the European constitution. They are as salubrious, and generally cooler than a great portion of Australia. Europeans can, if they choose, work in the open air, in proof of which it is stated that the strongest built house at one of the hill stations was constructed entirely by European soldiers, without any native aid whatever.

The offspring of pure European parents brought up in the hills does not degenerate. Ample proof exists in many fine young men and women now in the country.

East Indians do not degenerate in the hills; on the contrary, they improve. Those not confined to the desk have often a fine colour in their cheeks.

In Australia, there is no navigable river with the exception of the Murray, to a limited extent, few running streams, no water power, very little fertile soil, the climate is arid, the whole continent does not produce one single indigenous edible fruit, root, or grain, the very timber is so heavy and hard that it sinks in water, and turns the edge of carpenters' tools not specially made for the purpose.

The Kangra and many other valleys of the Himalayas are of great fertility. In them we see the astonishing spectacle of the productions of the temperate and torrid zones growing side by side, the creeping rose intertwining its branches with the bamboo, and the wild violet and tulip flowering round the roots of the plantain. Further in the interior, there are inexhaustible forests of pine; a rich vegetable loam, on which all the fruits and vegetables of Europe will thrive in perfection. In Kanawur, the vine unpruned, uncultivated, growing like a bramble in the hedges, yields a grape unequalled in the world. Water power everywhere abounds. The wool trade might be increased to any amount. Gold is found in fine dust, but only at the confluence of certain streams. What is still more valuable than gold,—iron and coal exist in the hills; the former in extraordinary abundance. Following the lead of the Government, European enterprise has already made some progress in the cultivation of the tea plant in the hilly regions of India.

Along the Himalaya range, there is not a hill slope from 3,000 to 6,000 feet in elevation, which is not more or less adapted for tea cultivation. India can, and will, one day, supply the world with that commodity.

From Deyrah to Kashmere, various localities present themselves in every sense calculated for the growth of the tea plant. Simla and Kussowlie, already possessing during the summer a considerable number of residents, would afford a limited market on the spot. The vegetation here resembles that of the locality where the plant is found growing spontaneously, and the climate is, in my opinion, from a considerable experience, not to be surpassed.

The great drawback to investments in the cultivation of the tea plant is the circumstance that no return can be expected for the first five years, the plant requiring that time to arrive at maturity. Those having other resources might, however, venture with every prospect of obtaining a profitable return. Located in these favoured regions and surrounded by all the charms of rural life, a few Europeans might in time become holders of extensive tracts of land, which would, by improved modes of irrigation and cultivation, enable them to realise considerable profits. Government is always ready to facilitate the settlement of European families at any point of this extensive chain of mountains; and some measures, we believe, have been adopted by the government of the Punjaub for affording Europeans every assistance in settling down near Kangra, or in the lesser ranges, where the fir, chestnut, and plane abound.

The number of chests of tea brought to the hammer at Almora in December, 1855, amounted to 908, containing 9,612 lbs. and 6 ozs. Of these, 537 chests were purchased by Europeans, and 371 by natives. One hundred and three chests were bought by residents in the Punjaub, where the new teas are especially appreciated; 96 for the North Western Provinces; 16 for Nainee Tal; and 322 for Almora and its visitors. The natives who bought were all residents of Almora or Nainee Tal. Three kinds of green tea (gunpowder, young Hyson, and Hysonskin) and three kinds of black (Souchong, Pouchong, and Bohea) were sold at Almora, and fetched *per pound*:—

	High.			*Low.*			*Aver.*			
Gunpowder	Rs.	4	12	Rs.	4	8	Rs.	4	8	2
Young Hyson ..	„	4	8	„	1	8	„	2	14	5
Hyson skin	„	0	7	„	0	5	„	0	8	20
Souchong	„	2	15	„	1	1	„	2	9	11
Pouchong	„	1	11	„	0	14	„	1	2	10
Bohea	„	0	9	„	0	7	„	0	7	10

The quantity sold at Deyra amounted to 308 chests, containing 3,588 lbs. 8 ozs., of which 290 chests were bought by Europeans, and 18 only by natives. None but black tea (Souchong and Pouchong) was offered, and realized very high prices, viz.:—

	High.			Low.			Aver.		
Souchong ..	Rs. 5	4	0	Rs. 2	4	0	Rs. 2	8	11
Pouchong ..	„ 2	12	0	„ 1	5	0	„ 1	10	2

Nearly all the second class or cheap teas were purchased by natives, showing that all that is wanted are sufficiently low prices to create a great demand. Those that now rule are still too high for natives, and must continue to be called "fancy" ones, so that the speculation must pay handsomely.

The Kangra teas were disposed of at Hoosheearpoor in the month of January, 1856.

The following information regarding the cultivation of tea in the Kangra Hills is taken from the Report of the Administration of the Punjaub for 1855-56:—

"The cultivation of tea by Government in the Kangra Hills is flourishing under the superintendence of Doctor Jameson; the article is of good quality, and is eagerly bought up at high prices. The following is the result of the sales (held in the spring) for the two last years:—

	lbs.		Rs.	A.	P.
1854-55 .	1,628		3,140	10	8
		or	£ 314	0	0
1855-56 .	5,077		6,854	3	10
		or	£ 685	0	0

	Rs. A. P.		£ s. d.
Average price per lb. .	1 5 7	.	0 2 8¼
Expenditure	Rupees 8,502	or	£850 per annum.

There is a large quantity of land in the Kangra district fit for this culture, and efforts are being made to induce the peasants to undertake the cultivation." *

It is exactly seventy years since the first settlers landed on the shores of Sydney Cove. They had for many years to struggle against a host of troubles. Amongst other

* Respecting Grants of Land *vide* Appendix D.

difficulties, they were frequently threatened with starvation. Aged men tell the stranger how, in their boyhood, the inhabitants of Sydney were placed on a daily allowance of biscuits and salt pork, how tea was sold for its weight in silver, the silver being put in one scale and the tea in the other.

How then does it come to pass that Australia has become the most valuable of our colonies; that she exports more wool than all the rest of the world put together; that she has immense vineyards and hop gardens; that she is cultivating cotton with success; that she has glass houses and potteries; that she manufactures woollen fabrics; while in that part of India most fit for colonization, the traveller meets with few marks of European civilization?

The reason is simply this, that in Australia emigration has been encouraged and rewarded by Government, while in India it has been until lately dreaded and repressed.

In Australia, up to the year 1830, every free immigrant who could show that he had brought out to the colony money, or property of any description, to the value of £500, received a free grant in perpetuity of a section of 640 acres of land. After a certain lapse of time, all improvements, such as clearing, stumping, fences, building, &c., were valued; if of £500 valuation, he received another section of the same size; if of £1,000, two sections; and so on. He likewise received convict labour free of all charge, except the ordinary rations; and many other advantages. Many half pay and retired officers of the army and navy were made Magistrates, or received small appointments under Government, which brought them in from £100 to £300 per annum.

In India, up to the year 1833, no white man could settle

without a license from the East India Company. The license was removable, and the holder subject to deportation at the will and pleasure of Government. This law, I am told, still applies, although never enforced, in our newly-acquired provinces, viz., the Punjaub, Nagpore, Burmah, Oude.

So recent is our acquaintance with those portions of our widely-extended dominions best adapted for the residence of Europeans that at the neighbouring stations of Bareilly, Moradabad, and Shahjehanpore, the existence of the beautiful lake at Nainee Tal was as much a mystery, up to 15 years ago, as were the sources of the Niger.

Perhaps there is no part of India which approximates so much to a European colony as Simla, which is about 8,000 feet above the level of the sea, and situated on the lower Himalayas, overlooking the extensive plains watered and bounded by the Sutlej and Jumna.

As we ascend the first elevation towards Simla, flowers and shrubs of our own land surround us till we descend the precipitous road to Sabathoo. Here the fir-fringed forests, which form so striking a feature in the Kussowlie Hills, disappear; and we pass through barren rocks here and there dotted with some solitary specimen of the vegetable world. Approaching Simla, the shades and appearances of the vegetation which abound at Kussowlie, with slight variations, again appear; and as we enter Simla, nothing can exceed the pleasing variety which greets the traveller from the plains. Varieties of the pine, including the gigantic deodar or Himalayan cedar, the oak, and many other timber trees—the apricot, the apple, the cherry, and other fruit trees are natives of the soil interspersed with black currant and raspberry bushes, and amongst the flowering shrubs, the rhododendron is the most conspicuous, which here attains to the size of a tree, and in the months of April and May, covered with large crimson blossoms, and growing in groves along the hill-sides, adds at once a novel and beautiful feature to the scene. Simla is a paradise as to climate compared with the heat of the plains between April and June. There, amid cloud and the grateful shade of fir-fringed elevations, the exhausted frame inhales the fresh breeze from the broad snow belt of the Hindoo Koosh, and one insensibly forgets all about the fever heat of Delhi or Agra. The bazaar at Simla is well supplied at all seasons ; and living, although expensive compared to the cheapness of the Dooab, is less than one-half the sum at which similar comforts could be secured in Europe. The scenery during a fine day is magnificent, the plains, 7,000 feet below, and at 30 miles distance, appear like a map, while the devious course of the river Sutlej is discernible as far as the eye can reach. Fields and villages appear distinctly marked out in the landscape. Here and there a blue line of mist, following the irregular course of the lateral ridges which extend into the plain, marks the course of some pure spring whose sweet waters are pouring down to cool the parched sufferers below. From the sub-Himalayan range, the great Saul Forest descends into the plain of Bengal, and affords another quarter inviting enterprise. The area of this forest has been roughly estimated at fifteen hundred miles. This is truly a land of promise, looking to the demand for timber for the Punjaub and other Railways, and the steady market throughout the year for local requirements.

At Simla, a resident pays much more in yearly ground rent for his land than he could buy it for, out and out, in many of the English colonies, and is hampered by many restrictions as to cutting down timber on his own estate; and pays for labour at a rate much above what it not only costs in the neighbouring native states, but in the adjoining British possessions.

It is a strange anomaly that the East India Company should, with their usual liberality, have obtained for their officers privileges in regard to land in certain of the English colonies, which privileges they partly withhold in their own dominions. By general orders of the Governor General in Council, dated the 18th January, 1854, a remission in the purchase of land is granted according to the following scale:—

Field Officers, of 25 years' service . . .	£600	0	0
Do. do. of 20 „ . . .	500	0	0
Do. do. of 15, or less	400	0	0
Captains of 20 years' service, or upwards .	400	0	0
Captains of 15, or less	300	0	0
Subalterns of 20, or upwards	300	0	0
Subalterns of 7, or upwards	200	0	0

In a little work called "*The Settler's Home*," the price of land is stated as follows in the under-mentioned colonies:—

			£	*s.*	*d.*
Nova Scotia	per acre.	. . .	0	1	9
Cape Breton	„	. . .	0	1	9
New Brunswick	„	. . .	0	2	8
Canada	„	. . .	0	5	0
The Cape	„	. . .	0	2	0
Natal	„	. . .	0	2	0
New Zealand	„	. . .	2	0	0
Australia	„	. . .	1	0	0
Van Dieman's Land	„	. . .	1	0	0

The upset price in Ceylon is also £1 per acre; and in the United States of America, it is a dollar.

In India, however moderate the nominal price of land might be, while the purchase in fee-simple is impossible, the number of Englishmen of capital and enterprise will be comparatively few who will select the most highly favoured regions for their Lares and Penates, where neither they nor their descendants could ever become the undoubted lords of the soil they themselves might reclaim from the wilderness.

But even under existing circumstances cotton-planters and agents would find in the plains profitable occupation—while tea-planters, timber-merchants, and dealers in wool would have in the hills an ample scope for their capital and energy.

The policy of the East India Company was no doubt dictated formerly by a praiseworthy and benevolent desire to protect the *mild* Hindoo from European oppression, and also perhaps, they had the example of the rebellion of the United States of America before their eyes.

It is now admitted that the extensive introduction of railways and other improved means of communication are essential not only to the defence and peaceful possession of India, but to the development of her resources, and the influx of white emigration with European capital and enterprise would, it is apparent, vastly increase the value of these modern improvements, and enhance the power of the state to overawe the disaffected, and to encourage the well-affected and industrious. The railways would make the action of government, whether for punishment or protection, equally prompt and efficacious, while the moral influence of the skill and enterprise of the European settlers would powerfully promote the development of the resources of the soil, and the progress of the people in commerce and civilization.

Europeans can live anywhere in India, but in the Himalayan regions alone can they live and enjoy life as they do in England. Railways once properly established one hundred thousand Europeans located in the hills might alike defy native treason at Delhi, and Russian aggression from the steppes of Asia. Many European officers and soldiers, men with large families are willing to spend the remainder of their lives on the Himalayan slopes. Give them but the same privileges granted to them in the colonies, and all difficulties in the way of colonization will speedily disappear.

The saving of life, and therefore of money, that would accrue by having the reserve of the European army cantoned in the hills is evident.

Great good would also result from settling in the hill regions, time-expired men of European regiments. The veteran soldiers who as invalids perform garrison duty in the plains, and end their days at such places as Buxar and Chunar, in comparative idleness and discomfort, might lead pleasant and useful lives in the hills, where not only would their own existence be prolonged, but their children might be reared to supply the place of their fathers in the effective ranks of their countrymen.

Should the passing cloud of the Sepoy mutiny have aroused the heart and mind of England to the greatness of her mission in the East, the blood of our countrymen will not have been shed in vain, and greater and more enduring triumphs will be achieved than even the capture of Delhi or the relief of Lucknow.

APPENDIX.

EQUIVALENTS IN INDIAN AND ENGLISH CURRENCY.

12 Pie	=	1 Anna	=	1½d.
16 Annas	=	1 Rupee	=	2s.
100,000 Rupees	=	1 Lac	=	£10,000.
100 Lacs	=	1 Crore	=	£1,000,000.

EQUIVALENTS IN INDIAN AND ENGLISH WEIGHTS.

80 Tolas	=	1 Seer	=	2 lbs.
40 Seers	=	1 Maund	=	80 lbs.
28 Maunds	=	2240 lbs.	=	1 ton.

APPENDIX A.

MEMORANDA ON THE EXTERNAL TRADE OF SCINDE FOR 1856-57,

With a Sketch of its Progress since the Conquest, by the Deputy Collector of Customs.

---

1. The external trade of Scinde for the past official year (1856-57) is distinguished by some encouraging features highly promising to the commerce of the province.

The value of the aggregate trade, exclusive of Government stores, amounts to Rs. 1,42,01,879, shewing an increase over the previous year's trade, valued at Rs. 1,23,42,537, of Rs. 18,59,342, equivalent to 15 per cent., and detailed as follows :—

IMPORTS.

Merchandize	Rs. 66,47,169	
Treasure	2,09,488	
		56,657
Which compared with the import value of the previous year		Rs. 62,98,134
Exhibits an increase of		5,58,523
Or 9 per cent.		

EXPORTS.

Merchandize	Rs. 73,46,406	
Treasure	98,816	
		74,45,222
Which compared with the export value of the previous year		60,44,403
Shews an increase of		14,00,819
Or 22 per cent.		

2. Contrasting the value of the trade of 1856-57 with its value, on an average of the five preceding years, there is an increase in imports of Rs. 13,79,229, or 25 per cent.,

and in exports of Rs. 34,51,014, or 88 per cent., equivalent in the aggregate to 52 per cent.

3. The following are Abstract Comparative Statements of the Chief Articles of Import and Export in the past and preceding years, shewing the increases and decreases thereon :—

	1855-56.	1856-57.	Increase.	Decrease.	Per Cent. in Increase.	Per Cent. in Decrease.
Apparel	1,52,184	1,01,763	..	50,421	..	33
Cotton Piece Goods.						
Coloured	4,51,554	4,47,360	..	4,194	..	1
Plain	22,17,957	21,72,070	..	45,887	..	2
Other kinds....	75,545	59,109	..	16,436	..	24
Twist and Thread	2,03,227	1,91,481	..	11,746	..	5
Grain.............	2,32,947	3,37,569	1,04,622	..	45	..
Metals, Raw	2,16,952	3,17,247	1,00,295	..	45	..
„ Manufactured .	1,06,458	95,881	..	10,572	..	10
Silk, Raw	1,47,794	56,577	..	91,217	..	63
Silk and Wool P. Goods	1,36,704	85,697	..	51,007	..	80
Spices	1,57,155	2,49,945	92,790	..	59	..
Sugar.............	2,15,959	1,64,776	..	51,183	..	24
Wines and Spirits....	1,94,590	2,63,247	68,657	..	85	..
Treasure	3,00,878	2,09,488	..	90,890	..	30
Fruit, Dry..........	1,81,060	2,56,283	1,25,223	..	96	..
Railway Stores	..	5,63,462	5,63,462	..	..	..
Total......	49,40,459	55,71,955	10,55,049	..	9	..

The principal articles of our export trade are as follows:—

	1855-56.	1856-57.	Increase.	Decrease.	Per Cent. in Increase.	Per Cent. in Decrease.
	Rs.	Rs.	Rs.	Rs.		
Horses	3,39,060	4,38,150	99,090	..	29	..
Indigo	4,23,881	3,54,655	..	69,226	..	16
Munjeet......... ...	68,944	4,40,552	3,71,608	..	539	..
Drugs.............	1,60,675	1,30,949	..	29,726	..	19
Wheat	3,08,299	10,672	..	2,97,627	..	97
Other kinds of Grain	2,56,193	1,57,337	..	98,856	..	39
Ghee	2,33,672	1,56,107	..	77,565	..	31
Saltpetre	2,12,004	3,75,472	1,63,468	..	86	..
Jingly	5,91,215	8,37,472	2,46.257	..	42	..
Sursee	4,76,335	3,18,600	..	1,57,735	..	33
Other kinds of Seeds	3,32,013	91,606	..	2,40,407	..	72
Silk, raw	3,761	3,20,174	3,16,413	..	8,393	..
Wool, sheeps'	22,13,108	31,15,903	9,02,795	..	41	..
Total .	56,19,160	67,47,649	20,99,631	..	22	..

4. **The countries in commercial connection with Scinde and the value of the trade with each are as follow :—**

	IMPORTS.		EXPORTS.	
	1855-56.	1856-57.	1855-56.	1856-57.
	Rs.	Rs.	Rs.	Rs.
Bombay	55,81,212	52,27,429	58,74,320	66,97,546
Calcutta	..	..	..	13,074
Concan	2,464	4,510	..	..
Cutch	74,986	72,425	1,12,401	1,38,310
England	1,57,800	7,73,835	35,139	1,446
France	..	..	..	93,390
Goa and Demaun	4,532	10,064	..	231
Guzerat	57,608	1,41,787	11,747	15,647
Katiawar	1,29,322	2,01,954	1,21,485	64,597
Malabar	97,632	90,388	1,69,154	1,45,933
Mauritius	1,894	8,930	17,568	28,538
Mekran	11,065	13,328	35,895	24,062
Persian Gulf	1,79,619	3,12,007	1,66,694	1,32,445
Total	62,98,134	68,56,657	60,44,408	73,55,219

5. The result of the past year's trade which these tables exhibit, cannot be viewed otherwise than as very satisfactory, when it is considered that the trade of the preceding year, 1855-56, with which it is compared, had, by the circumstances of war, been stimulated into unusual activity; to such a degree that the value of the exports in 1855-56 exceeded by 74 per cent. the value of the exports of the year preceding.

6. Had there been, therefore, no improvement in the past year's trade, it would not have been remarkable, as it would have been only reasonable to expect that, when the trade should no longer be influenced by unnatural causes, it would gradually relapse into its normal condition.

7. It is not improbable that the effects of the shock which Russian commerce and agriculture had sustained will, for some time to come, continue to act favorably on Indian trade; and had not counteracting influences arisen, owing to the disturbed state of Afghanistan and the Persian war, exciting distrust and alarm in the mind of the trader, it is extremely probable that the trade of the past year would have shown a very much larger increase.

8. By the removal of some of these by river steamers to the Persian Gulf, steam communication by the Indus was, for a time, entirely suspended, causing further interruption to commerce.

9. But the trade with Afghanistan shews, nevertheless, considerable improvement. In the articles Wool and Munjeet, there is an increase in the former of Rs. 9,02,795, and in the latter Rs. 3,71,608; and the trader states that had the peace of the country not been disturbed, the trade, from the encouraging state of the markets, must have been very great, independent of the general backwardness of the season.

10. Although a fact, that the quantity of land occupied in the production of Oil Seed has been immensely increased in Scinde and the Punjaub, the value of Oil Seed exported in the past year falls short of the value of the previous year's export by Rs. 1,51,936 or 11 per cent.

11. This can only be accounted for by supposing that the produce of the Punjaub did not find exit by the Indus. In the previous year Government were the purchasers of the Punjaub Linseed Crop, which was forwarded to Kurrachee.

12. In Saltpetre the increase is Rs. 1,63,468 or 86 per cent.

13. The articles of decreased import are Indigo, Drugs, and Grain. The former suffered by the interruption of the river communication by steamers.

14. During the activity of the Russian War a large quantity of Scinde Wheat was exported to England *via* Bombay. Peace probably rendered further speculation in the article unremunerative.

15. With a large increased export in the products which seek a European market, there is a simultaneous falling off in the import of British manufactures; viz., in piece goods, of Cotton, Silk, and Woollen, amounting to Rs. 1,31,370; and in manufactured metals, Rs. 10,572. The disturbed state of Afghanistan may be considered as the chief cause of this decrease.

16. The decrease in the importation of Sugar may be attributed to increased production in Scinde and the Punjaub; and of raw Silk, to a large increased supply chiefly from Bokhara, whence an extensive trade in the article has suddenly sprung up, placing Scinde in the position of an exporter of raw Silk instead of an importer, as heretofore.

17. In Salt the decrease in the export to Calcutta is to be attributed to the high rates of freight prevailing at Bombay, in consequence of the Government demand for tonnage to the Persian Gulf

18. A remarkable, because novel, feature in the past year's trade, is the fact of the exports exceeding the imports by Rs. 4,88,565 or 7 per cent.

19. With an export trade, which in the course of two years has considerably more than doubled itself, without improved facilities of communication;—and it would be a bold undertaking to attempt to smooth the rugged mountain passes, across which the greater portion of the trade of Scinde is borne;—what may we not expect when these where practicable shall have been introduced. Though railways may not yet awhile ascend into Afghanistan, they will divert the Afghan from his mountain track into the valley of the Indus; there relieve him of his burthen; and save him a further tedious journey of some hundred miles.

20. To doubt the immediate effect of roads and railroads on the commerce of the country, would be equivalent to denying that diminution in the price of commodities would have no tendency to increase consumption.

21. The earliest period for which there are records of the entire trade of Scinde dates from 1847-48. From the conquest in 1843, up to that time, no exact estimate of the extent of the trade can be formed; but as, from 1847-48, we find that about three-fourths of the export trade of Scinde went to Bombay, it may be reasonably inferred that a like proportion took the same direction from the period of the conquest, forward.

22. Admitting this to have been the case, a sufficiently

approximate estimate of the value of the trade during the above interval can be formed from the Bombay returns of trade, which show the value of the imports from, and exports to Scinde, from Bombay, to have been from 1843 to 1857, as follows:—

Statement showing the Trade of Scinde with Bombay since 1843-44.

Years.	Exports from Bombay to Scinde.	Imports into Bombay from Scinde.	
	Rs.	Rs.	
1843-44	13,91,743	1,87,054	As per Bombay Returns.
1844-45	21,78,388	3,66,464	
1845-46	31,31,164	6,91,939	
1846-47	29,45,550	13,88,222	
1847-48	22,98,108	13,86,113	Includes trade with Guzerat.
1848-49	27,74,906	9,17,519	
1849-50	35,87,995	9,07,656	
1850-51	38,36,765	14,34,350	
1851-52	43,97,389	16,76,828	As per Kurrachee Returns.
1852-53	48,18,547	31,61,112	
1853-54	45,46,422	33,62,907	
1854-55	51,76,193	27,02,680	
1855-56	55,81,212	53,74,320	
1856-57	52,27,429	66,97,546	

23. From this table we find that in 1843-44, the value of the exports from Scinde to Bombay amounted to 1,87,054; and the imports to Rs. 13,91,743; by adding to it a fourth as the probable proportion of the trade of Scinde with other places, we have Rs. 2,33,817, as the probable value of the general export trade of the province in 1843-44, and Rs. 17,39,679 as its import value.

24. In 1847-48, four years thereafter, when the registration of the trade of Scinde commenced, the value of the

exports to all places had risen to Rs. 15,47,308, or 562 per cent.; and the imports to Rs. 28,78,720, or 71 per cent., during the four years. In the two succeeding years, there is a considerable falling off in the exports; but a more than counterbalancing increase in the value of imports.

25. In 1851-52, the export trade again revives, its value amounting in that year to Rs. 24,41,228, or 58 per cent., in excess of the exports of 1847-48; and the imports to Rs. 48,92,202, or 70 per cent. over the imports of the same year.

26. In the following year, 1852-53, the trade, particularly in exports, shows an extraordinary improvement, these having risen in value to Rs. 37,63,376, or 54 per cent. over the exports of the year preceding, whilst the imports show an increase of only 10 per cent.

27. In 1853-54, there is no improvement in the export trade; it nevertheless maintains itself, whilst the imports show a falling off of 5 per cent.

28. In 1854-55, the value of the exports diminishes 8 per cent., whilst the imports show an increase of 13 per cent.

29. In 1855-56, the trade again takes an extraordinary leap, the value of the exports having risen to Rs. 60,44,403, and the imports to Rs. 62,98,134; the former equivalent to an increase of 74, and the latter of 9 per cent over the trade of the year preceding.

30. In 1856-57, there is a still further increase; the value of the exports in this year, having risen to Rs. 73,45,222, or 22 per cent. in excess of the year preceding; and the imports to Rs. 68,56,657, or 9 per cent excess.

31. The following is a tabular statement of the value of the import and export trade with all places, since 1847-48:—

Years.	Imports.	Exports.	Total.
	Rs.	Rs.	Rs.
1847-48	28,78,720	15,47,308	44,26,028
1848-49	34,97,157	10,71,339	45,68,496
1849-50	41,94,141	11,43,783	53,37,924
1850-51	42,58,316	19,64,618	62,22,934
1851-52	48,92,202	24,41,228	73,33,430
1852-53	53,56,908	37,63,376	91,20,284
1853-54	50,87,934	37,63,107	88,51,041
1854-55	37,51,967	34,68,937	72,20,904
1855-56	62,98,134	60,44,403	1,23,42,537
1856-57	68,56,657	73,45,222	1,42,01,879

32. On what may be considered good data, it has been shown, that the estimated value of the general export trade of Scinde in 1843-44, the period of the conquest, was Rs. 2,33,817; and its registered value in 1856-57, Rs. 73,45,222; an increase equivalent to 3,050 per cent. The value of the import trade with Bombay in 1843-44, was Rs. 13,91,743, and its registered value in 1856-57, Rs. 52,27,429, showing an increase of 247 per cent.

33. It has been supposed that our occupation of Scinde had the effect of diverting to Kurrachee a large portion of the trade of Sonmeanee in Mekran, to which port it was understood the Afghan merchants resorted with their wool and other produce, to avoid the exorbitant exactions of the Ameers. Such, however, would not appear to have been the case, as we find from the Bombay Returns

of Trade, that the value of the imports from Sonmeanee into Bombay, in 1843-44, amounted to Rs. 11,126 only, or, on an average of four years from 1843, to Rs. 6,917. The present value of the trade of Sonmeanee, including other ports in Mekran, with Bombay, is, exports Rs. 3,22,572, and imports, Rs. 1,36,539. The trade of Scinde, then, with reference at least to Sonmeanee, has not been diverted, but created.

34. There are few circumstances connected with India more remarkable than the rapidity with which a trade can be increased, notwithstanding the many obstacles, both physical and moral, which oppose its progress; yet a slight increase of demand, and consequently of price, oftentimes increases, in a wonderful degree, the export of some particular commodities.

35. There are two periods by which, under different circumstances, though in effect the same, the export trade of Scinde is distinguished in a peculiar degree, demonstrating the above proposition.

36. In 1852-53, without, apparently, the existence of any unusual demand for any particular produce in the home market, the exports from Scinde rose from Rs. 24,41,228 in 1851-52, to Rs. 37,63,376, or 54 per cent. in 1852-53.

37. In looking for the cause of so extraordinary an increase in one year, it seems to be discovered in the hope held out to the traders by the proclamation of the Fairs, which, had they met with the encouragement they unquestionably merited, would have enabled the traders to dispose of their produce at Kurrachee, in exchange for British manufactures; but the Afghan, who showed so ready an appreciation of the advantage of markets within

the province, was not rewarded, on arrival at the expected marts, by any display of British goods; so that the benefit he had expected to reap by disposing of his goods at Kurrachee, was lost by the obligation forced upon him to proceed to Bombay, thereby increasing the value of his produce by a further journey to a distant market, and consequently diminishing the profits of his investments.

38. Though failure had marked the first year of the Fairs, through the backwardness of the Bombay dealers, their eventual success would seem still to have been cherished, as the exports of the succeeding year, though they had not increased, still maintained their position; but in the third year of disappointment, that is, 1854-55, the exports fell off from Rs. 37,63,107 to Rs. 34,68,937, the only year since 1849-50 which does not show a progressive annual increase; and may we not find in this fact a practical manifestation of the prejudicial effects of crushed energy and enterprise?

39. Again, when the Russian war gave a stimulus to trade, the exports in 1854-55 took a still more extraordinary leap, having risen to Rs. 60,44,403 in 1855-56, or 74 per cent.

In the following year they further rose to Rs. 73,45,222, or 22 per cent.

40. It has been shown that, within the period of two years, the export trade of Scinde has risen in value from Rs. 34,68,937, in 1854-55, to Rs. 73,45,222, in 1856-57, an increase equivalent to 112 per cent., or 56 per cent. in each of the two years.

41. Scinde became a British province in 1843; the value of its trade at that time is shown to have been Rs. 233,817. The value of the trade of Bombay was in the

same year, exclusive of treasure, Rs. 11,74,54,884. In 1855-56, twelve years thereafter, it amounted to Rs. 15,54,68,229, being an increase in thirteen years of Rs. 3,80,13,345, or 33 per cent.

42. In the same period the value of the trade of Scinde has increased Rs. 1,13,69,041, or 575 per cent.

43. But, as formerly remarked, more than three-fourths of the trade of Scinde passes through Bombay; Bombay is indebted to Scinde for upwards of 119 lacs of Rupees, or nearly a million and a quarter sterling of this increase. Deducting which from the value of her trade in 1855-56—the Bombay returns for 1856-57 have not yet been received—the increase in her trade during the above period is reduced to 23 per cent.

44. Whilst, then, the trade of Scinde, despite the difficulties which encompass it, has advanced since the conquest 575 per cent., the trade of Bombay, notwithstanding the many improvements that have taken place in the interior of the country, and other advantages, has not increased, within the same period, more than 33 per cent., including her trade with Scinde.

45. In the past year it has been seen, that the exports of raw silk from Scinde have increased from Rs. 3,761 to Rs. 3,16,413, or 90 fold, derived from a new and unexpected source, Bokhara; having once taken the direction of the Indus, this trade will not probably depart from it; and having once established itself, may, if properly fostered, be increased to an incredible degree. Take wool for an example: the value of the exports five years ago, amounted to Rs. 7,57,162; it now amounts to Rs. 31,15,903, an increase equivalent to 312 per cent.

46. So also, in other products. Oil seeds, the export

value of which, five years ago, was Rs. 1,49,029, now amounts to Rs. 12,47,827, or 737 per cent.; and had the produce of the Punjaub in the past year taken the route of the Indus, the value of oil seeds, exported, would probably have been double that amount, 24,000 acres of land having, we are informed, been under linseed cultivation.

47. Without any additional facilities, but rather under adverse circumstances, it is apparent that the commerce of Scinde is taking root and expanding in a surprising degree; and it is extremely probable that the present unhappy state of the North-west Provinces and Bengal, will have the effect of directing the attention of the trader to the peaceful valley of the Indus. Let commerce be once diverted from its old route, and, if there be any advantages in the new, it will not readily forsake it; the difficulty lies in turning it out of its ancient channel.

48. It is gratifying to see that Kurrachee, as a place of trade, is now beginning to attract the attention of mercantile men, two respectable mercantile firms having lately established themselves at Kurrachee.

49. One is very successfully directing his attention to the raw produce of the province, and has made extensive purchases of wool, seeds, hides, horns and saltpetre—these, cleaned, picked and assorted, have been hitherto forwarded to Bombay for shipment thence to England; but direct shipments are now being made from Kurrachee. The "Samuel Boddington" is now loading with a variety of produce, including wool pressed by a screw constructed by the firm of Messrs. Warwick and Co.; wool it is found can be picked and assorted at Kurrachee at a cost 15 per

cent. cheaper than at Bombay, the wages of labour being less.

50. These firms have expressed themselves much pleased with the prospects of trade before them. Amongst other things, their attention is being directed to the refining of saltpetre, with which the province abounds; and a gentleman of capital has been invited from England, who is practically acquainted with the manufacture of indigo, which it is believed could be successfully prosecuted in the province, without the risks, from excessive moisture, which attends its cultivation in Bengal.

51. The cotton wool of Cutch, which adjoins the province of Scinde, whose last year's exports to Bombay amounted to upwards of one-sixth the produce of the Bombay presidency, will probably eventually be imported into Kurrachee as being the nearest market.

52. Two hydraulic presses adapted for the compression of any description of produce have lately been imported from England, so that we have now the means of packing at Kurrachee, which will afford increased facilities to direct exportation.

53. A large quantity of Manchester piece goods of the value of £8,000, has lately been imported direct from Manchester. Had they arrived a month earlier than they did, it is believed that the whole of the consignment could have been speedily sold. But the season had gone by. The importer seems very sanguine of success; he says he will soon show the Afghans that they can purchase cheaper from him, than by proceeding to Bombay. He has sold a considerable portion of his goods at satisfactory prices to both parties.

54. The traders seem to be much pleased at the prospect of a market at Kurrachee. They, the Afghans, say, "we have been in the habit of coming to Kurrachee only once a year; but if we can find a market there, we shall be able to come two or three times during the year; and that the snow only will prevent us from doing so."

55. Two vessels for Marseilles, and two for the Mauritius, have been lately laden at Kurrachee, direct to these ports. One for London, and another for Bourbon, direct, are now being laden; the former with a general cargo; the latter with wheat, ghee, grain, dholl, oil and salt fish.

56. That Kurrachee must eventually become a great commercial entrepot, few who have given any attention to the subject will be disposed to doubt. It has been suggested that the inducement of a market at Kurrachee, held out by the proclamation of the fairs, at once raised the value of exports 54 per cent.; and that a little advance in the price of certain descriptions of produce has had the effect in these past two years, of considerably more than doubling the trade.

57. Let Kurrachee export her produce direct to the countries which consume it, and it will soon be seen that the resources of the countries east and west of the Indus, are but in the dawn of development.

58. It has been remarked that the effects of the Russian war gave an impetus to the trade of India; and there can be no doubt that the commerce of Scinde benefitted by that impetus; but a more healthful, because natural, and permanent influence is now beginning to develop itself, which will soon take root and fructify,

doing more for the improvement and extension of her commerce than could be effected by any temporary or adventitious aid.

59. That influence lies in the independence of the commerce of Scinde, which is to be attained by British merchants becoming resident in the province, by applying capital to the development of the vast mineral and vegetable resources of the country; and exporting its produce direct to Europe. The immediate effect of this would be to increase the price of produce to the producer, and, consequently the supply; for if 17 per cent.,—and there exists practical proof of its being so,—be the difference between shipping produce at Kurrachee direct to Europe, and sending it to Bombay for shipment thence, to that degree would the trade be encouraged, just as if the price of produce in England were to rise 17 per cent., or more, and so soon as the traders find that they can procure as cheap and equally good articles at Kurrachee as at Bombay, so surely will they abandon the latter market.

60. The value of the trade of Scinde now amounts to a million and a half sterling, exclusive of the value of government stores. If it progress within the next four years in the ratio of the past two, in 1860, even under present circumstances, it will exceed three millions and a half sterling, or three-tenths, the present value of the trade of Bombay, deducting the value (Rs. 3,13,27,682) of her imports re-exported,—Scinde having no such feature in her trade, of any consequence, to give it a fictitious value,—and when the lines of railway in the Punjaub and Scinde shall be open to traffic; the river communication improved by convenient and powerful steamers; and the harbour made eligible for vessels of

deeper draft; and though last, not least, the abolition of transit duties in foreign territory, particularly in Afghanistan,—Kurrachee cannot fail to become one of the chief commercial cities of the empire.

P. M. DALZELL,
Deputy Collector of Customs.

KURRACHEE CUSTOM HOUSE,
9th September, 1857.

APPENDIX B.

TRADE WITH SCINDE AND CENTRAL ASIA.

Despatch from East India Company to the Governor of Bombay.

"Attaching as we do, (say the Honourable Court of Directors) great importance to the development of the trade with Scinde, which the experience of a very few years gives reason to believe may be increased to an extent which at one time could scarcely have been anticipated, we have reserved for the present despatch our remarks on the information contained in your letters of the dates noted at foot.*

1852-53.		1853-54.	
Camel loads.	Estimated value.	Camel loads.	Estimated value.
	Rs.		Rs.
7,759½	6,47,429	11,900	9,24,371

* Letters dated 14th Sept. (No. 49), 1854; 27th Sept. (No. 51) 1854; 2nd April (No 35), 1855; 13th August (No. 75), 1855.

" A comparison of the amount of goods brought from Khorasan, Lus. Bayla, Sonmeeanee, &c., indicates that the merchants of Beloochistan and Central Asia are quite alive to the advantage of meeting a ready sale for their produce at Kurrachee. Their enterprise has, however, received a temporary check in not finding supplies of English commodities at the fair of 1854, which compelled them to carry their goods to Bombay. We fear that this discouraging feature is not likely immediately to be remedied, for we find it stated that the merchants at Bombay are not disposed to establish agencies at Kurrachee, or contribute to the success of the fair by forwarding their goods, and this not from any jealousy of the improving trade of Scinde, but because their hands are so full as to render any extension of their commercial relations inconvenient. Only two English merchants from Bombay attended, with small parcels of goods, little varied, and ill-calculated to suit the tastes of the foreign traders. Their visit seemed to be more for the purpose of inquiry than of sale or purchase, and so far may be productive of future utility. The direction of their inquiries was principally as to the amount of supply likely to be obtained in oil seeds, and it may be remarked that the soil and climate of Scinde are peculiarly adapted to the cultivation of linseed, and that in a few years it will probably afford a large supply for exportation.

" The invitation given in 1852 to the merchants of Manchester, to turn their attention to this promising mart was not responded to, as not a single bale of goods appeared at the fair direct from England. We must, therefore, again endeavour to stimulate the enterprise of parties to supply the requirements of Central Asia, by affording more enlarged statistical information for the commercial classes of this country relative to the demand in Scinde for British fabrics. It is to a direct intercourse with England that Scinde must look for the enlargement of her commerce. Even with such returns as she can at present make (and we find the supply fully keeping pace with the demand), a fair prospect of advantage is afforded to the enterprise of British merchants embarking in this trade. The progressive improvement in trade at the port of Kurrachee is shown in the following statement :—

	Imports.	Exports.	
	Rs.	Rs.	
1850-1	42,54,446	19,59,699	
1851-2	48,78,105	24,32,418	exclusive of treasure.
1852-3	53,21,862	37,58,851	

"Mr. Dalzell, the Deputy Collector of Customs at Kurrachee, points out, as one of the most striking features of trade, the greatly increased exportation of wool, amounting to 90 per cent. over the supply of the previous years,—an increase which may, in the absence of all other influencing causes, be attributed to the operation of the fair, affording proof that with a market at Kurrachee to receive the produce and meet the wants of Central Asia, an influx of this valuable commodity is likely to follow to a greatly increased extent.*

"Mr. Dalzell draws a comparative statement of the trade

* Articles of Export.—Wool, Saltpetre, Indigo, Munjeet, Assafœtida, Hides and Skins, Tallow, Jungly seeds, Bees'-wax, Mustard, Linseed, Cotton. Gums, Ivory. Silk, raw, Cloves, brought from Muscat and Zanzibar.

R 2

of the port, showing an increase in the exports for the past three years, over the year preceding the proclamation of the fair, to the extent of Rs. 17,94,152, equivalent to 92 per cent., and in imports of Rs. 10,76,416, or 25 per cent., affording additional evidence that the commerce has been stimulated by the fair. It has attracted shiploads of horses from Bushire, produce from the coast of Mekran, and ships from Zanzibar and Muscat, bearing gums, ivory, raw silk, and cloves, all novel imports; and it has given the stamp of a commercial mart to Kurrachee, which will hereafter attract increasing numbers of traders.

" It is questioned by some who have taken part in the correspondence submitted to us, whether the establishment of fairs may not be regarded in the light of an artificial stimulus to commerce. The fair of Kurrachee cannot be thus regarded; it is a most legitimate aid to a newly opening trade. The principal object of its institution was to enable the merchants of Central Asia periodically visiting Kurrachee, who have an aversion to voyages by sea, to barter their produce at a mart less remote from their homes than Bombay. It affords to them a most encouraging and unobjectionable accommodation, and enables them to extend their operations further and faster than they otherwise could. Mr. Frere very justly disclaims " any idea that it is possible by fairs, or by any other means, to create commerce. When men meet, and have goods to exchange, commerce will exist. When they have none, no fairs will make a trade."

" In the actual condition of Scinde, as shown by the returns, we have only to promote, and not to create, a trade. Looking to the article of wool alone, the amount of its importation from Candahar and Khelat in 1843 was to the value only of Rs. 559. The people of Central Asia did not know it was sought for. They have found it to be an acceptable article of barter; and in 1851 an increase of this valuable staple took place to the extent of 2,185 camel loads, valued at Rs. 2,54,430.

"If the access to Kurrachee were difficult or dangerous, the prospect of improvement to the trade would, indeed, be unpromising; but 'Kurrachee has a good harbour always accessible, and, according to the opinions of the commanders of the several English vessels that entered it in 1853-54, capable at present of holding from twenty-five to thirty vessels of from 500 to 1,000 tons burthen; and, if moorings were laid down, and the channels kept clear by an efficient dredging-machine, would be equal to the accommodation of nearly 100 vessels, with facilities for landing and shipping goods, moderate charges, and charts of the coast.'* That a port so easily approachable, and affording such an extensive field for the dissemination of British manufactures, should not have attracted the attention of English merchants, is remarkable, and can only be attributed to the advantages of its position not being sufficiently known.

"We will now review what has been done to aid the extension of the trade, and what is in progress to advance the same desirable end. Considerable sums of money, have been most usefully expended in the improvement of the port, and in facilitating the landing and embarkation of goods. Charts of the coast have been published; the frontier duties have been abolished; and the active exertions of Major Jacob and the Collector of Shikarpore, and

* Mr. Dalzell's Report, 16th March, 1854.

of their assistants, have secured an improved state of the roads on the great commercial lines, which has led to the general result of greatly increased intercourse. Mr. Pruce emphatically observes, 'Good roads are the very arteries of commerce, without which commerce could no more thrive than man could exist without blood-vessels.' Major Jacob is not satisfied with what has been done. He thinks the exertions of Government should be directed to the improvement of the roads even as far as the city of Candahar. He represents that, although the advice tendered to the Khan of Khelat has been productive of the establishment of security on the line of transit through his districts, the state of the roads has been in no way cared for. Considering the present desire of the Khan of Khelat to conciliate the good-will of the British Government, he might, perhaps, be induced to take some measures for this purpose, and we would wish you to try the influence, of persuasion on his mind. From Khelat to Candahar Major Jacob represents the state of the roads or paths as greatly impeding the progress of commerce, and that they are, moreover, infested by robbers. Any appeal, however, to the Chief of Candahar must be made under the direction of the Governor-General in Council, to whom we shall transmit a copy of this despatch.

"With a view to the removal of shoals, &c., in the vicinity of Kurrachee, and at the mouths of the Indus, we directed you to place at the disposal of the Commissioner of Scinde the steam dredge, which, until lately, has not been made use of at the port of Bombay. You have represented that it is advantageously employed for local purposes, that it is not sea-worthy, and could not with safety be towed to so distant a port as Kurrachee. We have recently sent two steam dredges for the service of Scinde in the manner and by the ships noted at bottom; and as the Commissioner is very urgent in his request for this aid, we direct that no time may be lost in forwarding them to their destination.*

"The construction of a permanent Serai at Kurrachee, and of buildings and enclosures at the different halting-places on the great commercial lines, which much facilitate the operations and convenience of merchants, and is a legitimate aid to trade. The sovereigns and rulers of Asia have practically admitted the policy of affording such accommodation, and we are glad that you have recognised the value of the Commissioners' suggestion.

"In addition to the measures already mentioned, which have been adopted to improve the trade of the province we may allude to the plan now in course of organization for constructing a line of railroad from Kurrachee to Kotree on the Indus. This is calculated to give a powerful impetus to trade on the river, since it will remove the great obstacle which has hitherto impeded commercial transit to the Punjaub, arising from the difficulties attending the entrance to the mouths of the Indus.

"Your letter of the 2nd of April, 1855, does not throw much light on the progress of the trade we are now reviewing. Mr. Dalzell, the deputy-collector of Customs, observes :—'On the general trade I might have ventured on a few observations; but, from the imperfect returns, I shall abstain from saying more than that there are sufficient indications of a greatly improving trade.'†

* The hulls per the *Swarthmore* and *Bona Ventura* in October last from Liverpool

The dredges and machinery on the *Haddington* in January last from London.

† Memorandum on the frontier trade of Scinde for 1853-54, in Mr. Frere's letter, dated 2nd March, 1855.

" It behoves us to be watchful to obtain all possible information of the commodities which suit the markets of Afghanistan. British fabrics have been introduced at Trebizond, on the south-east extremity of the Black Sea, in lieu of the circuitous route by the Cape, Bombay, and the Persian Gulf, with perfect success; and, with similar enterprise on the part of British merchants, we may safely look to a propitious result in Central Asia.

" We proceed to make a few observations on the progress of trade in the direction of the Punjaub. It has assumed a character of importance which there was hardly reason to expect; and it is shown in the official documents now before us that the increase in the value of imports from the Punjaub, in 1853-4 nearly equals the increase in that of those from Afghanistan, the former amounting to Rs. 3,60,260, and the latter to Rs.3,97,806.* The steamers fill equally well up and down the Indus, and are not in

* Imports from Afghanistan and other countries west of the Indus:—

1852-3	Rs.	17,64,575
1853-4	„	21,62,381
Increase	„	3,97,806

Imports from Punjaub and adjacent British possessions:—

1852-3	Rs.	11,58,674
1853-4	„	18,18,934
Apparent increase	„	6,60,260
Deduct estimated value of river traffic by steamers not registered in 1852-3	Rs.	3,00,000
Real increase	„	3,60,260

sufficient number to meet the increasing calls of the public; and without additional means of transport on the river; increased intercourse is evidently precluded. It is very desirable that the deficiency should be supplied by the enterprise of private associations, which might have the effect, also, of reducing the price of freightage, which is much complained of.

" Mr. Dalzell observes, with much appearance of probability, that the countries adjacent to the Indus will in time draw the whole of their supplies from the nearest point, *i. e.* Kurrachee. The merchants of the Punjaub and the places on the banks of the Indus will also be induced to resort to Kurrachee, in preference to the circuitous route by the Ganges; and the Europeans in those parts already draw their supplies by the former river. By this route also we now send our troops and recruits for the Upper Provinces, and the transmission of military stores by the same channel is annually on the increase. Aided by the railroad, and by increased accommodation on the river, commerce will necessarily follow the same direction; and so numerous are the staple commodities of the Punjaub, and so earnest are the endeavours to suit them to the wants of the English market, that there is a satisfactory prospect of ample returns.

" Mr. Edgeworth the Commissioner, points out that Moultan itself holds out excellent prospects as an emporium of goods for the Cabul and Punjaub markets, and states that the country under his supervision admits of an indefinite extension of indigo, sugar, and cotton as agricultural products, while wool, saltpetre, and barilla, from the uncultivated tracts, give a large field for exports in return for British fabrics: and he has been assured by two native firms of their ability at the present moment to send raw produce, of the nature stated below, to the value of three lacs of rupees; but, as there are no capitalists at Kurrachee prepared to purchase, they cannot enter on so hazardous a speculation.*

"Mr. Edgeworth states that a large quantity of cotton might be sent down the river from Moultan, but its bulk is so great from imperfect pressure that it cannot be stowed away in the steamers. He earnestly begs that, as an encouragement to the growth of cotton, a screw-press may be established at Moultan, the working of which might in the first instance be farmed out, and a suitable opportunity be hereafter taken of selling it. Mr. Frere makes the same requisition for Kurrachee, and we think that, in consideration of the special circumstances of the case, the want should be supplied to both places: and in the event of a screw-press not having yet been established at Moultan, we desire that steps be immediately taken to afford to the trade there, as well as at Kurrachee, this aid which is so greatly needed.

"Mr. Dalzell draws his conclusions as to the amount of exports from India to Central Asia, *viâ* the Punjaub, from the returns of trade quoted by *The Friend of India*, which, he says, may be supposed to be correct, as they were registered under the native Government for the levy of duties; and supposing them not to have increased since 1849, the entire annual trade of India with Central Asia would not average thirty lacs of rupees, an amount

* Wool, cotton, indigo, barilla, tamarisk galls, saltpetre, and sundries.

scarcely exceeding the value of exports from Bombay to the small province of Cutch; 'a trade so trifling,' he observes, 'considering the vast regions over which it is supposed to be dispersed, as to give colour to the probability that the Russian manufactures are successfully competing with the productions of England,—in countries, too, approaching our Indian frontier.'"

"Mr. Dalzell regrets that the Punjaub returns of trade should not have been kept up: he observes that, taken in conjunction with those of Scinde, they would have been most useful and interesting records, not only as completing the chain of information in regard to the nature and extent of our entire exports beyond the Indus and imports from the Punjaub, but as illustrative of the extent to which the old routes are still adhered to by the traders, and the degree in which they may be giving way to the Indus route; which, as it is naturally, so must it practically become, the great high road to Upper Western India.

"We cannot conclude without expressing our sense of the very great ability which has marked the administration of the Commissioner, Mr. H. B. E. Frere, in fostering the great commercial interests we have now passed under review. His judgment and zeal have been alike conspicuous, and he seems to have imparted his energy to the officers of the province, by whom he has been most ably supported."

APPENDIX C.

SONMEEANEE—AS IT WAS,—AND IS.

Information of a trustworthy character regarding Sonmeeanee appeared desirable from the statements which were made sometime ago in the public papers as to the success of the trade opened by the Americans in *domestics* with this place, and the injurious effect that this success was thought likely to produce on the progress of British commerce in that part of the world. Sonmeeanee, properly Soumeeanee, in Beloochistan, is a fishing station, with a bad harbour, on the shore of the Arabian Sea, about 50 miles to the west of Kurrachee, latitude 24° 27′, longitude 66° 39′. It consists of about 250 huts, built of matting or mud, each adorned with a turret for ventilation, has a population of about 1,000 inhabitants, and is dignified, by English gazetteers, into a small town. Sonmeeanee and the neighbouring territory rejoice in an Iam or chief, who holds his dusty principality under the Khan of Khelat, the right trusty friend and ally of the British.

The following notes on the port and commerce of Sonmeeanee may be relied upon as conveying the latest and most authentic information, collected on the spot by a late lamented and able uncovenanted civil servant of the East India Company, Mr. Macleod, late Deputy Collector of Kurrachee, and who died before their transmission to Government.

"Soumeeanee has gradually sunk in importance since the British occupied Kurrachee. The *first* serious blow it received was in the diversion of the Afghan trade in the time of Sir Charles Napier; this was mainly caused by the exertions of Khan Mahomed Mingul, the chief of Wudd, and the facilities which presented themselves at Kurrachee in accommodation, and ready freight for goods to Bombay, decided the traders in preferring Kurrachee as their port of export. A *second* blow was inflicted when interportal duties were abolished; as goods arriving in Bombay or any other British port from a British possession were admitted duty free—though this made a difference of but *three per cent.* in favour of Kurrachee over Soumeeanee, it had its effect; and that it was the more felt as the Customs' forms on dutiable goods are strictly carried into operation in Bombay. The *third* and finishing stroke was the abolition of frontier customs in Scinde. Every man now who has produce takes it to Kurrachee, as there he not only finds a good market, but he is better able to invest his money in return goods suited to the people of Lus. To all these must be added the difficulties under which traders labour, where there is no settled government. The Jam's man of business is paid rupees ten per mensem *(Luckee-sir)*; he collects the revenue, which is mainly derived from the Customs, and he is also the head of the police—if such an establishment can be said to exist. There are a few sepoys, never exceeding four in number, who receive rations but no pay, and to their agency is attributed all the robberies which occur, and which have of late, owing to the unsettled state of the country, been very numerous. He has another duty, that of supplying the Jam's sepoys and other retainers with food during their stay in the town, whenever business induces them to visit it. As they have no money and he has no state resources, the merchants are indented on, with a promise of reimbursement, for food for themselves and their horses. The customs levied on imports and also on exports at Soumeeanee is *three per cent.* on value: the vessel's manifest or the merchant's advices being produced, no other formality is thought of, and there is nothing like an examination to test the correctness of these documents —this is so far to the advantage of commerce.

"According to Lieutenant Pottinger, Soumeeanee was plundered and burned to the ground by the Joasmee pirates in 1808. It was recovering when he visited it in 1811, it then contained 250 huts, and had, for its appearance of poverty, a considerable trade; it must have fluctuated considerably since then. It is not to appearance of one-half the importance it was in 1844. According to the best accounts that can be obtained, the revenue of the town from all sources in 1838 was between Rs. 40 and 45,000; it fell to Rs. 15,000 in 1844-45; and at the present date the receipts for the year do not exceed Rs. 4 or 5,000. The vessels belonging to the port of Soumeeanee are

The Futtay Shaee of	250	Candies.
Sullamut Savoy	175	,,
Meerapooree	250	,,
Aorsee	150	,,
Putton	60	,,
Wachera	40	,,
Looto	50	,,
Sullamůt Savoy (2nd)	175	,,
Ashrafee	175	,,
Do. (2nd)	60	,,

"All these vessels are sailed under the British flag and possess British registers. There is not much employment for them just now: the ports with which a traffic is kept up are Bombay, Muskat, Mandavie, and Kurrachee. The first seven boats belong to Hemraj, a Hindoo merchant, who has been ruined through his transactions with the Jam, and is now at Kurrachee, where he will in all probability settle. The next belongs to Sett Katin, a Kojaha merchant, the next following to Rungoo, a Banian; the next to Versee, and the last Dingee to Khemchund Bubhoo.

"SOUMEEANEE FISHERY.—There are Rachuns of the largest size and ten or twelve Buttels. The Koolee population amount to about one hundred men and boys of sufficient age to enable their taking a place in the boats—the mode of fishery is precisely that under adoption in Kurrachee. The fins of the sharks are sent to Bombay for the China market, as are also the maws (as they are called) of the seal. The rawus which afford the maws on the coast of Scinde and Kutch, are not found here. The flesh of the shark is salted for the Bombay market, and the smaller fish is consumed in the town, or carried off in a salted state by the inhabitants of the surrounding countries. The fishermen pay the Government ten fish in the every hundred they catch—they have no other direct taxation, and have but one cause of complaint, which is that they cannot find sale for all they catch, for which they believe themselves to be far worse off than their brothers of Kurrachee.

"There are now of inhabited houses, and which are here considered permanent—that is,

Built of mud	145
Of Jopras or mat houses	107
	252

" Which, at four persons to a house, will give the number of inhabitants 1,008. There are 100 of uninhabited houses in the town, the owners of which have emigrated, and 106 ruins of tenements, the destruction of which must be attributable to the same cause. All, or nearly all, these people who once inhabited these houses have taken up their residence in Kurrachee. The present population of Soumeeanee is computed as follows :—

Kojahas	250
Banians	342
Koolees	250
Labourers, dyers, and artificers . .	200
	1,042

" The Jam at times visits the place when his attention is devoted to the wives of his Hindoo subjects, and to the extraction of money from the Banians and other merchants. Since the late disturbance he has drawn in ready money ; first a sum of Rs. 500 then Rs. 300, and but a few days back he sent an order on his kardar for Rs. 1,000. This sum the people declined to give, but made a contribution to the extent of between Rs. 300 and 400, which has not yet been dispatched, for this he has promised a remission of taxes, and will perhaps grant it.

" Under such circumstances it is not a matter of surprise that the town should be in a ruinous condition, that the revenue should so seriously diminish. Soumeeanee will fall yet lower in condition as Kurrachee gathers strength, the traffic now carried on with Bombay will be superseded by one with Kurrachee and that by land in lieu of by water."

APPENDIX D.

GRANTS OF LAND—CONDITIONS OF—FOR TEA CULTIVATION.

Grants of land, on conditions similar to those recently conceded for tea cultivation in the province of Kumaon, would rapidly extend in the country of the five rivers, the cultivation of cotton, wheat, tea, flax,* hemp, and the mulberry. What these terms are the following official document will show.

CONDITIONS OF GRANTS OF LAND FOR TEA CULTIVATION.

Revenue Department, 26th Sept., 1855.

Notification.—Grants of land for tea cultivation, in the Kumaon and Gurhwal districts of the Kumaon province, will be made on the following conditions, on application to the Senior Assistant Commissioner of the district.

2nd.—Each grant will be of not less than 200, or more than 2000 acres. More than one grant may be taken by one person or Company, on the applicant's satisfying the local authorities, acting under the usual control in the revenue department, of their possessing sufficient means and capital to undertake an extended cultivation and manufacture of tea.

* Linseed. — Eleven hundred bags of Punjaub linseed were sold at Kurrachee on the 26th September, 1855. The average price was 4rs. 8a. a maund. Seven hundred bags, not yet arrived, were sold at 4rs. 10a., and an offer to sell all that might arrive before October, brought 4rs. 5a. a maund. A quantity of Scinde linseed was also sold at 4rs. 6a. a maund. These prices are extremely profitable to the growers.

3rd.—One-fourth of the land in the grant will be given free from assessment, in perpetuity, on fulfilment of the conditions below stated.

4th.—The term of first lease will be for twenty years. For the first four years, the grant will be rent-free: in the fifth year, one anna per acre will be charged on three-fourths, or the assessable portion of the grant; two annas per acre in the 6th year; three annas in the 7th year, and so on, one more anna being added in each year, till, in the last year, the maximum rate is reached, of one rupee per acre.—The full assessment, on a grant of 2000 acres, will thus not exceed 1500 rupees per annum.

5th.—The following are the prescribed conditions of clearance:—

At the close of the 5th year, from the date of grant, a twentieth part of the assessable area; at the close of the 10th year, one-fifth of the assessable area; at the close of the 15th year, half of the assessable area; and at the close of the last year, three-fourths of the assessable area is to be cleared, and well stocked with tea plants.

6th.—In the twenty-first year, on the fulfilment of the above conditions, the proprietary right in the grant, and the right of engagement with Government, shall vest in the grantee, his heirs, executors or assigns, under the conditions generally applicable to the owners of estates in Kumaon; and the rate of assessment on the lands in the grant, in whatever manner cultivated, shall never exceed the average rate on grain-crops in lands in the same locality.

7th.—On failure of payment of the prescribed assessment in any year, or of any of the above conditions, (the fact of which failure shall, after local enquiry, conducted by the Senior Assistant Commissioner, be finally determined by the Sudder Board of Revenue,) the entire grant shall be liable to resumption, at the discretion of the Government, with exception to the portion of the assessable area which may be *bonâ fide* under tea cultivation, and to a further portion of land, which shall be allowed in perpetuity, free of assessment, to the extent of one fourth of such cultivated area. The portions, so exempted, will remain in the possession of the grantee, subject to the usual rates and rules of assessment in the district.

8th.—Grantees shall be bound to erect boundary pillars at convenient points round the circuit of a grant, within six months from its date, failing which, such pillars will be put up by the Government officers, and the cost thereof shall be recoverable from the grantee, in the same manner as the regulated rate of assessment.

9th.—No claim to the right and interest in a grant on any transfer by the original grantee will be recognised as valid, unless on registry of the transferee in the office of the Senior Assistant Commissioner.

10th.—So long as Government establishments for the experimental growth and manufacture of tea shall be maintained in the province, supplies of seeds and plants will be given gratis to grantees, on application to the Superintendent, Botanical Gardens, North Western Provinces, as far as may be in his power.

By order of the Honourable the Lieutenant-Governor, North Western Provinces.

(Signed) W. MUIR,

Secretary to the Govt. N. W. P.

APPENDIX E.

FIGHTING STRENGTH OF FRONTIER CLANS.

"We have, from time to time, described the policy adopted by the British Government towards these clans, and its success appears at last to be acknowledged. We question, however, whether the magnitude of that success is even yet thoroughly appreciated. The immense length of the territory to be watched, the barbarous names of the clans who from time to time descend upon the plains, and the apparent want of connection in our own movements—perplex and weary the most attentive. The public think of the 'frontier,' much as if it were an outlying station in some danger from the tribes around. We have seen some statistics which will, we think, tend to diminish this delusion. They show that the clans whom we have compelled to respect our territory, can turn out a force greater than the whole army of Bengal. That they require even now an army of observation greater than the force which defended the Peninsula. That the Government has in fact placed the chain upon tribes as wild and almost as numerous as those who have for centuries maintained the independence of Arabia.

"The numbers stand as follows. Beyond British territory we have—

	Fighting men
"Tribes on Huzara Frontier and near the Indus—North of Peshawur	8,000
Swat and its dependencies	20,000
Momunds	12,000
Afreedies	20,000
Oruckzyes and other tribes in Kohat Frontier	30,000
Wuzeeries	20,000
Sheoranees and other in Dehra Ismael Khan District	5,000
Belooch Tribes on Dehra Khazee Khan border	20,000
Total . . .	135,000

"Besides the above, there are other warlike tribes within British Territory with the following number of

	Fighting men.
Turnoulees (including Jehandad)	8,000
Other Tribes of Huzara	10,000
Eusufzye	25,000
Khuttucks	12,000
Bungushes	15,000
Derajat Tribes	10,000
Total	60,000

"These men are all, be it remembered, trained from boyhood to the use of arms. All can use the tulwar, the long assassin's knife, and the long and heavy matchlock. All are fanatic Mussalmans, clinging like mountaineers everywhere to the worst dogma of their faith, that the slaughter of an infidel is the readiest road to heaven. All, too, are accustomed to consider plunder the easiest source of income, and robbery the only profession worthy of an honourable man. Add to these facts, that they have for ages regarded the people of the plains as serfs born to till for the benefit of the mountain, and that these serfs can be attacked through all the passes of ranges which extend for eight hundred miles, and the task of the Government may be partially comprehended. The figures, too, may serve to explain the necessity for the great force which is now concentrated in the frontier stations :—

	Regular.	Irregular.	Total.
Huzara		1,884	1,884
Peshawur	10,754	2,538	13,202
Kohat	67	3,559	3,626
Dehra Ismael Khan		3,204	3,204
Dehra Ghazee Khan		1,615	1,615
Total,	10,821	12,800	23,621

"It is fortunate, if not for the existence, at least for the stability of our rule that these tribes are incapable of combination. They live in incessant blood-shedding feuds. Life for life is the universal law of the mountain, and the feud once commenced can end only with the destruction of one clan or the other. They have but one common bond, the hatred of the infidel, which from time to time urges individuals to acts of homicidal frenzy. That bond, however, is sufficiently powerful to give rise to some apprehension. A union among these tribes is considered in the Punjaub an impossibility. Feuds as deadly were pacified in Arabia, when tribes equally wild and not more fanatic united for the conquest of the Oriental world." *

* Friend of India.

FOURTH REPORT OF DIRECTORS OF SCINDE RAILWAY COMPANY.

APPENDIX F.

FOURTH REPORT OF DIRECTORS OF SCINDE RAILWAY COMPANY,

With Proceedings of General Meeting of 18th February, 1858.

THE Directors in their Report submitted at the ANNUAL GENERAL MEETING, held in February, 1857, informed the proprietors that they shortly expected to learn the decision of the Government of Bombay regarding the course of the line. They have now the satisfaction of stating that in September last, the Bombay Government approved of the line originally proposed by the Company. Scinde.

On receipt of this intelligence, your Directors lost no time in entering into a contract for the execution of the works between Kurrachee and Kotree, the port of Hyderabad, with Messrs. Bray and Company; and a member of that firm, accompanied by an efficient staff, sailed for Kurrachee by the last steamer; previous to which, in order to accommodate the pressing wants of Government and the immense local traffic, they deemed it advisable to commence operations by constructing the four miles of the line between the Harbour and Kurrachee.

Since the last Report, thirty miles of permanent way material, making with that previously shipped, 60 miles, with a portion of the rolling stock, has been dispatched, and a further quantity is now being forwarded.

The Directors have received intelligence that Coal, adapted for the use of locomotives, has been discovered near the upper terminus of the Scinde Railway, which cannot fail, by decreasing the working expenses, to have a Coal.

beneficial influence on the remunerative character of the undertaking. This Coal has been successfully tried by the Honourable East India Company's Steamers on the Indus.

Harbour.

Your Directors continue to receive most favourable accounts of the depth of water in the harbour of Kurrachee. The Agent of the Scinde Railway in a letter to the Chairman, dated 28th September last, states, "that several merchant captains went on board the 'Hugh Lindsay,' while towing a ship out, and they never had soundings less than 26 feet; and Captain Darke, of the 'Hugh Lindsay,' holds and expresses a very strong opinion that it is impossible to find any high tide throughout the year, when soundings would be less than 26 feet in the main channel." The advantages of having so good a harbour at the terminus of the Railway are apparent, both for the immediate facilities afforded for landing the stores of the Company, and for the powerful effect which it will necessarily have in developing the commerce of Upper and North Western India, and also in enhancing the value and importance of all the undertakings of this Company.

External Trade of Scinde.

An estimate may be formed of the progress of the external trade of Scinde from the official returns of the value of the import and export trade of the Port of Kurrachee, from 1st May, 1852, to 30th April, 1857.

The steadiness of the rate of increase is not less remarkable than its large amount, as the following table shows:—

YEAR.	IMPORTS.	EXPORTS.	TOTAL.
1852-53	£535,690	£376,337	£912,027
1853-54	508,793	376,310	885,103
1854-55	575,196	346,893	922,089
1855-56	629,813	604,400	1,234,253
1856-57	685,665	734,522	1,420,187

The most striking circumstance shown in the preceding returns is that the increase of 74 per cent. in the value of exports during 1855-56, caused by the Russian war, has been followed by a further increase of 22 per cent. during the past year.

Surveys to Dadur and Deesa.

The authorities in Scinde have recommended that your Directors be authorised to survey a branch line from Sukkur, *viâ* Shikarpoor and Jacobabad to Dadur, near the Bolan Pass, with the view to secure to the Scinde Railway the trade of Afghanistan and adjacent countries. They have also recommended the survey of a branch line from Hyderabad to Deesa, which, when executed, will place Kurrachee in direct railway communication with Bombay, and eventually with Calcutta, the Bombay Baroda and Central India Railway Company being about to extend their line to Deesa.

According to the last advices, the survey of the former of these branches had already been completed as far as Jacobabad, a distance of sixty miles.

With reference to these branch lines, that distinguished public officer, Mr. Bartle Frere, the Commissioner in Scinde, in a despatch to the Governor of Bombay, dated 21st July last, states, "that both the lines referred to appear of the very greatest importance, not only in a commercial, but in a military and political point of view. It seems almost superfluous to argue this point with regard to the line from Sukkur, *viâ* Shikarpoor and Jacobabad, in the direction of the Bolan Pass. Its necessity has been repeatedly insisted on by General Jacob, and it is obviously essential to secure rapid means of communication between the river and the important frontier towards the Bolan Pass. The country is a dead level, the canals and water

Dadur.

courses have been bridged, the road has been carried in perfectly straight lines of from ten to twenty miles without turning or angle, and the portions subject to inundation have been raised." In the same despatch, the Commissioner, referring to the branch to Deesa, remarks, that "hardly less important is a line which would connect Scinde with Guzerat or Rajpootana. We are at this moment receiving a terrible lesson of the danger of depending in so extended an empire on single lines of communication. Emergent requisitions for reinforcements have been received here from the northern division of the army, and owing to the want of roads, it is at this moment doubtful whether the reinforcements we have sent will be able to reach Deesa."

Deesa.

Indus Steam Flotilla.

In June last, the Directors received the sanction of the Honourable East India Company to issue £250,000 of Capital upon the same terms and conditions as those granted to the Railway Company, for the purpose of establishing steam vessels on the Indus, between Hyderabad, the upper terminus of the Scinde Railway, and Moultan, the lower terminus of the Punjaub Railway. The shares in this new Capital were offered to the Proprietors of the Scinde Railway, and have all been allotted, and a first call of £4 per share is now in course of payment.

In July last, the East India Company appointed Major Crawford, Superintending Engineer to the Government of Bombay, Captain Balfour, Indian Navy, and Mr. Winter, a Marine Engineer, as a Commission to examine the boats used on the Danube and other rivers in Europe, with the view to obtain the most recent information as to the description of boat best adapted for the navigation of Indian rivers, and their Report has been just forwarded by the

Honourable Court for the information of the Directors of this Company.

The survey of the Punjaub Railway has been most satisfactorily completed, the plans and sections have been received in this country, and the East India Company have sanctioned the issue of £1,500,000 of capital, on which they will guarantee 5 per cent. interest upon the usual terms, which will give three shares in the guaranteed capital for every five shares in the £2,500,000 for which scrip has been issued. The military and political importance of this Railway cannot be over-estimated. It will be constructed at a very moderate expense, and from the great existing traffic, the Directors have every expectation that the line will prove most remunerative.

Punjaub Railway.

The Government of the Punjaub, in their despatch on the Railway from Moultan to Lahore and Umritsir, state that "So far as the commercial and material interests of the Punjaub are concerned, there is a proposed line from the North-East to South-West, which is of greater consequence to the country than any public work, or any number of works that could be specified. A glance at the accompanying rough Sketch Map will show that Northern India has two natural divisions—*first*, the Provinces of the Ganges and its tributaries; *second*, the Provinces of the Indus and its tributaries. In the first or Easterly division, the stream of trade and wealth must ever flow down the valley of the Ganges to the natural outlet of Calcutta. In the second or Westerly division, if the power of Art and Science be brought to the aid of nature, the commerce could follow the direction of the Punjaub rivers to the Indus, then down the valley of the Indus towards the rising port of Kurrachee, which is destined to be, to the

North-West of India, what Calcutta is to the North-East. *A line drawn North to South, somewhere near Agra and Delhi, will form the probable boundary of the two natural sub-divisions. And if the same facilities were created Westward, which exist Eastward, then all the commerce West of the line would follow the Indus to Kurrachee, in the same manner as the commerce on the east follows the Ganges to Calcutta.* At present, however, the major part of the commerce of the extreme North-West travels eastward merely from the want of a more direct route. But if the great route of the Indus were to be thoroughly opened, this commerce would go straight to Kurrachee. To this port there would then come the products from the North-Western India, and from the Central Asian countries beyond that frontier, and in exchange for these, the products of European countries. In this same direction there would also arrive the vast quantities of Government stores and material for the military and public establishments in that quarter, and large numbers of European travellers would frequent this line (in preference to the Eastern route), on account of its comparative shortness and proximity to overland passage to Europe."

"The details, commercial and otherwise, are of great variety and interest, and will be treated of in a separate report; but if the arguments urged should (as it is fully believed they will) be supported by statistical facts and data, then it were superfluous to dilate on the importance of a scheme which will affect the trade of all North-Western India, will give birth to a new commerce yet undeveloped, will be carried out with unusual facility, will prove financially profitable in a high degree, will vitally concern the best material interests of twenty-one millions of industrious people, and will conduce more than any other circumstance that could be named, to the future prosperity of the Punjaub."

Appended to this Report is a letter, under date 21st October, 1857, from the officiating Secretary to the Chief Commissioner of the Punjaub to the Government of India, embodying the views of that eminent statesman, Sir John Lawrence, on the urgency and pressing necessity which exist for the immediate construction of the Punjaub Railway.

Survey from Lahore to Peshawur.

The survey of a line of Railway from Lahore to Peshawur, near the Khyber Pass, has been recommended by the Government of India, and authorised by the East India Company, and the execution of it entrusted to the Engineering Staff of the Punjaub Railway.

A statement of accounts for the past year is appended to this Report, which, with the books of the Company have been examined by the Auditors, and also by the Accountants' Department of the East India Company.

By the provisions of the Act the following Directors and Auditor retire from office at this Meeting :—

W. P. ANDREW, Esq.
HARRY BORRADAILE, Esq. } *Directors.*

AND

MAJOR J. A. MOORE, *Auditor.*

And being eligible for re-election, offer themselves accordingly.

W. P. ANDREW, *Chairman.*

SCINDE RAILWAY COMPANY.

Dr. *Statement of Total Receipts and Disbursements in England to 31st December, 1857, and at Kurrachee to 30th September, 1857.* **Cr.**

	England. To 31st Dec. £ s. d.	India. To 30th Sept. £ s. d.	Total. £ s. d.
To Amount received on Shares as per last Account to 31st December, 1856 ..	308,350 0 0	10,650 4 9	319,000 4 9
„ Do. do. do.	52,885 0 0	900 0 6	53,785 0 6
„ Amount received as Transfer fees to 31st December, 1856 ..	65 18 0	0 9 2	66 7 2
„ Do. do. do.	16 0 6	1 0 7	17 1 1
„ Interest received on Calls to 31st December, 1856	8 10 11	0 7 2	8 18 1
„ Do. do. do.	1 14 2	2 0 6	3 14 8
„ Amount received of the Honourable East India Company in excess of payments into their Treasury in India	.. ..	17,531 5 1	17,531 5 1
£	361,327 3 7	29,085 7 9	390,412 11 4
To the Honourable East India Company on account of Interest ....£	27,452 13 4	806 0 10	28,258 14 2
£	388,779 16 11	29,891 8 7	418,671 5 6

	England. To 31st Dec. £ s. d.	India. To 30th Sept. £ s. d.	Total. £ s. d.
By Amount Expended to 31st December, 1856, as per last Account	90,100 0 2	9,362 10 4	99,462 10 6
„ Law and Parliamentary charges	529 13 0	.. ..	529 13 0
„ Establishment charges, including Stationery, Rent, Advertising, Allowance to Directors, Salaries, Furniture, Office Expenses, &c.	2,394 3 0	1,631 19 4	4,026 2 4
„ Engineering and Surveying	655 4 7	9,342 10 6	9,997 15 1
„ Freight and Insurance	19,527 14 4	.. ..	19,527 14 4
„ Warehouse and Shipping charges ..	1,528 19 0	.. ..	1,528 19 0
„ Permanent Way	90,051 19 4	.. ..	90,051 19 4
„ Punjaub Survey	536 0 8	4,154 17 4	4,690 18 0
„ Stores Department at Kurrachee....	.. ..	4,127 13 5	4,127 13 5
„ Salaries for Indian Establishment ..	1,188 6 9	.. ..	1,188 6 9
„ Stationery for ditto ditto ..	130 5 8	.. ..	130 5 8
„ Engineering ditto ditto ..	246 4 9	.. ..	246 4 9
„ Passage	115 0 0	.. ..	115 0 0
„ Indus Steam Flotilla	355 18 5	.. ..	355 18 5
„ Works Account	.. ..	79 8 6	79 8 6
£	207,359 9 8	28,698 19 5	236,058 9 1
By Interest paid to Proprietors........	27,425 2 4	791 17 2	28,216 19 6
„ Balance at Bankers, Petty Cash, and in Agents' hands	2,475 1 3	400 12 0	2,875 13 3
„ Amount with the Hon. East India Company	151,520 3 8	.. ..	151,520 3 8
	388,779 16 11	29,891 8 7	418,671 5 6

Amount in the hands of the Honourable East India Company in England £151,520 3 8
Less amount advanced by do. do. in India.......................... 17,531 5 1

Net amount in hands of the Honourable East India Company.....................£133,988 18 7

We hereby certify that we have examined the accounts, of which the above is a summary, and we declare the same correct.

(Signed) T. H. MADDOCK, H. BORRADAILE, } DIRECTORS. W. P. ANDREW, CHAIRMAN.

(Signed) ALEX. MACKENZIE, J. A. MOORE, } AUDITORS.

London, 1st February, 1858.

The following resolutions were carried unanimously :—

1. Proposed by the Chairman, seconded by Sir Herbert Maddock,—

> "That this Meeting receive and adopt the report and accounts of the Directors."

2. Proposed by Sir Herbert Maddock, and seconded by George L. Browne, Esq.,—

> "That W. P. Andrew and Harry Borradaile, Esquires, be re-elected Directors of this Company."

3. Proposed by George L. Browne, Esq., seconded by the Rev. C. Ibbotson,—

> "That Major John Arthur Moore be re-elected an Auditor of this Company."

The meeting was then made special, pursuant to notice.

4. Proposed by the Chairman, seconded by Sir Herbert Maddock,—

> "That the Directors be, and are hereby authorised to issue £1,500,000 of capital in 75,000 shares of £20 each, for the construction of the Punjaub Railway, upon which the Honourable East India Company have guaranteed 5 per cent. interest, upon the usual terms; and that three shares in this guaranteed capital be given for every five shares in the £2,500,000, for which scrip has been issued."

5. Proposed by Frederick Warren, Esq., seconded by Chas. Norris Wilde, Esq.,—

"That the best thanks of this Meeting be tendered to the Chairman and Directors for the able and energetic manner in which they have conducted the important negotiations confided to them, and for the ability and zeal they have brought to bear upon the general affairs of the Company."

6. Proposed by Thomas Williamson Ramsay, Esq., and seconded by Charles Norris Wilde, Esq.,—

"That the cordial thanks of this Meeting are due to W. P. Andrew, Esq., the Chairman, for his unwearied attention to the interests of the Company, and for his courteous conduct in the chair this day."

W. P. ANDREW, *Chairman.*
THOS. BURNELL, *Secretary.*

From W. P. ANDREW, Esq., Chairman of Scinde Railway Company, to Sir JAMES C. MELVILL, K.C.B.

SCINDE RAILWAY COMPANY, GRESHAM HOUSE,
Old Broad Street, Jan. 14, 1858.

SIR,

In continuation of my letter, No. 212, dated 14th of December last, requesting permission for this Company to take the necessary steps for raising the capital for the construction of the railway from Moultan to Lahore and Umritsir, I have now the honour to transmit herewith copy of a letter just received through the agent of the Company, addressed by the officiating Secretary to the Chief Commissioner of the Punjaub to the Secretary of the Government of India, Public Works Department, which cannot but be highly satisfactory to the Court, as the letter in question embodies the views of that distinguished statesman, Sir John Lawrence, as to the importance and urgency of the work.

I have the honour to be, &c.,
(Signed) W. P. ANDREW, *Chairman.*

Sir J. C. MELVILL, K.C.B., &c.

From Lieut. E. H. PASKE, Officiating Secretary to Chief Commissioner in the Punjaub, to Colonel W. E. BAKER, Secretary to the Government of India, Public Works Department, Fort William.

Lahore, October 21, 1857.

SIR,

In compliance with the invitation conveyed in your letter, No. 224, dated 19th January, 1856, the Chief Commissioner laid fully before the Supreme Government, in Mr. Temple's letter to your address, No. 278, dated 26th August,

1856, his views in regard to the desirableness of a railway connecting Umritsir with Moultan, and I have now the honour to submit, by the Chief Commissioner's direction, copies of the documents noted in the margin,* which show that the scheme has passed from the stage of speculation to that of action, and that the approval and sanction of the authorities in England are now alone required to admit of the work of construction being at once and vigorously proceeded with.

2. The plans, maps, and sections of the above railway which accompanied Mr. Brunton's report, were despatched from Lahore on the 27th August last, and reached Moultan the subsequent day. Inquiry will be made regarding their arrival at Kurrachee and transmission onwards, the result of which will be communicated. The Chief Commissioner regrets that, by some mistake in his office, these documents were not sent to the Bombay Government as was intended. At that time a great pressure existed in every department, and the Chief Commissioner himself had just started for Jullander to ascertain the feeling of the Jammoo troops, and push them on as fast as possible to Delhi.

3. As a Company has been formed for carrying out the above project, the Directors of which have placed themselves in communication with the authorities in London, matters are now in the best position for ensuring a successful prosecution of the undertaking. But the Chief Commissioner has nevertheless deemed it his duty to keep the supreme Government informed, as far as is in his power, of the progress which is being made on the spot,

* 1. Letter to the address of my predecessor from Mr. J. Neville Warren, agent for the Scinde Railway Company, dated 11th February, 1857, No. 51, inclosing prospectus of Punjaub Railway Company.

2. My predecessor's reply, No. 546, dated 3rd March, 1857.

3. Letter addressed by William Brunton, Esq., to the Directors of the above Company, dated 16th June, 1857, reporting on the survey for a line of Railway between Umritsir and Moultan, effected under his supervision as their chief Engineer.

4. Estimate of probable cost of constructing the above Railway with rolling stock, &c.

and to offer such suggestions or remarks as may appear to him likely to be useful at the present time.

4. In the 19th paragraph of Mr. Temple's letter, above referred to, it was assumed that two millions sterling would probably be required for the completion of a double line of rail from Umritsir to Moultan. From the accompanying documents it will be seen that the Company propose to lay down a single line only, for reasons which, though not therein stated, have doubtless been considered valid by competent parties, after fully considering all that can be said in favour of either course. The maximum cost, as estimated by Mr. Brunton, is £1,676,295, and the Chief Commissioner has reason to believe that the actual outlay is not expected to reach this amount if the work be carried out judiciously and with economy.

5. Mr. Brunton's report and the plans which accompany it abundantly corroborate the opinions expressed in Mr. Temple's letter, in regard to the unusually favourable character of the country to be traversed, for the laying down of a railroad. The slope of the surface is so slight as to be hardly deserving of consideration, while it is nearly uniform throughout; no elevation or hollows of importance occur in any portion of it. No stream or rivulets, save of the most insignificant character, have anywhere to be crossed, as the line keeps to the water shed throughout until it approaches Moultan, which is situated in the alluvial plain or kadir adjoining the Chenab, and even in that portion no engineering difficulties of importance occur. Some of the small inundation canals will have to be crossed, and some of the outlets of the Baree Doab Canal, but none of these will involve works of a costly character.

6. The Baree Doab Canal and proposed railway, it will be observed, run nearly parallel to one another, through the greater portion of the length of the latter. Each will in many ways be productive of advantage to the other, and both will lead in the most effective manner to civilise and supply with inhabitants a new tract which is at present, for the most part, the resort

exclusively of nomadic races of graziers and camel breeders. The natural adaptation of the line for the laying down of a railway is sufficiently indicated by the fact, that it is nearly identical with that independently selected for the course of the canal; and it is stated by Mr. Brunton that a portion of it, as laid down by him, exhibits a continuous straight line of greater length than can be found, he believes, in any European railway.

7. The returns to be expected from the railway, even at an early stage of its existence, as shown in the 21st paragraph of Mr. Temple's letter, were calculated at 9 per cent. gross income upon an outlay of two millions. The Chief Commissioner is not aware that the grounds on which these calculations were based have been in any way impugned, or that anything has occurred to show that they were erroneous; on the contrary, all the statistical data collected by parties interested in the question, as given in the several publications of Mr. Andrew, the chairman of this and other companies, tend in his opinion very strongly to indicate that a vast and increasing traffic may be calculated upon with confidence, while the rapidity with which the trade of Kurrachee has increased, the returns showing an aggregate value of exports and imports, in 1854, of £1,233,000 against £122,010 in 1843, attests the tendency of the traffic of these parts to expand, in proportion as it is facilitated and encouraged. If, then, so considerable a return was anticipated, on valid grounds, from an outlay of two millions, it seems not unreasonable to expect, that with an outlay reduced by one-fifth or one-sixth, the net return will amount to 6 per cent. at the least.

8. It may be further remarked, that the completion of the proposed line of railway has become the more important and essential, in consequence of the establishment of a company, to whom a remunerative rate of interest on their capital has been guaranteed, for the completion of a line of railway from Kurrachee to Kotree, with a powerful flotilla of steamers from thence to Moultan. The success of these undertakings, in a financial point of view, must mainly depend upon the amount of goods and

number of passengers passing to and from the Punjaub and other places beyond it, to which the proposed railway must afford an immense stimulus; when to this is added the exceeding importance to Government, of being enabled to convey troops and military stores to the capital of the Punjaub and stations beyond it with ease and rapidity, there can, the Chief Commissioner believes, be but one opinion as to the vast advantages to be anticipated from the carrying out of the undertaking now under consideration.

9. The experience of some of the railways heretofore opened in India appears to show that very considerable modifications in the form and arrangement of both the carriages employed and the railway stations erected on the lines in England are indispensable to adapt them to this country. It is, therefore, in the opinion of the Chief Commissioner, most desirable that prominent attention be directed at once to this point, and he is glad, therefore, to observe that Mr. Brunton urges the building of the carriages in this country, importing the iron-work only, a measure of the expediency of which he has no doubt. No plans have as yet been drawn for railway stations, as it is thought that this would be premature at the present stage. But the Chief Commissioner has seen a sketch, showing roughly the ground plan of the buildings Mr. Brunton recommends, which appear appropriate, and from Mr. Brunton's character, and the Indian experience now acquired by him and his assistants, it may be confidently anticipated that if a discretion be allowed him in these matters, all necessary points will be attended to.

10. The Chief Commissioner would further suggest, that the station-houses be so arranged as to render them easily defensible. Recent events have forcibly shown that this is a consideration which cannot be safely overlooked in any part of India, and this is more especially the case in a wild tract, such as that which will be traversed by a great part of the proposed line, the tribes inhabiting which are to some extent at the present time in a

state of rebellion. He thinks, also, that the fences which are to be placed along either side of the road should be of such materials and construction as to afford as little temptation as possible to the people of the country to remove them, or no ordinary vigilance will suffice for their protection. The planting of a hedge, as suggested by Mr. Brunton, would probably be found the best plan of all, and many thorny plants suitable for the purpose are indigenous to the country.

11. It is not necessary to refer in this place to the professional portions of Mr. Brunton's report. But in regard to his proposition that the Directors of the company should have a control over the erection of any buildings within a mile of each station, in order that all new villages may be constructed with regularity and a due regard to sanitary considerations, the Chief Commissioner would remark that this can apply to those portions only of the line, the country adjoining which is at present waste; and in such localities he will be quite prepared to direct district officers not to allow buildings to be erected within a reasonable limit, without the concurrence and advice of the officers of the Company, which will probably be the most appropriate mode of meeting Mr. Brunton's views. The question also mooted by him, whether or not the land required for the railway is to be given by the Government, and the owners compensated by it, for any property standing thereon, which may be destroyed, will doubtless be determined according to precedents supplied by existing railways in India, so that it is not necessary to enlarge upon it here.

12. There is another point adverted to by Mr. Brunton, on which the Chief Commissioner is desirous of offering an opinion, viz., the party by whom the work shall be executed. The Chief Commissioner doubts the expediency of entrusting it to contractors in England who are new to the country, its languages, and its population. If European contractors can be met with on the spot, possessed of capital and resources, they will probably be preferable to all others. But such persons are rare, especially in the Punjaub, while substantial native contractors

are ready to come forward to any required extent, and these men having an intimate acquaintance with all the resources of the country, many of them having acquired, as contractors in the canal and other engineering departments, experience in works analogous to those of the railway, must obviously possess immense advantages over persons arrived fresh from Europe, with no previously acquired Indian experience. It would indeed be quite indispensable for European contractors to employ this very class of men, so that by inviting such contractors we should be but creating a body of go-betweens, who would simply have to perform functions which could be equally well or better performed by the engineers themselves, seeing that these have now acquired considerable local experience. The Chief Commissioner has reason to believe that Mr. Brunton himself is pretty much of this opinion; and, indeed, as his estimates are based on existing local rates, it may be doubted whether they will afford a sufficient margin to remunerate a European contractor, in addition to the profits of the actual executors of the work.

13. It is understood that Mr. Brunton and his assistants are about to proceed shortly to Scinde, with a view to surveying a new line in contemplation in that province, as nothing further can be done in this quarter until sanction shall have been accorded by the authorities in England, and definitive orders shall have reached India. The delay resulting from this cause it is presumed cannot be avoided. But as every necessary inquiry has now been made and communicated to the Directors, the surveys completed, and the remarkable adaptation of the proposed line for railway purposes established beyond all room for doubt, the Chief Commissioner earnestly hopes that the requisite orders may be speedily issued, and (seeing that Mr. Brunton considers four years at least to be necessary, under the most favourable circumstances, for the completion of the Railway)—that this work, from which almost incalculable benefits may be anticipated for the Punjaub, may be commenced upon at the earliest practicable period.

14. In conclusion, I am directed to observe that the Chief Commissioner considers it due to Mr. Brunton and his assistants to give his testimony to the very satisfactory manner in which the work has been conducted thus far. On the professional merits of the survey it will be for others to decide; but as respects all that is of an administrative character, Mr. Brunton appears to the Chief Commissioner to have evinced throughout much judgment and firmness, as well as a very conciliatory spirit. There has been no clashing with the local authorities or with the people. The work entrusted to him has been carried on steadily, effectively, and unobtrusively, even throughout a period of most alarming excitement; and the conduct of all parties connected with the undertaking has, in the Chief Commissioner's opinion, been deserving of much commendation.

I have. &c.,

(Signed) E. H. PASKE,

Officiating Secretary to Chief Commissioner.

PROCEEDINGS of the THIRD ANNUAL GENERAL MEETING of the Shareholders of the SCINDE RAILWAY COMPANY, held February 18th, 1858.

The Third Annual General Meeeting of the Scinde Railway Company was held on Thursday, at their offices, Gresham House; W. P. Andrew, Esq.—the Chairman of this and other undertakings, designed to open up a communication between the port of Kurrachee and the north-western provinces by the route of the Indus—presiding.

The Secretary (Mr. Burnell) having read the advertisement convening the meeting, the report was taken as read:—

The Chairman said—You will observe that the business which we have to-day is both general and special, for the purpose, in the first instance, of disposing of the interesting matters which belong to the Scinde Railway undertaking; and, in the second, of asking your consent to the raising of capital for the construction of the Punjaub Railway, which is required by the conditions of the agreement entered into with the Honourable East India Company. When first he had the pleasure of meeting the shareholders, two years before, he explained that the Scinde Railway, from Kurrachee to the Indus, although having a great and defined object, was only the first link in the chain of steam communication from Peshawur to the sea, and the general design was subdivided in order more completely to meet the convenience of all interested in the undertaking. The capital for the Scinde Railway had been estimated at £750,000 in the first instance; but neither this Company, nor the East India Company, ever considered that this amount would be equal to the work to be performed. Nevertheless, the East India Company, as they were aware, came to a resolution authorising the creation of £500,000 only, upon which they guaranteed interest at the rate of 5 per cent. As he had previously observed, neither the East India Company nor the engineers of the company considered this enough, but as the East India Company thought it expedient to limit the guarantee to that amount, the financial position of the company was formed on that basis. Under the arrangement, the shareholders were invited to pay up the amount of the calls in advance if they thought proper, to a certain extent, and the recent call, now in course of payment, was on another £500,000 of capital having the guarantee.

The Report of the Directors had already been in the hands of the proprietors for some days, and it was scarcely necessary for him to detain the meeting by any lengthened observations on the present occasion, because the Report was so ample that the proprietors were in possession of all the important elements necessary to enable them to arrive at a just conclusion in reference to the value of the undertaking in which they had embarked. At the three special meetings of the company held last year, he had availed himself of the opportunity afforded of addressing the proprietors upon such subjects of interest as appeared to him most important; but he would, with the permission of the meeting, say a few words in confirmation of the remarks which he had on previous occasions thought it right to submit to the meeting.

And, in the first place, he would refer to the depth of water at the port of Kurrachee. This was a most important point to consider in reference to their project, and he was extremely happy to say that, in every statement which he had put forward on the subject, he had always been rather under than over the mark. Two years ago he stated that the depth of water on the bar was 17½ feet. Another year passed, and then he had the satisfaction of receiving from the most competent authorities, and upon the most careful examination, evidence to the effect that the depth of water was 21½ feet; and the proprietors would see from the printed report the evidence of the company's agent in Scinde, showing that the average depth at high tide throughout the year, was even then greatly understated. It was, in fact, 26 feet. The agent wrote, on the 20th of September last, "That several merchant captains went on board the 'Hugh Lindsay,' while towing a ship out, and they never had soundings less than 26 feet, and Captain Darke, of the 'Hugh Lindsay,' holds and expresses a very strong opinion that it is impossible to find any high tide throughout the year, when soundings would be less than 26 feet in the main channel." The depth was 26 feet over the bar, a depth which would admit of even the reception of the Leviathan in the port of Kurrachee, if the Leviathan should be chartered to that port. (Hear hear).

At a previous meeting he mentioned to the proprietors that considerable delay had taken place in settling the course of the line. He was now happy to inform them that the line had been agreed to by the Bombay Government; that in September last the works were being proceeded with with great energy. The effect of the delay to which he referred had been, to divert the labours of their staff out in India from their immediate object. At the same time he was glad to say that although their engineers had directed their attention to other quarters, they had made surveys for various extensions which promised to become of importance in the future operations of the company. In reference, however, to the portion of the line between Keeamaree and Kurrachee —which, he might observe, was not a branch line, but a section of the trunk line—he would remind the proprietors that when they last met, he had stated to them the opinion of Mr. Bartle Frere, and represented to them how very valuable the traffic of this small section of railway would prove to the company; and he had recently received from that gentleman, who had always taken a very earnest interest in the undertaking, a statistical return showing the actual traffic which now passed over this portion of line, which, although only 4 miles in length, would nevertheless, surpass any other section of the line in its remunerative returns. In the year 1856, the traffic embraced 107,066 carts, 14,914 carriages, 46,251 horses, and above 900,000 passengers, European and native. In short, the traffic was surprising. This was for the year 1856; and if they reflected for a moment on the activity which had been given to that port by the amount of munitions of war and military stores which had been sent out during the past year for the purpose of putting down the unhappy rebellion in our Indian possessions, they might estimate the increasing importance and value of the port of Kurrachee. (Hear, hear).

Taking, however, a more general view of the commercial value of the undertaking, it would no doubt be interesting to the meeting to know that, from official returns which had been furnished to him, the commerce of the valley of the Indus had increased from £358,400 to £1,420,187 in the course of the last ten years; and that the article of silk, from the market of Bokhara, which, in the previous year only figured for £376, last year represented £32,017; the export of wool in 1847 amounted to £18,159, and last year to £311,590. These were very remarkable facts, which he thought it would be agreeable to the meeting to be made acquainted with; and he thought they would agree with him that it was not out of place to give attention to such matters, upon which the ultimate success of a great undertaking must depend.

There was another matter also to which he begged to refer, as likely to exercise considerable influence on their property. He alluded to the discovery of coal on the Indus. (Hear, hear). And he had the satisfaction of stating that experiments had been made with the coal on board the East India Company's steam-ship, the Nimrod, and with the best success, by the officers of the Steam Flotilla. [The hon. gentleman read the official communication which he had received on this subject].

He would here also take an opportunity of stating that the directors had entered into a contract with Messrs. Bray for the construction of the line from Kurrachee to Kotree; and there would be no doubt, from the high character of these gentlemen, and the reputation they had already earned for themselves in the construction of works on the Great Indian Peninsula line, that the contract would be completed within two years and three months, to the great satisfaction of the company and their own credit. At the same time every precaution had been taken in the drawing up of the contract, that no inducement should be wanting to the energetic prosecution of the works; on the one hand, a sort of bonus was to be given for every week saved in the construction within the time fixed, and, on the other, a penalty or forfeiture for every week's delay beyond the same time.

A PROPRIETOR.—Perhaps the chairman would be good enough to state the amount of the contract.

The CHAIRMAN said he was unable to do that. The contract was upon a schedule of prices.

Another PROPRIETOR.—What quantity of land have we in possession?

The CHAIRMAN—The company have all the necessary land given by the Government. The land from Keeamaree to Kurrachee is now in possession, and on which the works are being proceeded with.

He would now say a few words in reference to the Indus Steam Flotilla and the Punjaub Railway, which were so intimately connected with this undertaking. The proprietors would remember that when parliamentary authority was obtained for the establishment of that Flotilla, it was arranged that the Scinde Company should raise the necessary capital, but that the capital was to be specially applicable to the Flotilla, and should not interfere, or be mixed up with, the separate capital of the Scinde Railway, but that the capital of each undertaking should be employed separately, and stand in separate accounts, and that each undertaking should stand upon its own merits, and that all new shares belonging to each should be offered in the first instance to the proprietors of each individual project. The capital and revenue accounts were to be kept entirely distinct, and the only interest in common between the three companies was that there should be one management, and that mutual dependence which the geographical connection and commercial relations of the three undertakings involved. The deposit on the shares in the Flotilla had been paid, the first call was in course of payment, and no time would be lost in prosecuting the undertaking. The East India Company appointed a commission for the purpose of examining and determining upon the best form of boat for the navigation of the Indus, consisting of gentlemen of known ability, Major Crawford, Consulting Engineer to the Government of Bombay, Captain Balfour, of the Indian Navy, and a marine engineer of experience; and their report, which had been printed for our information and guidance, fully supported the views entertained by the engineers of this company, in almost every particular. (Hear, hear).

As to the Punjaub Railway, which comprehended 248 miles of line from Moultan to Lahore and Umritsir, it was satisfactory to know that, in an engineering point of view, it was remarkable for the easy character of the country through which it passed. There was not a single cutting or embankment of any extent. That distinguished statesman, Sir John Lawrence, who, as they were aware, was now not only placed at the head of the Punjaub, but of a large portion of Upper India, had warmly recommended the undertaking to the support of the authorities, and had taken occasion, in a manner which was extremely gratifying to the directors of the company, to record his testimony as to the energy and ability of Mr. Brunton and the engineering staff. The latter gentleman, writing from Lahore, especially mentioned the extraordinary adaptation of the surface of the country to railway purposes, and the presence of facilities for construction, which surpassed the advantages on the

Scinde line. Mr. Brunton and his staff assuredly deserved the greatest approbation which it was in the power of the company to bestow; for, engaged as they were in prosecuting engineering surveys in a country agitated by the mutiny of the Bengal army, and where they actually performed military duty, and were drilled twice a day, they nevertheless exhibited an energy, and produced results, which could not have been surpassed had their labours been exercised in the pleasant and peaceful fields of England. The whole line of the Punjaub Railway was surveyed, too, in seven months. (Hear, hear).

Sir John Lawrence, as would be seen by reference to the correspondence published at the close of the report, pressed upon the authorities the necessity of a speedy completion of the line, as of the highest importance, both in a political and commercial point of view. Such testimony was most valuable. (Hear, hear).

Since the survey of the Punjaub was completed, the directors received authority to continue their surveys on to Peshawur, a distance of 256 miles.

There were also other surveys authorised to Deesa and to Dadur, at the mouth of the Bolan Pass. Both these extensions had been very strongly recommended by Mr. Frere, and by General Jacob. The line to Dadur was about 160 miles in length, and had been already surveyed by our engineers from Sukkur *via* Shikarpore to Jacobabad, a distance of 50 or 60 miles, and taken in conjunction with the line to Peshawur and the intervening steam route, it was obvious that an invading force attempting either of the great passes, would be liable to be taken by us either in flank or rear. The proprietors had already heard in that room the opinions of his distinguished friend, Mr. Frere, as to the importance of our commanding these passes; and it was now incontestible that, in order to confirm the imperial grasp upon India, we must have strategical possession of that country. It was under this latter view that the line of communication up the valley of the Indus assumed its most important aspect. It presented the shortest and most direct road for the conveyance of troops to North-Western India, inhabited by brave and hardy races, who nevertheless were vain and presumptuous, but who, though now our allies, gave this country much trouble in a recent campaign, and it would be found necessary to impress upon them the fact, by the presence of European troops, that we were not dependent alone on *their* thews and sinews, for the possession of the Punjaub and Upper India. He alluded more especially to the Sikhs, who might justly be termed the Paladins of the East. (Hear, hear).

Deesa was on the other side of the Indus, at a distance of about 260 miles; but an extension in that direction would be of immense value, because by means of that line the Scinde would become connected with the Bombay line, and give them an entrance into Rahjpootana and Central India, and lead to a union of the opposite sides of the peninsula by steam transit. These, however, were matters to which he should have occasion to draw their attention at some future time, and he now begged to move the adoption of the report and accounts.

Sir Herbert Maddock seconded the resolution.

A Proprietor drew the attention of the chairman to the alteration which had taken place in the arrangement for the construction of the Moultan line. At first it was stated that it was intended originally to make the line a double line, and now it appeared that it was to be only a single line. According to the estimate of the chairman, no doubt seemed to be entertained that the traffic would be very large; and it therefore struck him that if the line were constructed as a double line in the first instance, it would be a considerable saving to the company. There was another point to which he would also venture to direct the attention of the chairman—namely, that, looking at the red line as laid down on the map, indicating the proposed extension to the Khyber Pass, the line seemed to describe a very wide curve, which, unless there were some very good reason to the contrary, would be better served by a more direct line.

The CHAIRMAN said it was to be taken into consideration that, although the traffic on the Moultan, Lahore, and Umritsir line would, no doubt, be very great, yet the largest proportion of the traffic would be through traffic; and after carefully considering the amount of accommodation that could be afforded, the professional advisers and staff of the Company had decided upon a single line of rails throughout, with very ample and commodious sidings, with bridges and other masonry works for a double line. It was not improbable, also, that in some parts the line would be made double, and this would very likely be the case between Umritsir and Lahore. In reference to the considerable bend which the line appeared to take, and which the honourable proprietor seemed to think would admit of improvement, it was absolutely essential that the line should touch the important cities of Lahore and Umritsir—Lahore was the capital and a great military station, and Umritsir was a great commercial emporium with a trade of between two and three millions a-year; and, in order to accommodate these points, as well as to afford the most convenient extension to Peshawur, the curve was necessary, and, for the most part, the line followed the present high road. If they had adopted a more direct line, and hugged the banks of the Indus, they would have lost sight of the principal towns and the great objects they had in view. The line, as laid down, appeared to be the best, both for political and commercial considerations.

A Proprietor said he should be glad to know if the company intended to employ native contractors for the Punjaub Railway.

The Chairman said it was the intention of the Company to do so. In the first place, the native contractors were, for the most part, very wealthy and reliable men, and had had great experience in the construction of public works, and in the Punjaub particularly, of several hundred miles of canal. It was also considered by himself and his colleagues at the Board, to be judicious policy to induce the natives to take an active interest in the line. The system to be pursued would be the employment of native contractors under the supervision of the Company's staff.

Mr. Wilde referred to the arrangement originally determined upon for keeping the capital of the several undertakings, namely, the Scinde, the Flotilla and the Punjaub, distinct as to capital and revenue. He thought this a very salutary regulation, but he saw in the present accounts some charges on account of the Punjaub debited to the Scinde Company. Upon this point he should be glad of some explanation. He desired also to say a few words upon the amount of money in the hands of the East India Company. They held about £150,000, upon which no interest was allowed, which appeared to be scarcely fair, seeing that they charged against the Company every penny which they paid in the shape of interest on the paid-up capital in the shares. There was another minor point to which he would call attention. He alluded to the custom of inviting the proprietors to these meetings by circular as well as by advertisement. On a recent occasion the circular was not sent. He thought, also, by a friendly arrangement between the Secretaries of the Indian Railway Companies, the inconvenience of two Indian Railway Companies meeting on the same day might be avoided. This, however, was the case with the Madras and the Scinde Company.

The Chairman said the Scinde had always held their meeting on the 18th February, but the matter should be attended to. In answer to the question as to the items of expenditure on the Indus and Punjaub accounts, they were part of preliminary expenses which were paid by the Scinde Company, and were placed to a suspense account until the separate accounts were opened. The expense of the survey of the Punjaub was paid by the Scinde Company and placed to a separate account. As to the amount in the hands of the East India Company not bearing interest, it was the object, of course, of this Company to prevent any large accumulation in their hands, but the East India Company would not permit them to enter into any contracts without money being previously paid into their hands; so that they could not avoid making payments, and were practically in this matter in the hands of the East India Company.

The Chairman, without pledging himself, gave, as his own impression, the following information regarding calls.

—The first call on the Punjaub would be £4 16s. 8d., payable on the 27th March. On the first issues of the Scinde shares, £5, payable on the 28th May; second call on the Flotilla shares of £5 on the 28th June; call of £5 on the second issue of the Scinde shares on the 10th July; fourth call on the first issue of Scinde shares of £5, payable on the 27th September; and a third call on the Flotilla, due the 28th of October. These calls were no doubt heavy, but the Directors had no alternative.

After some further discussion, in the course of which a very strong opinion was expressed as to the injustice and unreasonableness of the East India Company retaining so large an amount of money to meet contracts for which they were in no way liable,—

The resolution for the adoption of the Report and accounts was put and carried unanimously.

The retiring Directors, namely, Mr. Andrew, the Chairman, and Mr. Harry Borradaile, were then re-elected, and Major Moore was re-elected Auditor; and the business of the General Meeting being concluded,—

The Meeting was made special, for the purpose of authorising the creation of £1,500,000, in shares of £20 each, upon which the Honourable the East India Company guaranteed interest at the rate of five per cent.

The Chairman, in submitting the formal resolution to the adoption of the meeting, explained that the original estimate was £2,500,000, but the Company's Engineer who surveyed the line, put the figure at £1,600,000. This, however, was thought to be excessive by Sir John Lawrence, and at length the East India Company determined upon the sum of £1,500,000 as the amount upon which they would grant the guarantee. The Directors, however, did not acquiesce in this estimate. They did not consider it adequate. There were many details of expense connected with the undertaking, which did not appear to have been fully appreciated, either by their own engineers in the Punjaub, or by the East India Company; and there were many subjects, such as freight, upon which the Directors in London were in a position to exercise a correct judgment. A further capital would, no doubt, be necessary, but for the present they were limited to the £1,500,000. As to the value of the line when made, the proprietors would remember the interesting statistics and statesmanlike views which Mr. Frere laid before them in that room; and also on a subsequent occasion, they would recollect the graphic description which Mr. Temple gave of the traffic and resources of the Punjaub and neighbouring territories, confirming all that has been previously said of the profitable results which were anticipated to flow from the undertaking. The Chairman then proceeded to give a slight sketch of the history of the line, and of the formation of the Punjaub Railway Company, which would now merge in the Scinde Company, and stated that the scrip now out for the Punjaub represented £2,500,000, but as the capital had been reduced to three-fifths of the original estimates, the arrangement proposed was, that three new shares would exchange against every five of the old. The call would be £4 16s. 8d., making, with the deposits, £5 paid. The Chairman also read the letter of the East India Company, rendering it imperative to pay up 25 per cent. of the capital on or before the end of March next.

The formal resolution was then put, and carried unanimously.

Mr. GOODLIFFE said, supposing the present capital

should prove inadequate, he presumed the East India Company would not refuse a guarantee on such additional capital.

The CHAIRMAN said, the East India Company would not permit them to spend more capital than that guaranteed, and he had no doubt that all the capital required would be guaranteed, as the guarantee was given on the *usual terms.*

A PROPRIETOR said, the Chairman, if he remembered rightly, proposed, in a pamphlet written by him, to commence at Umritsir.

The CHAIRMAN said it was true that, years ago, he might have expressed an opinion to that effect. But at that time their project had not assumed its present vast proportions. Such a scheme would then have frightened the East India Company (A laugh). It was now proposed to commence at various points—in fact, all along.

The CHAIRMAN, in answer to questions put by Sir Charles Douglas and other proprietors, replied that as to calls, the call about to be made on the Punjaub would not very soon be followed by another, but this would depend in a great measure on the amount paid up in anticipation. Not a moment would be lost to push on the construction of the Flotilla, and no delay was expected, since they were cordially supported by the authorities, both at home and abroad. Six vessels would be ready in 18 months. The distance between Lahore and Umritsir was 32 miles. The Punjaub line would be 250 miles in length.

In answer to questions as to the effect which any change in the government of India might have on the security of the Company.

The CHAIRMAN said it would affect not the nature of

the security. The security was the revenue of India, whether administered by the Crown or the East India Company. In explanation, also, of the course to be pursued in the distribution of any further capital which may be created in respect of branch lines or extensions, it was stated that the shares would be allotted to the holders of shares in the particular undertaking from which the extension proceeded, as, for instance: — Suppose a line to Deesa, it would spring from the Scinde Railway proper; and that to Peshawur would be given to the Punjaub. If any extension of capital should be determined upon for the purpose of building boats, either to augment the Flotilla at present proposed, or for the purpose of navigating the smaller tributary streams of the Punjaub, such shares would of right belong to the then holders in the Steam Flotilla; and the local authorities were at this moment collecting data to be placed in his hands for the latter purpose.

The resolution was then passed unanimously.

A vote of thanks was then moved to the Chairman, and carried by acclamation, with many compliments to the Chairman upon the singular energy and distinguished ability with which he had conducted the affairs of the Company.

The CHAIRMAN briefly acknowledged the compliment, and congratulated the proprietors that the projects which a few years since were only shadowed forth, had now assumed a distinct form; and, with the assistance of the contributions of the shareholders, would speedily become flourishing realities.

The meeting then separated.

APPENDIX G.

EUPHRATES AND INDUS ROUTE TO CENTRAL ASIA.

A Deputation in favour of 'the Government guaranteeing a minimum rate of interest on the Euphrates Valley Railway, had an interview with Viscount Palmerston, 22nd June, 1857.

The deputation consisted of the Earl of Shaftesbury, Mr. W. P. Andrew (chairman of the Euphrates Valley Railway), Mr. P. Anstruther, Mr. W. Ainsworth, Sir F. L. Arthur, Bart., Mr. A. F. Bellasis, Sir W. Colebrooke, C.B., the Earl of Chichester, the Earl of Carnarvon, Major-General Chesney, R.A., Mr. F. Ellis, M.P., Mr. Sotheron Estcourt, M.P., Mr. A. S. Finlay, M.P., Lord Goderich, Mr. H. Gladstone, Mr. W. Hutt, M.P., Mr. Thos. Headlam, M.P., Mr. T. B. Horsfall, M.P., Col. Harvey, Mr. T. K. Lynch, Mr. John Laird, Mr. Macgregor Laird, Mr. James Merry, M.P., Sir H. Maddock, Major Moore, Sir D. Norreys, M.P., Colonel W. Pinney, M.P., Mr. F. W. Russell, M.P., Sir Justin Sheil, K.C.B., Count Strylecki, Col. Steinbach, Gen. Sabine, Lord Talbot de Malahide, the Lord Mayor, Mr. Matthew Uzielli, Mr. W. Vansittart, M.P., Sir W. F. Williams of Kars, Mr. T. A. Yarrow, Mr. Wickham, M.P., Hon. A. Kinnaird, M.P., Mr. Arthur Otway, the Earl of Albemarle, Lord Ashley, Mr. Thomas Alcock, M.P., Mr. J. E. Anderdon, Viscount Bangor, M. W. Buchanan, M.P., Mr. F. B.

Beamish, M.P., Mr. G. Bowyer, M.P., Dr. Boyd, M.P., Major C. Bruce, M.P., Lord Colchester, Lord Cloncurry, Lord Cremorne, Lord R. Clinton, Sir Edw. Colebrooke, M.P., the Hon. H. Cole, M.P., Alderman Copeland, M P., the Bishop of Durham, Lord Dufferin, the Earl of Donoughmore, Mr. R. Davison, M.P., Colonel Dunne, M.P., Sir James Duke, M.P., the Earl of Enniskillen, Earl of Erne, Lord Elcho, Sir De Lacy Evans, M.P., Mr. J. C. Ewart, M.P., Sir J. Elphinstone, M.P., Mr. W. Fagan, M.P., Sir R. Ferguson, M.P., Sir G. Foster, M.P., Mr. C. Fortescue, M.P., Mr. F. French, M.P., Lord Robert Grosvenor, M.P., Mr. E. Grogan, M.P., Mr. S. Gregson, M.P., Mr. G. Hamilton, M.P., Mr. J. H. Hamilton, M.P., Colonel Harvey, Mr. A. Hastie, M.P., Mr. H. Ingram, M.P , Mr. W. Kirk, M.P., Mr. T. Longman, Lord Monteagle, the Earl of Mayo, Mr. J. R. Mowbray, M.P., Mr. R. Monckton Milnes, M.P., Sir John Macneill, Mr. H. A. Mackinnon, Sir Roderick Murchison, Mr. G. Macartney, M.P., Mr. J. M'Cann, M.P., Mr. J. M'Clintock, M.P., Mr. M'Evory, M.P., Mr. P.W. Martin, Mr. C. W. Martin. Mr. G. G. M'Pherson, Mr. F. North, M.P., Colonel North, M.P., the Right Hon. J. Napier, M.P., Mr. C. Newdegate, M.P., Sir George Pollock, G C.B., Mr. J. Pritchard, M.P., the Earl of Roden, Lord Rossmore, Lord Sandon, the Bishop of St. David's, Mr. R. Slaney, Mr. W. Sowerby, Mr. A. Turner, M.P., Colonel Taylor, M.P., Mr. W. Tollemache, M.P., Sir H. Verney, Lord Wrottesley, Mr. Whiteside, M.P., Mr. Thos. Williams, Mr. J. A. Warre, M.P.*

Lord Shaftesbury introduced the deputation to Lord

* *Times*, 23rd June, 1857.

Palmerston, and pointed out, in forcible language, the vast importance to this country of securing an alternative route to India, and the great interest generally felt throughout the country in this great undertaking, so calculated to promote commerce, civilization, and Christianity, and stated that Mr. Andrew, the Chairman of the company, would submit to his Lordship more detailed information.

Mr. Andrew, after expressing his regret for the unavoidable absence of Lord Stanley, said that for some years it had been considered a great national object to secure an alternative short route to India, but that recently the establishment of the route by the Euphrates had become more and more necessary, and more especially since it had been determined to open up the Valley of the Indus by the application of steam. The great traffic which would pour down this valley from Central Asia and the Punjaub, once flowing towards Kurrachee, would naturally seek an outlet by the sister valley of the Euphrates, at least the lighter and more valuable products, as well as the mails and passengers; but the support of the Government was not sought on commercial grounds. That support was sought alone on the ground of the political importance of this ancient line of communication. The grand object was to connect England with the north-west frontier of India, by steam transit through the Euphrates and Indus Valleys. The latter would render movable to either the Kyber or the Bolan, the two gates of India, the flower of the British army cantoned in the Punjaub, and connected by the Euphrates line by means of steamers, the flank and rear would be threatened of any force advancing through Persia towards India. So that the invasion of India by this great scheme would be placed beyond even speculation; and it would be evident, by the great army of India of 300,000 men being united by this means to the army in England, the mutual support they would render each other would quadruple the power and ascendancy of this country, and promote powerfully the progress, the freedom, and the peace of the world. The countries to be traversed were the richest and most ancient in the world, and might again become the granaries of Europe, and not only supply us with wheat, but with cotton of excellent quality; and his gallant friend, General Chesney, who had recently visited these regions, would tell them that there were thousands of camel-loads of this valuable commodity rotting on the ground from the want of the means of transport. Sir W. F. Williams, of Kars, would tell them there was no difficulty in dealing with the Arabs, if they were fairly treated. The Lord Mayor, who had had intimate commercial relations with the East, and Mr. Lynch, of Bagdad, who had for many years traded with the Arabs, would speak to the honesty and trustworthiness of the Arab. As to physical difficulty there was none—the line had been surveyed and proved to be singularly easy. Her Majesty's Government had given their powerful influence and support in obtaining the firman and concession. They had placed Her Majesty's ship, Stromboli, at the disposal of General Chesney and Sir John M'Neill, and the engineering staff; and Lord Stratford de Redcliffe had lent his powerful advocacy with the Porte. He (Mr. Andrew) was deeply grateful for the assistance thus far afforded them; but they had now arrived at that point when something more was absolutely necessary, and that was the pecuniary support of Government to enable the capital to be raised for the prosecution of the work. It was not a matter for private individuals to undertake. If they wanted an investment for their funds, they would certainly not choose Turkish Arabia. The establishment of a steam route by the Euphrates had been placed before the public and the Government. Many Chambers of Commerce and other influential associations had already memorialized the Government in favour of granting pecuniary aid; and it was believed the country was anxious that this route should be carried out by Englishmen; and it now rested with the Government to say whether they concurred in the importance of the work, and if so, whether they would be prepared to recommend such an amount of pecuniary assistance, whether by guarantee or otherwise, as would enable this, the most important undertaking ever submitted to their consideration, to be proceeded with.

Sir W. F. Williams, of Kars, stated that during his long residence amongst the Arabs, he experienced no difficulty in dealing with them, or in procuring, during his excavations in Susa, any number of workmen he might require; and he also pointed out the great importance of the proposed harbour of Seleucia, as there was not a single good harbour on the Syrian coast.

Count Strylecki briefly addressed his lordship on the support of successive Turkish Governments to the undertaking, viewing it as of incalculable political importance to England in relation to her Indian possessions.

Mr. Finlay, M.P., speaking from personal acquaintance with the country to be traversed, dwelt on the great capacity for development, if only the means of transport were afforded.

General Chesney gave full explanations regarding the harbour, as to its exact position, capacity, &c.

Sir Justin Sheil, late ambassador in Persia, dwelt on the

political importance of the line, and stated that it would shorten the distance to Kurrachee, the European port of India, by 1,400 miles.

The Lord Mayor had had (through his agents) extensive commercial transactions with the Arabs, and had found them most reliable and honest, and he considered they were as much alive to their own interests as any other race, and would be in favour of the railway because it would at once give them employment and afford them an outlet for their products.

Mr. Lynch, of Bagdad, from long residence, fully confirmed his lordship's views.

Mr. Horsfall, M.P., assured his lordship that the undertaking was viewed with great interest in the manufacturing districts generally, and placed in his lordship's hands a memorial from the Chamber of Commerce of Liverpool, praying that the Government would extend the necessary pecuniary aid to the Euphrates Valley Railway Company.

Lord Palmerston assured the deputation that the Government were fully alive to the great importance of the Euphrates route; that they had supported and would continue to support it; but he could not give an opinion as to giving the guarantee on the capital without consulting his colleagues, and requested Mr. Andrew, to put his proposition in writing, and that it should have a proper amount of consideration, and that Government would be happy to aid it, if in their power.

Mr. Andrew having thanked his lordship for the courteous reception afforded to the deputation, the deputation withdrew, much gratified by the manner in which they had been received.*

* *Morning Herald*, 23rd June, 1857.